UPON THIS ROCK

UPON THIS ROCK

The Story of
Nicholas Rivett-Carnac
and St Mark's Church, Kennington

Jenny Cooke

Foreword by Ronald Bowlby
Bishop of Southwark

HODDER AND STOUGHTON
LONDON SYDNEY AUCKLAND TORONTO

British Library Cataloguing in Publication Data

Cooke, Jenny
  Upon this rock: the story of Nicholas Rivett-Carnac and
St. Mark's Church, Kennington.
  1. Christian life. Faith
  I. Title
  248.4

ISBN 0-340-49678-9

Dedicated to the people of St Mark's Church, past and present. Some of them are mentioned by name in the text. Many are not. But each and every one has played an important part in the history of the church. They are beloved by God and important to Kennington. Without them there would be no church. For a church is its people; and without them it is nothing but an empty shell.

Jesus said:

Why do you call me, 'Lord, Lord,' and do not do what I say? I will show you what he is like who comes to me and hears my words and puts them into practice. He is like a man building a house, who dug down deep and laid the foundation on rock. When the flood came, the torrent struck that house but could not shake it, because it was well built. But the one who hears my words and does not put them into practice is like a man who built a house on the ground without a foundation. The moment the torrent struck that house, it collapsed and its destruction was complete.

Luke 6:46–49 NIV

Contents

Part IV Thy Will Be Done

Foreword

Reading this book has been a strange experience for me, as well as a very moving one at times. I have discovered much that I did not know about St Mark's in Kennington, and about its present Vicar and his wife. That may sound surprising, coming from their Diocesan Bishop: but Southwark is one of the largest dioceses, and there is no way by which one person can begin to know everything that God does among the people and parishes committed to his care.

Each reader will draw his or her own particular nourishment from the story of this remarkable church. I can only share with you some of the things which have come to me on reading it, and which I hope you may discover too.

First, in thinking about the ministry of Nicholas Rivett-Carnac (shared so closely with Marigold in recent years) I do see links with St Francis, as the author suggests. There is the same mixture of gentle manner with tough obedience; a deep compassion and concern for those on the margin or broken down; the same commitment to prayer and the cross, as a necessary and not optional part of discipleship.

Second, life-changing experiences are expected at St Mark's, and they happen. There is a deep trust that God will lead and sustain, however difficult it seems at times; a trust rooted in the Word of God and the life of the Spirit.

Third, this is not a narrow book. By that I mean that we are not left feeling that there is only one way to God, and that is to be found at St Mark's, Kennington! While much of what happens in worship and ministry springs from a particular tradition with its own language and emphasis, other experiences and expressions of faith are recognised and valued. Narrow churches do not allow people to grow.

Fourth, here is a true *parish* church, part of a diocese, wanting to serve the community who live around; giving and receiving. It has therefore been a bridge across which many people have crossed, people who are now working in the name of Christ in many parts of the world and in many different ways.

I hope this story will help many to grow in faith, as it has helped me.

St Peter's Day 1988   Ronald Bowlby
                                                  Bishop of Southwark

Note

This is a true story. In certain cases names of individuals and minor details of their circumstances have been changed to protect their anonymity.

Prologue

People begin to rise from their seats. They walk forward,
dignified and in quiet disarray: the old and the young;
the tall and the short; the wealthy and the poor; the
immigrant and the person whose family has lived in
Britain century upon century. Children dance and
chirrup, clinging on to adults' hands. Piano music
surges and then threads through the morning air.
Sometimes a child's whine or cry ascends with the music
up to the stained-glass dome. And through the windows
streams light that rests on the table in their midst.

Still the people come, moving towards the old round
family table, polished and set now with a simple bowl of
pink carnations, earthen chalices of wine and hunks of
fresh white bread. There are jugs too, and an opened
prayer book propped on a white cloth. The people come
and stand quietly, a glad crowd waiting round the table.
Some have rapt faces, some are thoughtful, a few are sad
and searching. But all may come freely, to the only true
place of equality on the earth. They come to the feet of
Jesus, where all men and all women may share in the
Holy Communion.

And so, like a real family meal, people eat and drink
and are satisfied. All their memories, griefs and joys,
their very beings offered up in a moment of true
worship.

Nicholas, their vicar, who moments before had
opened his arms wide in a gesture of something more
than welcome and cried, 'He opened wide his arms for
us on the cross; he put an end to death by dying for us

and revealed the resurrection by rising to new life',[1] now
walks forward. His eyes rest for a second on the table. He
remembers it from his grandmother's house in Scotland,
gleaming with another welcome all those years ago,
piled high with raspberry jam, scones, cream and a
china tea service. Even though it was wartime then, it
had been like paradise playing with his brother and
sister in the garden that overlooked the Moray Firth and
waiting for the excitement of seeing the car bring his
parents on their rare visits from London. It had been
good too, in later years, to bring that family table and
place it here in the body of the church.

Now as he looks round the church he sees the people;
he knows them; he enters into their lives. He sighs with a
sudden weight of joy. For at this time and in this place in
a church in the broken inner city it is like a foretaste of
heaven. He bows his head and his lips move in silent
thankfulness. He waits as the last person slips back to
their seat. And still the words from the majestic service
hang in the air:

Send the Holy Spirit on your people
and gather into one in your kingdom
all who share this one bread and one cup,
so that we, in the company of all the saints,
may praise and glorify you for ever,
through him from whom all good things come,
Jesus Christ our Lord.[2]

Nicholas looks up in welcome and recognition. All his
years of pilgrimage have led him to this place and to
these people. This is truly an intimation of heaven, he
thinks. A taste of the kingdom of Christ on earth, where
all are united. And there is no division. Never need there
be any division between class and colour in the family of
Christ. All are united in him, the rock of our salvation.

[1]Third Eucharistic prayer in the Alternative Service Book.
[2]ibid.

Part I
The Divided Kingdom

The tragedy of Britain seemed to me to be fairly easy
to pinpoint. We are a divided nation. Management
and workers, black and white, North and South,
upper-class and lower-class . . . one could go on. This
characteristic goes right back into our history. The
divisions seem to be growing deeper at the moment,
but many do not recognise the sadness of our
situation.

Nigel Swinford on Movement Three
of his composition *Symphony of Nations*
(concert programme)

1

Lennox Gardens

Trying on his father's shoes.

Nicholas ran down the steps outside his front door and raced across the road to the gardens across the square. All at once his steps faltered. He turned round. There was Nanny Macintosh standing on the top step with a coat in her hand.

'Come back,' she called. 'And make sure you look when you cross the road.'

Nicholas glanced vaguely to the left and right. He occasionally saw a car glide by but it was more likely he would see his friends from Number One come shooting round the corner on their bicycles.

'Nanny, can I have my bike out today?'

She smiled. 'All right.' Then she bent down and whispered, 'There's someone special coming to see you after tea, isn't there!'

For a moment his blue eyes were blank and then his whole face lit up. He flushed slightly and turned away. After a few moments he said, 'Can I have my bike now please?'

Later, as he and his older sister Isla tore round Lennox Gardens on their bicycles, he shouted louder than the rest and was more daring than usual in the games. But his heart beat a bit faster as he hugged that special knowledge to himself that someone was coming to see him. Someone who was not usually there. Someone who let him sit on his knee and play with the big gold watch and chain and slip it in and out of his waistcoat pockets. Someone whom Mamma said was in the navy and 'at sea'. Nicholas knew what it was like at sea because he and Isla and Mamma had been on a great big ship for days and days until they got to somewhere called China and he and Isla had had a ride on a rickshaw. He remembered that. But it all seemed hazy in his mind now. China and the Chinese men with pigtails that they rolled up quickly when a foreigner went past, and Chinese prisoners who wore masks at the carnival because Mamma said something called a prison was near their house.

'Come on!' called Isla. 'You're daydreaming! We're playing Red Indians behind those laurel bushes!'

Obediently he threw himself into the game, becoming louder and noisier than the rest. But always at the back of his mind was the thought that someone special would be waiting to see him after tea.

At last it was time to leave the gardens and Nanny Macintosh was telling them to get their things together. Isla trod on his foot by accident and he shouted back and reached out to pull her hair. But Nanny quelled him with one of her looks. So, tired and dirty, they trooped across the road, pushing the bicycles now, and were about to climb the steps when they heard a tinkling bell.

'Muffins!' cried Nanny. 'Wait a minute.' And she trotted off to the corner where the muffin man had pushed his cart.

Nicholas scratched the back of his leg with his other foot. He wished she would hurry up. Who wanted muffins anyway? Why couldn't they just rush inside and not bother with washing hands and get tea over quickly so he could come downstairs to the drawing-room for that special hour with Mamma, which was going to be so extra special today. He turned round and scowled at Isla.

But Nanny Macintosh was not to be hurried. First the

bicycles had to be put away. Then the coats. Then the climb up the four flights of stairs. Then hands washed. Then tea and toasted muffins to be eaten. He endured it all. Even though he could not tell the time he kept glancing up at the clock, like Nanny did sometimes.

All at once it was six o'clock and suddenly, for some unaccountable reason, he held back.

'Come on,' called Nanny. 'Isla will get there first if you don't hurry up.'

He trailed down the first long flight of stairs just in earshot of Isla and her excited chatter. Then he stopped. The whole staircase seemed to glow white in the sunlight that poured in through the window. The whole house seemed full of light and laughter and happiness, as if waiting for something. For someone. He looked quickly to the right and to the left and then darted across the landing to his parents' bedroom. He reached up and opened the door. Inside it was lighter and brighter and happier even than on the landing. The sun seemed to be bursting out all over the room. Hastily he tiptoed across and opened another door.

He stopped dead. Yes! There they were, as he knew somehow they must be, all black and shining and resplendent. He waited a few seconds and then crept across the carpet and reached out his hand. Quivering, his fingers touched the shining shoes. Usually they were not there and the dressing-room was empty. But today they *were* there. He hardly noticed all the suitcases and suits and uniforms hanging up. He only had eyes for the shoes. Suddenly he sat down and pulled off his own shoes. This was hard because the laces got stuck and by the time he had finished pulling and tugging they were in a real knot. But today he did not care. Eventually he threw the shoes down and, trembling with excitement, pulled the large shining shoes towards him.

At first he tried putting them on sitting down but that was no good because he could not stand up again. Then he stood up and put both his feet into the shoes and wriggled his toes. He tried walking but they were so big it was like paddling in the sea.

Suddenly a shout of laughter shot through the room.
He started and tried to turn round but the shoes stopped
him. It was Nanny of course, and behind her Mamma.

'Oh, that's where you are!' cried Nanny.

But it was Mamma he looked at and Mamma's eyes
that filled with laughter as she bent down to him.

'What are you doing?' she said. 'Your Dad's
downstairs in the drawing-room waiting for you. And
you are up here!' She smiled and helped Nanny untie
the knotted laces. Then her blue eyes looked straight at
him and her lovely brooch caught all the sunlight in the
room.

'My darling, funny little son,' she whispered and
ruffled his hair. 'Fancy you putting your Dad's shoes on
like that. You must have been trying to walk in his
footsteps.'

Once the shoes were off and tidied away and his own
shoes laced up again he followed his mother downstairs,
shy now and half hiding behind her skirt until the great
drawing-room door of the London house in the gracious
square called Lennox Gardens opened. And he heard
his father's voice and saw him standing on the rug. His
knees wobbled slightly as he crossed the carpet and he
tried to greet his father seriously as he had heard grown-
ups do. But then his father laughed and lifted him high
in the air and Mamma laughed and Isla laughed too,
the memory of the scowl quite forgotten. Everything
was wonderful again.

'And I'll be here for your fifth birthday this year,' said
his father. 'Would you like to go to the Royal
Tournament since you and King George V share the
same birthday?'

'Oh, yes!'

'And what's all this I hear about you trying my naval
shoes on, eh?'

Nicholas hid his face in his father's shoulder. And as
he did so his mother's words seemed to hang in the air:
walking in his father's footsteps.

2

War

In September 1941 another convoy of nine trans-
ports came through, with the loss of only one under a
very strong escort comprising the battleships *Prince of
Wales* and *Rodney*, the *Ark Royal*, five cruisers and
eighteen destroyers... Please convey my compli-
ments to the Admirals, all officers and men engaged
in the magnificent crash through of supplies to
Malta... which cannot fail to have an important
influence on the immediate future of the war in the
Mediterranean.

Winston S. Churchill
from *The Second World War*,
vols III, IV
(1951 Cassell plc.)

Nicholas woke up with a start. He sat up in bed, wide
awake, the noise of the air-raid siren wailing in the
room. All round the dormitory boys were pulling on
their jumpers, trousers and shoes. A master suddenly
appeared in the doorway.

'All set, boys. Quick march down to the basement and
then to the air-raid shelter. No running. No, don't
bother with ties.'

'Sir!'

'No, not now,' said the master. If he was weary he did
not show it.

Nicholas nearly tripped over in his excitement. He

knew there would be books and sweets in the shelter and really it was jolly good fun in an air raid.

Once down there the boys settled in their places. The Head stood up and said, 'I'm proud of you Lambrook boys. No panic and no pushing. Nice and sensible.' He permitted a hum of conversation to develop and Nicholas began talking to his friend, Tony.

'Do you think there's bombing near Slough tonight?'

'Yes! The aeroplanes seem to drop down a bit near here.'

'Is your father in the war, Tony?'

'Yes. In the army. Is yours?'

Nicholas's back went a little straighter. 'Oh, mine's in the navy. He's a captain.'

'Gosh,' said Tony, 'how exciting. Does he tell you all about sea battles and things?'

Nicholas thought about this for a while. He had to admit it. 'No, he doesn't say much. He's got medals though, from the First World War on the convoys to Russia. He's got a DSC.'

After a pause Tony said, 'I thought you came to this school before?'

'Yes. I did. For two years. Then my father went to New Zealand so we went too. And we were in Malta before that. With my father being in the navy we have to move around a lot.'

'Jolly exciting!'

Nicholas did not answer. He supposed it was, only moving about so much meant he had got behind in his school work and that was becoming more and more of a problem, especially as that important exam was coming up. He pushed this thought to the back of his mind and promptly forgot it.

'And that new boy in the first form, is he your brother?'

'Yes,' said Nicholas with pride. 'That's Miles. He's five years younger than me.'

It was funny though, he thought as the buzz of conversation gradually lulled, how being five years older meant he hardly used to notice Miles, until his parents had told him to look after him at school. And now he was really proud of his young brother. Nicholas yawned and his eyes began to close.

The all clear woke them up with a start. Nicholas and Tony forgot all about everything in the race to be first back in bed in the dormitory.

Later that term the same master called Nicholas out of his class one day. He cleared his throat. 'Er, look,' he said at last, 'Nicholas, I'm afraid I've got some bad news for you. You've not passed the entrance exam for Dartmouth.'

Nicholas stared at the master, unable to take it in at first. Not passed the entrance exam to Dartmouth?

The master said kindly, 'You can sit this term for the common entrance and try and get into public school.'

'But...'

'Go back to class now. We'll tell your parents. Don't worry. It'll be all right.'

Nicholas went back to the classroom in a daze. He sat quite still at the desk and appeared to be concentrating but his mind was a jousting of questions. What ever would his father say? His father had been to Dartmouth Naval College so obviously he had not failed the entrance exam. No, said another part of his mind, but he was very lonely there and used to watch the trains passing by and wish he was on them going home. And his mother died of consumption when he was twelve. Nicholas stared at his fountain pen. The drone of the lesson went on around him but he was unable to take it in. What on earth was he going to tell his parents and his classmates?

But when it came to it his classmates were not in the least bothered about his failure, just as long as he continued to play soccer and rugby for the school. And when the holidays came and he had to see his mother and father they did not seem to mind much either, or at least they did not make him feel as if they did.

His father said simply, 'What on earth does it matter!

We'll get you in somewhere else.'

His mother said, 'I don't mind if I've got a son who hates lessons but I do hope I've got a son who's good at games and who loves them.'

'Yes, I do,' cried Nicholas, jumping up. 'I'm in the cricket eleven next term!'

'Jolly good,' said his father. 'You must be taking after my father,' and then he lapsed into silence.

Nicholas looked up at him and his eyes shone brightly. He had heard all about the time in 1875 when his grandfather had bowled out the bearded and jovial cricketer W.G. Grace for a duck.

However the fact of not getting into Dartmouth was not allowed to become a bit thing in the family. His parents hardly ever mentioned it and it was only to Nicholas himself that it was still a big thing. Big, that was, until he heard that he had passed the common entrance for Marlborough public school.

When he wrote and told his mother the news she replied at once. 'You've done very well. We are very proud of you. Now we have got some news for you. I'm going to be staying on in London while your father takes command of HMS *Rodney*. Although he is going to miss us, he is really pleased as he has been longing to get back to sea.'

The shadow of the Second World War did not really touch Nicholas very much at Marlborough. Of course he knew it was serious. He and his brother and sister had to spend their holidays at their grandmother's in Scotland because of the bombing, and his parents came up to see them when they could.

One day the geography master pointed to Malta on the map and suddenly went very tight-lipped and said it was a jolly good thing Malta had not fallen because its strategic importance was inestimable. It kept the Eastern Mediterranean sea routes open, otherwise we would only be able to use the Cape route.

'Hitler wants Malta,' said the master gravely. His eyes seemed to bore straight into Nicholas. 'And some very brave and gallant men are sailing in the convoys to get supplies to the Maltese people.'

A slight cheer rippled round the classroom. Nicholas flushed and bent his head. He knew his father was the captain of HMS *Rodney*. But of course no one ever really talked about it at home. He had a sudden picture in his mind's eye of his father standing strong and alone on the captain's bridge. Smart in every detail, right down to the shining black naval shoes.

'Come on now,' said the master at his elbow. 'Let's get on.' His words were stern but when Nicholas glanced up at him his eyes were sad and kind all at the same time.

In the main, however, life at Marlborough was one long ache of struggling through lessons and waiting impatiently for the next session at games. Lessons often ended with him having to stand up and mumble that he did not understand the question. Could the master please repeat it. The form's laughter, tinged with a little malice and thankfulness that they *could* answer the question, always seemed to accompany Nicholas. But all that was forgotten during games. His friends and comrades clapped him on the back and only ever laughed with him then. He was the captain of his house rugby team. The McWhirter twins were also in the team and when one year their house won the inter-house rugger competition they were all thrilled. As well as rugby Nicholas did athletics, tennis, running and cycling. He loved running, the feeling of the ground pounding beneath his feet, the agony in his chest, the sweet knowledge of victory at the end, with the cheers echoing round the sports field.

In his last year he scraped through the General Certificate and the form's laughter was quieted for ever. One evening he and a friend called John decided to go to chapel, a voluntary privilege reserved for older boys. Nicholas much preferred these voluntary services as the whole atmosphere seemed different from the compulsory ones. This particular evening the service was much as usual, with God somewhere in the scheme of things, the benevolent schoolmaster who, if you did your bit and did not cheat and were loyal, would somehow keep in his omnipotent and gentlemanly place, well in the background.

Nicholas chuckled as they left and began walking back under the stars. 'It was quite good tonight. Better than those awful services we had to go to when I was younger!' He remembered the dour puritanical services when he was on holiday with the family at his grandmother's house in Scotland, the gloomy singing and the dreary building, the unending wait to escape into the fresh air.

'Do you believe in God?' asked John suddenly and unexpectedly.

Nicholas was surprised. He had never thought of questioning it. 'Yes, of course I do.'

That night in bed Nicholas remembered he had been half aware of a great dome of black sky above him spangled with stars, a myriad of lights, during the walk back to school. The sky's mystery and strange purpose seemed to beckon him, calling almost imperceptibly that life was full of wonder and God much, much more than a benevolent schoolmaster. He lay awake for a while and for the first time became aware of questions in his mind. How had all those stars come into being? Had they been created? Was God there? Who *was* God? He yawned and relaxed back into the pillows. No doubt he could think about it in the morning. But when morning came he had forgotten all about it.

In 1944 the Allied forces landed on the Normandy beaches. Nicholas's father had been involved with the planning of the invasion for a year and was appointed Rear-Admiral in charge of the beaches. He was loved and respected by his naval colleagues, and not least for his service on HMS *Rodney*.

The following year Nicholas left school and because the family had Scottish connections decided to join the Scots Guards. It was not exactly in his father's footsteps, but was certainly the next best thing.

3

The Army

I had never seen such fine acting before, but seeing it
and staying the weekend and meeting the Oliviers as
ordinary people made me think about my own role
as the traditional soldier: how when in full dress I was
no longer myself as an individual, but purely a
reminder to others of history and tradition; something the public wanted to see, something they liked
and which entertained them, but nothing real. It was
not me on parade but the uniform and all the pomp
and glory that went with it. I was not, like the
Laurence Oliviers, creating parts: I was just filling
them – and probably not all that well at that.
Perhaps this influenced me in my decision later to
leave the Army.

Richard Carr-Gomm
from *Push on the Door*
The Carr-Gomm Society, 1982

Nicholas began army life as a recruit at Hobbs Barracks
by the Lingfield racecourse. Because he was still under
eighteen he had to queue up for extra milk and put up
with great laughter from everyone and a chorus of
'Youngsters better go for their milk!' Then he went on to
officer training at what would once have been
Sandhurst but was now Aldershot because of the war.
He got a regular commission when he left and became a
captain in the Scots Guards.

Everything about army life suited him. He enjoyed
the comradeship, the close friendships, the adventure,

the team work, the discipline, the physical fitness required, the sense of belonging to something orderly and organised with everything in its place. He felt at home with the army's standards and the standards of the other officers. They were after all what had made Britain great, the standards of Empire and the upper classes. He never questioned them but accepted them whole-heartedly. He fitted into them as neatly as hand fits a glove, as a foot slides into a well-polished shoe.

'What do you want to do eventually?' his mother asked him one Saturday afternoon when they were relaxing with a glass of lemonade after a game of tennis. 'Do you want to stay in the army?'

'Oh, yes,' said Nicholas. 'It's a good life,' and he laughed. Except for exams though, said a little thought in his mind. He had always been weak at them and to stay for life in the army meant staff college exams had to be passed. 'Well anyway, perhaps I will and perhaps I won't. There's another five years before I need to decide. And there's Malaya in between.'

She stared at him bright-eyed and he now saw with a pang a few grey hairs in the brown curls. 'So now you are off to Malaya?' she said.

He grinned. 'Yes. Got to set the citizens of Malaya free from the Communist tyranny!'

'I'm very proud of you, darling. You'll do well, I know you will. I'm very proud of all my children.' She kissed him and he waved goodbye, the adventure of sailing to Malaya already filling his mind.

He never questioned the rightness of Great Britain fighting a guerrilla war in the Malayan swamps and jungles. He had grown up with such a loyalty to his country that it never occurred to him that it might be wrong. One took the view that England was right, almost like the kingdom of heaven really. The country was right about everything. So for fifteen months as platoon commander he led his men alone into the jungle. They were all professional soldiers, skilled, courageous and careful. They coped with the humid

climate, wild animals, snakes, insects and the rough
sleeping conditions. Some of them got killed. Once he
wrote home, 'The leeches are the worst. They really are
awful.' Then shyly, almost as an afterthought, 'I believe
I've been mentioned in dispatches'. He found great
satisfaction in leading his men, in the comradeship that
grew up between them and in the way he knew
instinctively that his men related to him and wanted to
follow his leadership.

At the end of the fifteen months they sailed home and
Nicholas was posted to Wellington Barracks opposite
Buckingham Palace. He found himself on the St James's
Palace rota when the soldiers took it in turns to do guard
duty at Buckingham Palace.

'It's not really a guard, Mum,' he told her when he
got home. 'It's more ceremonial. I've got to do the same
thing on the Windsor Castle rota as well.'

And she smiled back at him, trusting, accepting and
lovely as ever.

On coronation day in June 1953 Nicholas was
immaculate in his red and gold Scots Guards dress
uniform. He held his bearskin under his arm ready –
then they set off, uniforms glowing, ceremonial swords
swinging, heads held high, gold braid as rich as Empire
on their collars and cuffs. Five regiments of the Brigade
of Guards marched down the Mall that day: Grenadiers,
Coldstream, Scots, Irish and Welsh. There were miles of
processions and somewhere in among them marched
Nicholas at the head of his men. It was all so perfect and
so fitting, that traditional connection between the upper
classes, royalty and the services. He was proud to be part
of it. He was so proud, wasn't he? So very happy. He
underlined the words firmly to himself so that there was
no room for any doubt at all.

Later that evening and on many such evenings he and
his friends took off their uniforms and put on dark suits
ready for the fun to begin. The code of practice Nicholas
lived by said it was all right to get drunk and gamble and
see girls, just as long as you were not disloyal. Loyalty

meant everything. It was a strict code in its way and had its honourable side which was to bear fruit in his life. The pattern of the evenings was much the same. Plenty of drink flowing, too much in fact at the incessant drinks parties, and several girls joining in. Then they got into the car and drove off very fast, tearing over crossroads with all the horns down, and no thought for the consequences. Other people got caught perhaps, but never the crowd Nicholas had fun with. They liked being upper-class tearaways and he had no bad conscience over it.

In the racing season a party of them used to go to the races by car. They loved the Grand National, particularly the biggest jump, Becher's Brook. Many a horse and rider came a cropper there. But some went on to win. There was a simple philosophy behind it all. If you doubled up on the bets you could make enough money to pay for the day and drink champagne after the last race. Sometimes you did win enough. And sometimes you lost. One day Nicholas realised with a shock that he had gone through some thousands of pounds in gambling at the races and on the Stock Exchange. His little amount of capital was almost gone. But none of that worried his wealthy friends. Such things were common in their group. And if you were trying to escape into a pleasurable life, then why not? It was not so much the money that he longed for but the life of the wealthy set. And he was completely accepted into it, right bang in the centre of that rosy whisky-filled atmosphere.

One morning as Nicholas was driving his car he happened to switch on the radio. An American accent filled the air and, intrigued, he listened carefully, quite unable to switch off. The next day found him twiddling the knobs and checking his watch to make sure he did not miss hearing the American again. This happened several times. He discovered the American was called Billy Graham and that he was a famous preacher visiting London from the United States. He has really

got something, thought Nicholas by the end of the week.
I wish I could go and hear him. Even so he was surprised
to be given two tickets the same day to a private party
Billy Graham was attending in Wellington Barracks.
'Richard Carr-Gomm will be there,' said the officer who
handed him the invitation card. 'Why don't you come
along and bring a friend?'

'Oh,' said Nicholas. Richard Carr-Gomm, a major in
the Coldstream Guards, was a friend of his. 'Well,
thanks, I will.'

When the time came he went to the Officers' Mess,
ordered a glass of whisky from the waiter and began to
invite one friend after another. As he did so he became
aware that there were pauses among the comfortable
armchairs.

'No thanks.'

'Sorry, Nicholas.'

'Not today.'

'Sorry.'

'Sorry.'

'What on earth do you want to hear Billy Graham for!
Don't tell me you're getting religious!'

At last he gave up, sat down feeling increasingly
embarrassed and drained the whisky. If only someone
would come with him, it would be easy to go. But no one
would. And somehow he lacked the courage to go on his
own. Anything to do with Christianity had been firmly
left behind at school. The memory of the starry night at
Marlborough was almost forgotten. He had not thought
deeply about God since his schooldays. So now he was
left gazing into his empty whisky glass while a feeling of
blankness and disappointment crept up on him and an
uncomfortable truth nudged him in the spine. He had
not had the courage to stick his neck out. He had been
brave enough to go to Malaya but he did not want to be
different from his set of friends. He sighed and ordered
another whisky.

It seemed that in no time at all Nicholas's ten-year
stint in the army was drawing to a close. Although he

was a captain he had decided not to stay in the army. He was going to leave, as so many others did at that point, with the thousand pound gratuity and begin life as a ship-broker in the City. The tradition was to make enough money to have the same living standards as one's parents, live a good life, settle down, get married, have a family and serve the community.

And yet something was wrong. It was so faint, so small, smaller than a tiny cloud in a brilliant summer sky and quite as unnoticeable unless you looked for it. Something niggled at him and he found it difficult to put it into words. He was not a failure, he knew that. Despite the loss of the Dartmouth place he knew his parents were pleased with him. He had followed as best he could in his father's footsteps, done and said and thought everything that was required of him. Perhaps that was the trouble. His whole life had been measured in terms of discipline and orders and doing what was expected of him. Army life had followed on so neatly from Marlborough that it was almost like an extension of the same thing. There had always been a goal to strive for, another rung up the ladder to reach for. And now, suddenly in the City office, life was not like that any more.

A thought startling in its originality and clarity, began to grow in him. It said that perhaps he was not cut out for such a stereotyped life after all. That had been all right in his immature young man's days. But perhaps, now he was twenty-seven, the real Nicholas was beginning to emerge; a person with different gifts that were not being tapped. He sighed and stared into the middle distance at his City desk. The top was littered with papers covered in figures. The phone was ringing again. He answered it mechanically, still half in a daydream. What am I doing all this for, he wondered, as he gazed out of the window. Was he going to spend the rest of his life putting oil tanker owners in touch with oil company producers and hoping to make a decent commission out of it? Was that all there was to life? All there was going to be to *his* life? No, he thought suddenly and quite vehemently. Life MUST be more than that!

As he made his way home that evening to the flat he shared with his sister Isla and to the lovely welcome and glass of sherry she often gave him, he had a moment of insight. The truth was that he was not much good at being a ship-broker. And he did not enjoy it much. If he stayed on he would either be a failure or at best inadequate. If that was the case then he would have to do something else. But what could he do? He frowned. He simply did not know. He had spent nearly thirty years as a loyal son of the Establishment, doggedly following in its pattern and footsteps. Now he wanted something else: if only he could work out what it was.

When he mentioned this to his parents they were as supportive as ever and seemed to think his idea of taking six months off to think things through, and to read and write, was a good one. Then even this had to be postponed because the Suez crisis erupted. British and French troops had invaded Egypt and their aeroplanes bombed Cairo, in an attempt to regain control of the Suez Canal which had been nationalised by the Egyptian government. Nicholas was called up as a reservist, promoted a major and ordered to get his group of men into good heart and discipline, ready for action if necessary. He enjoyed it so much that he wondered briefly if he should have left the army. He had been so deeply rooted there. His men, at first disgruntled at being called up from their new civilian jobs, left his care a happy group. Major Nicholas Rivett-Carnac had been good for them.

The Suez crisis blew over, the battalions were disbanded and Sir Anthony Eden resigned. Nicholas, out of the army, decided not to go back to the City. Instead he made up his mind to go to Spain and wait for inspiration on how to run his life and what to do next. He was looking forward to it and to reading and writing thrillers. And if nothing worked out he knew he could still come back to the City.

If he had but known it, this was to be the beginning of the conflict.

4

The Great Divide

St Francis of Assisi was the son of a rich cloth
merchant. He loved life and pleasure and was the
leader of all the young men in the town. In 1202 he
became a soldier, fighting in the wars between the
City States and was taken prisoner for a year.
Afterwards he tried to become a knight and take part
in further battles, but at Spoleto he had a vision or a
dream telling him to return home and wait for a call
to a new kind of knighthood.

> After *Encyclopaedia Britannica*
> and Julien Green, *God's Fool*
> (Hodder & Stoughton, 1986)

By the time Nicholas disembarked from the boat to
Spain he felt as if all his limbs were gradually uncurling
and relaxing from the cramped discipline of ten years of
army life. He stretched and yawned in the small hotel
room he had rented and his hands reached for yet
another book to read.

He had told his friends before coming away that he
was going to try his hand at writing thrillers. But
somehow the novels in the Ian Fleming style never quite
got off the ground, their chapters never quite reached
double figures. His manuscripts slowly disappeared
under a pile of anything and everything to read.

It was strange after so many years of being extrovert
and gregarious, conforming to his class group, to find

himself on his own. Strange but satisfying. It was as if the surface of things was being peeled back and he could not get enough of contemplating the depths beneath.

For the umpteenth time he read further into Bertrand Russell's *History of Western Philosophy*. He did not understand it all but found he could not put it down. Russell's section on the history of the Church fascinated him. Nicholas kept on thinking, this man calls himself an atheist and says that life has no meaning, but if the history of the Church is as important as seen through his cynical eyes, then there must be something in it.

He finally put the book down and stared unseeingly at the wall. The small thing that he had discerned as being wrong before, as small as a tiny cloud, was now filling his whole horizon. If only he could find the meaning. What did his life *mean* now he saw it as so much more than an Establishment pattern? With these thoughts came a darkness, a confusion, that settled on his back and made him hang his head slightly.

After a moment his back straightened. He shook his head as if to clear it. Of course he believed in God. He had been brought up to believe, without it being put into so many words, that God was the head of the Established way of doing things. God might be remote and possibly irrelevant, but none the less he was the necessary head of all things. Nicholas sighed deeply. That much at least he could accept from his parents' example. Then as he strode restlessly up and down the room, the question of meaning came shooting back. What was the meaning of life for *him*? That was what he had to find out.

One morning he awoke at first light and lay for a moment or two trying to gather his senses. Before he had come to properly his body suddenly felt weightless and a marvellous peace and joy rolled all over him. For a couple of minutes he lay perfectly still in this state. And while one part of him knew that God, the almighty and ineffable, was in this mystery, the other part relaxed totally into the hundred per cent feeling of physical, mental, emotional and spiritual wholeness. He sparkled with joy. He recognised instinctively that this was a foretaste of some future joy and that from somewhere deep in his unconscious mind he was responding to something. No, to someone. Then the joy faded.

In no time, it seemed, he was back at home, and searching to come into that intimacy of God's presence again as he had done in Spain. And yet if his heart was settled his mind was not. For he found himself still questioning the meaning of life and longing to find some answers. If his parents were concerned they did not show it but still loved and accepted the new Nicholas as they had the old. The only trouble was he did not feel new inside, only very bewildered.

One day, without really thinking too much about it, he went to see a test match at Lords. While hovering about in the refreshment room a hand clamped down on to his shoulder. Startled, he spun round.

'Hello there!'

'It's Richard Carr-Gomm!' said Nicholas. 'Hello.'

Richard laughed. 'Yes! The last time I saw you was in the Officers' Mess at Wellington Barracks. I heard you had left. What are you doing now?'

It passed through Nicholas's mind in a flash that Richard Carr-Gomm was the officer who had had the Billy Graham party to which he had not plucked up the courage to go.

'Well, I'm not sure. Actually, I've left the City.'

Richard raised his eyebrows. 'Left all that!'

'Yes. I'm trying to write thrillers!' Richard ran his hand through his hair. For a second his eyes seemed to try and read what lay behind Nicholas's words. Then his face relaxed and his brown eyes suddenly twinkled. 'I bet you don't know what I'm doing!'

'No?'

'I'm scrubbing floors in Bermondsey!'

Nicholas stared in frank surprise.

'I'm a home help. Unpaid! A scrubbing major!'

'What?'

'Yes. Really. Look, I live in Bermondsey now. You know my family owned property there for years and it got rather run down, and I, well, I'm trying to help some of the pensioners. There's over twelve thousand of them. Mostly poor. Nearly all lonely. Why don't you come and visit me and see. In fact you could come next week. It'll be good background for your books.'

Nicholas felt delighted with this invitation. 'I'll come tomorrow, if that's all right,' he said.

And so it was arranged.

Richard said as they parted, 'It's quite liberating coming south over the Thames, you know. You leave all that false nightclub, Knightsbridge life behind. You can forget all that pall of sophistication and that veneer. You come into a real community. Real warmth there. Bermondsey people are caught up in the straight-forward human struggle to survive.'

Nicholas's face flushed slightly. 'I'd like to come,' he said, 'so much.'

'Don't get too many rosy ideas,' called Richard behind him. 'I visited New Scotland Yard once and saw a map on the wall. It was covered with flags, each one representing a crime that had been committed. When I asked why Bermondsey was almost clear they chuckled and said, "Oh, all the criminals come from there. They leave home and go elsewhere to commit crime!"'

But Nicholas hardly heard him.

So it was that he went to visit Richard in Lady Gomm House in Bermondsey and was introduced to the warden of Bede House, a Christian settlement that was run there. Nicholas was interested in the work and the warden liked him. Eventually he was given a room at Bede House for nine months. In return he helped with the general work, leading prayers and running the many clubs: for teenagers, for dockers, for the unemployed and for pensioners. Over the weeks he got to know Stella Masterman the bursar, and Dorothy Furness the warden, quite well. He liked and respected them both.

Stella said, 'You know, I've been in Bermondsey forty years! It seems incredible. Of course when I first came things weren't at all as they are now. There was no park and none of those red-brick flats.'

Nicholas said, 'What was it like here in those days?'

She sighed. 'The living conditions were awful. They were cramped and appalling. Some of the worst slums in London were in Bermondsey. It was quite common then for people to live with rats in the rooms.'

'Rats!' Nicholas felt he could not have heard properly. 'Rats! But ...'

'Well, all that's gone now, thank goodness. The Bermondsey reformers did a good job between the wars. But I remember the General Strike. Those were grim days.'

'You mean families lived in rooms with rats?'

She nodded.

He stared at her. Unbidden the memory came to him of Number Five Lennox Gardens: it's gracious proportions, well-ordered rooms, beautiful meals. He remembered so vividly the pleasantness of it all, the rightness of growing up there. But if what Stella said was true, and it *must* be true, while he lived the life of luxury there, other little boys not five miles away lived with rats. It was unbelievable.

Stella said, 'When I was a child my parents had a gardener who always used to say, "I dread having to end my days in the workhouse." One day he collapsed in the garden. He was unable to go on working and was taken to one of those grim Victorian workhouses. He died there. This made such an impression on me that I decided there and then to spend my life doing anything I could to try and help people like him.'

Nicholas stared at her. Even though she was seventy her face was serene and beautiful. He suddenly realised what this work at Bede House meant to her and that indeed she had given her whole life to helping others.

She said, 'Of course things are better now. But older people who were children before the First World War remember running around with no shoes on. In fact some of them remember it as recently as the thirties.'

Nicholas went to his room that evening with his head in a whirl. He tossed and turned into the small hours but sleep would not come. At last he sat up in bed and stared into the darkness of his room. The unfairness of the class system gripped him and he became aware that his hands were tightly clenched beneath the sheets. His whole childhood and early life seemed to pass before his eyes. His great-great-grandfather had been the first chairman of the East India Company and the Governor of Bombay and had been created a baronet. The title passed from one generation to the next. One day he himself would inherit it. It was said that Rudyard Kipling had made the point that the Rivett-Carnacs were one of the four most important British families in India: if there was a loaf of bread to divide between four British families out there then one would be the Rivett-Carnacs. His mother's father had been at Harrow and was a wealthy landowner. His father's father had married a Miss Crabbe, the granddaughter of the poet Crabbe. Whichever way he looked at the family it was illustrious, brought up to serve its country by leading and being loyal. The power and weight of it all was so much that his head fell forward slightly on his breast. He found himself crying out to God to show him the way through. His mind shot back to Richard Carr-Gomm and his work with the elderly in Bermondsey; *he* seemed to have found a way through.

There was to be no answer for him that night however, and with a sigh of something like despair Nicholas flung himself down again in the bed and tried to go to sleep.

Next morning he decided he would start going to church. And later, in answer to his request, Richard recommended the nearby City Temple at Holborn. The following Sunday Nicholas went along and began listening to the preaching of Dr Leslie Weatherhead. As he listened he felt this preacher knew about the love of

God and could communicate it.

'After the service go out and walk under the stars and give your life to God,' cried the preacher.

Nicholas nodded to himself. As soon as he could he wandered across the park and gazed up at the night sky. I'll volunteer for active service, er, God, he thought. I'll give my life to God. I'll become ordained.

For a time this new purpose and resolve filled him with excitement and joy. It was like a light shining brightly and beckoning to him. But as the weeks went by the old darkness came back and with it his sense of confusion. What had seemed so clear to him after hearing Dr Weatherhead preach was now less real, as if the light had been covered by thick clouds.

Eventually he talked to a friendly clergyman about his feelings. This man listened closely and then gave him some advice. His eyes were kind but his words were adamant. 'You don't know enough about the church, nor about your call yet. Become a church member. And get some more experience of helping people. In fact, why don't you think about becoming a probation officer?'

Nicholas suddenly looked up. Why, yes! That was a good idea.

He was beginning to meet some of the dockers who lived in Bermondsey, and even some of the local Teddy boys who roamed around in gangs. Somehow it agonised him to imagine their lives, the poverty of their opportunity, the lack of almost everything that made life worth living. He had read accounts of people coming back from the war looking for a sense of purpose, but somehow they did not find one. So many of these people had been bombed out during the war, or fought overseas and come home either to unemployment or to repetitive work. He so desperately wanted them to have a sense of purpose – but he knew in his heart of hearts that he did not really have one himself.

He could not get rid of the knowledge of the contrast between the two groups of people who lived so close by, simply separated by the Thames. North lay the upper-class patch, until recently a patch he was totally at home in. And here, south of the river, was squalor and pain. As he walked and walked in every spare moment he had, he tried to assimilate the fact that the world he had known, loved and accepted was not the only world in Britain. In truth it was only a tiny part of the country's life. He buried his head in his hands one night by his bed. Everything within him seemed dark and full of perplexity. All his former life no longer seemed real, but an illusion, a passing grandeur. He had been brought up to serve others and there was a rightness in that. But, as he felt now, it had not gone far enough. He lifted his head and stared at his hands. As far as his parents had been able they had worked tirelessly and searched for goodness. He had been well brought up, he knew that. No one could have done more for him, nor given him more, than his parents had done.

As the days passed the agony of mind he was in grew no less. I was brought up, he thought, to live an honourable life, and to be loyal and to do my duty; and to have fun and smart clothes and status; to go to parties and be wealthy. While people here lived with rats. He had been in a golden group but it all seemed tarnished, mere gilding now. He had been taught about honesty, honour, loyalty, service and concern for others. But somehow the service and concern had not stretched far enough. It had excluded more than half the nation.

Stella pointed out to him that those awful living conditions no longer applied and that the dockers at least had plenty of money in their pay packets.

'But they don't know how to spend it,' he cried. 'Except on drink and gambling.' Just exactly like you did until recently, said an insistent thought at the back of his mind. But he hurried on, 'There's no one to tell them how to live a satisfying life. The church,' he flung his arms wide, 'seems at best totally irrelevant! It doesn't reach the people. It doesn't speak their language! Everything is so frustrating! Nothing seems to bridge the

gap for these people. It's all so, so unequal! If only...'
words failed him. The vast sea of human need, misery
and ignorance overwhelmed him. Everything seemed
hopeless.

He began to visit the Turner family regularly. The
father had been gassed in the First World War. The
mother was an invalid and spent all her days in an
armchair. One son was an epileptic and had violent fits.
Their daughter was brain-damaged. The other son was
brain-damaged too, but not so badly and was able to
play table tennis with Nicholas. Somehow the family
struggled on. There were so many sad cases, so many sad
people he had dealings with. And without realising it he
picked up the darkness and oppression and resentment
of the area. This weighed on his spirits and made him
feel guilty.

He carried on at Bede House for the full nine months
and worked hard, while the torrent of questions within
him grew to storm force. He no longer felt able to join his
old friends in what he now considered the unreality of
their lives. He had a growing awareness of the easy and
unconscious selfishness of the group he had been part of
until recently, so he cut himself off from them, buried
himself in his room or went to the park and tried to talk
to the gangs. Sometimes he wandered into pubs and
attempted to reach the gang leaders, trying to make
himself heard above the incessant noise of rock and roll
music. They listened. But nothing changed. It was the
blind leading the blind. For even with them he did not
feel as if he belonged. Their world was so different from
the disciplined life he had led in the army. In those days
things had been done according to the 'rules'. It had at
least been a fair fight. Here it was frightening. There
were no rules, simply youngsters running around with
broken bottles and people being terrified. He felt as if he
were on a journey through darkness, having left a false
light behind but with nothing to guide him now and no
beacon at the end of the road.

The worst agony was when he went home to see the

parents he loved. And they loved him. How could he
explain that he felt they were all victims of the class
situation, the terrible gap in British society, the
inequality, the divided kingdom? What could he say to
them in the gracious surroundings of Fornham House
where they now lived, and the lovely gardens? It was like
a great divide. How could he say anything when they
had done so much for him? So he became tongue-tied
and withdrawn. He knew he was hurting them and felt
even worse because of it.

His mother always ran out to meet him when he came
home, and welcomed him. She tried to draw him out,
listening when he spoke haltingly of his feelings, talking
to put him at his ease as they sat in the drawing-room.
She pushed away the historical novels and the
biographies she loved so much, and made him the centre
of her attention. Yet Nicholas knew he was retreating,
putting up a barrier. He hung his head and said
nothing.

Suddenly she said, 'I have a feeling, you know, that
some of your suffering is because of your background,
because of me. I hope that is not so.'

No, no, his whole being cried out, as he stiffly shook
his head. But the more he wanted to jump up and
reassure her the less he was able to do so.

She said, 'You only have to read Dickens to get a
picture of life in those slums.'

Charles Dickens? Nicholas thought with guilt of the
serious reading he might have done and the time he had
wasted on hundreds of thrillers.

'Dickens wrote about Bermondsey,' she said. 'I
believe the warehouses where Bill Sikes was finally
hounded down were on Jacob's Island there.'

But don't you see, he cried out silently, that is just the
point. Dickens wrote about it and not many of our class
did very much about it.

Instead he said, 'Yes, Mum.'

She sensed his anger and depression. 'Let's join Dad
for a glass of sherry,' she said at last.

He nodded. And if she was upset because the elder son of the house, who had followed so faithfully in his father's footsteps and was always at the centre of a group of young and smiling men in the photos in her album, was now so painfully alone and solitary, she did not show it.

But for once the afternoon ended more happily. He told his parents about Richard Carr-Gomm.

'Do you know what he told me last week, Mum? Apparently his grandfather was the chairman of the London Hospital Board at the end of Queen Victoria's reign. And he helped to befriend a young man who was so physically handicapped that he had been exhibited at fairs. Treated like an animal, only worse.'

'Really,' she said. 'Oh, do tell me more.'

'Well, this young man was quite intelligent and a lot of famous people began to visit him. He was known as the Elephant Man.'

So over the glass of sherry they chatted amicably, his darkness forgotten for a while.

Later though, as Nicholas made his way back to Bede House, he thought about the Elephant Man, a human being with all the sensibilities, frailties and subtleties everyone has. He thought about the down-at-heel Bermondsey mothers with lank greasy hair and dirty prams, and the drunken men being sick. They were all human beings made in God's image. And somehow, somehow he was going to try and atone for his previous failure to understand. He was going to find a way in which he could help. He would go into the probation service. And then, after some experience, he would become ordained. His pace quickened and by the time he got back to Bede House he was almost running.

5

Holy Trinity, Rotherhithe

One day at home St Francis went to the ruined chapel at San Damiano where, mysteriously, he seemed to hear the crucifix speak to him. 'Go, Francis, and repair my house.' He took the command literally, sold his father's cloth and horse without permission, attempting to raise money for the chapel repairs. His father was very angry and eventually brought him before the bishop. Francis stripped himself of all his clothes down to a hair shirt. He handed them back to his father and said, 'Until now I have called you my father on earth. But henceforth I can truly say: our Father who art in heaven...'

The early Franciscan rule of life, which has not survived, set as the aim of the new life: 'To follow the teachings of our Lord Jesus Christ and to walk in his footsteps.'

After *Encyclopaedia Britannica*
and Julien Green, *God's Fool*
(Hodder & Stoughton, 1986)

One morning as Nicholas was nearing the end of his time at Bede House he was tidying up his room. In a drawer he found a photograph of his father in naval white dress uniform complete with medals and white shoes. He gazed at it for some minutes. But he had got used to hiding his feelings, bottling up his sensitivity in the stiff-upper-lip army tradition, so now not a muscle in

his face moved. He took out other photographs and
looked at them for some time. He saw his mother and
sister and brother smiling in shiny black and white.
With sudden insight he knew just how much his family
meant to him. Then he put the photographs away
carefully, making sure none of the edges was creased. He
straightened his back and stood tall, almost to attention,
in the quietness of that room. He had quite made up his
mind. He was determined to stick to his inner vision,
cloudy and confused though it was for most of the time.
He now knew he found the class system intolerable.
Despite the suffering of loneliness he was going through
and not knowing where this journey would lead him, he
was rock sure. He would never in any way, through his
own actions, allow the divided kingdom to perpetuate
itself in his life. It meant he would never marry. Never
have any children to inherit the title – and the conflict.
He knew now that it was impossible for him as a
Christian to remain in that wealthy environment. For
Jesus had preached his gospel to the poor. He felt
haunted by the stories of the rich young ruler and of
Dives and Lazarus. What, he asked himself, did he have
to do to be saved? Words he had read in the parables
troubled him too: about outer darkness and wailing and
gnashing of teeth. Somehow he felt he had to find out the
truth and discover a rock upon which to place his feet.
Even though he did not really feel he knew God and
hardly felt worthy of the name of a Christian and did not
really understand the way he was taking, yet he was
determined not to retrace his footsteps. He half guessed
he was in a waking trauma, a nightmare, a permanent
shock. His confidence in himself, his achievements, his
place among the rulers of society, was broken.

At the time Nicholas did not realise the decision he
was making sprang from the very best tradition of his
background. The virtues of loyalty and honesty, so
much part of his particular Establishment-upbringing,
sprang from Christian roots of long ago. Brought up
always to tell the truth, he was now trying to follow the

real truth. It was not so much a case of abandoning his father's footsteps, as he genuinely thought, but of finding the heavenly Father's footsteps, the only true, real and worthwhile footsteps anybody can ever want to follow.

As the years rolled by a different Nicholas began to emerge, like a moth from a chrysalis. He joined the probation service, completed his training and did six months at Marylebone Magistrates Court. That was followed by eighteen months at the North London Juvenile Court. He had a high success rate with his clients and it struck him that this was more due to prayer than the careful questioning and listening techniques he had been taught, useful as these were. Over the months a thought grew in him, gradually becoming more and more insistent. 'The most important and worthwhile thing you can do,' it said, 'is to learn to pray and to teach others to pray.' So he went to Westcott House, an Anglican Theological College in Cambridge, where he trained to become a clergyman.

Yet still he did not feel entirely free of the old pain, darkness and bewilderment that weighed on him. Sometimes it was less than others, but it was always there. Perhaps, he thought, it was part of the oppression and pain of the world God was allowing him to feel, so that he would never forget how most people had to get through life. One or two friends even said to him, 'You're getting a bit of a stoop! Straighten your shoulders, man!' Which he did – until pressing worries made him forget again.

In many ways his two years at Westcott House, Cambridge were a disappointment. The lectures were more academic than devotional and he left without really learning how to pray better or having grasped properly what was the foundation, the rock, upon which lives should be built. However he made some good friendships and came to love and respect the principal, Peter Walker. In the holidays when Nicholas stayed with his parents at Fornham House and farm near Bury

St Edmunds, Peter used to visit them there.

Nicholas's father had retired from the navy after his appointment in Australia as Vice-Admiral of administration and was now able to enjoy country life. Nicholas leaned idly over the fence and watched the cows. How many times his father had looked forward to seeing some Jersey cows beyond the fence of his garden as he spent so many long hours on the bridge of his ship. They must have been long lonely nights watching for the enemy, protecting his country. What must he think of his son in his calling as a clergyman, he wondered? He sensed that although his father went out of his way to encourage him he was worried about it. Nicholas guessed that his worry was due to his own childhood: unhappy winter days spent in cold, damp Victorian vicarages with little money to make life inviting or comfortable. His father's mother had died when he was a boy and his clergyman father had been a slightly remote figure, communicating more of the severity of the gospels than the warmth, generosity and joy of Christ. Nicholas's mother said his father had accepted his calling. But all the same as Nicholas hung on into the evening and watched the light fading over the fields, he wondered very much.

When the time came for him to choose his first curacy it seemed the place chose itself for him. Rotherhithe was the next-door parish to Bermondsey, and an area of dockland much bombed during the war. The church, Holy Trinity, had been rebuilt afterwards and the vicarage garden was the only bit of greenery for miles around. Nicholas had attended the church while he was doing his two years in the probation service and helped to run the youth club. So now when Father Batty, the vicar, invited him to become his curate he accepted happily.

He watched Father Batty carefully and tried to learn from him. He was an elderly unmarried man and the local people knew and loved the black-cassocked figure as he strode round the parish. He visited constantly, particularly in the hospital. He opened the vicarage gardens for the children to come in and play whenever they wanted to.

'It's like a community church, almost village-like, only in the heart of dockland!' Nicholas explained to his mother one day. 'And I'm now known as Father Batty's friend!'

Once at a clergy training session the instructor rubbed his eyes wearily and said, 'None of us in the Church of England can find the link with the people. It's so difficult to get that link with the local people and get a good relationship with them. The Church has really lost touch with them since the industrial revolution.'

'But,' said Nicholas quickly, 'I think Father Batty's already doing it.'

Then Nicholas's parents gave him a car and he and Father Batty shared in the running expenses. They decided to pick up anyone they could at the local bus stop and in this way many a conversation opened about spiritual things. But after a while Nicholas found himself becoming worried and frustrated. The numbers coming to church never exceeded fifty, despite all Father Batty's love and friendship. Somehow he knew the message was not getting across to the several thousands in the parish. And he did not understand the how and the why of making it happen.

Then one day a large envelope arrived for him. When he opened it he discovered it was from the Billy Graham organisation, inviting clergy to become involved with another crusade. Enclosed was a book by Jim Packer, *Fundamentalism and the Word of God* (Eerdmans Publishing Co., 1958). This book was to open up the Bible to Nicholas in an exciting way. As he read he began to realise that here was the anchor, the rock, that he had been searching for.

Another book sent to Nicholas was *The Cross and the Switchblade* by David Wilkerson (Lakeland Publishers, 1964), and he could not put it down. As he read the stirring story of how drug addicts were being helped in New York by a young pastor called David Wilkerson, he felt for the first time that this ministry being described was what he had been searching for. He asked around if there was anything similar happening in this country and was told, yes, there is Vic Ramsey who is doing it in Orange Street, between Trafalgar Square and Leicester Square. So, often after Sunday evening services, he went up there and found himself in a basement room full of smoke and people taking drugs. One Sunday a lady was giving a brief talk. Nicholas watched her.

'You boys,' she was saying, 'you won't change your lives. You won't change. Your lives are going to destruction.'

As her words rang out her voice cracked. Her face broke into weeping. Nicholas stared. He had never seen anyone crying like this, weeping unashamedly out of love for drug addicts. And his heart was strangely warmed.

But this love was even more fully expressed when Vic stood up to preach the gospel. His preaching had a boldness and simplicity and power that Nicholas had not experienced before.

'For God so loved the world,' cried Vic, 'that he gave his one and only Son, that whoever believes in him shall not perish but have eternal life. For God did not send his Son into the world to condemn the world, but to save the world through him' (John 3:16–17 NIV).

'It's like this,' he said. 'It's an ABC: (A) Accept that you need to be forgiven and saved. (B) Believe that Jesus loves you personally and died on the cross for you so that you may be forgiven and saved from the power, guilt and punishment of sin, and brought into fellowship with God. (C) Choose to invite him to come into your heart as Saviour and Lord.'

Then Vic gave his appeal to come forward. Without hesitation Nicholas sprang towards him. Everything raced through his mind at once. All the time in Spain, at Bede House, in the probation service, at Westcott House and now at Rotherhithe, even at his confirmation as a boy, all his searching seemed to culminate at this point.

He was thrilled to go forward, thrilled to be identified with fellow sinners and drop-outs and drug addicts. At Westcott House the principal had told him that the sense of purpose and divine guidance would come to him when he made his confession. But it had not. It was as if everything was leading him to this point in a smoky basement. It felt as if he had been on a journey all his life and now he had reached his destination. The transcendent God whose love had been drawing him for so long had now slipped inside him. For Nicholas had made the choice and promise after Vic's words. He was born again.

Afterwards he and Vic became friends and he really committed himself to helping out regularly with the drug addicts. Now he had a quiet peace and a sense of drawing close to Jesus. But still, he felt, there must be something more. Had not George Bennett talked about the Holy Spirit when he came and gave that lecture at Westcott House about the healing Christ? Nicholas was plunged into thought again. Somehow he would find out more.

At first he wondered if he should join the order of Anglo-Catholic monks known as the Community of the Glorious Ascension. He knew deep down that the reason was because he had been so caught up in the class strife that he felt he needed to commit himself to being a bachelor. The monks lived very simply and he was drawn to the life. However in the end it was Father Batty who joined them and not Nicholas! But he had kept in touch with George Bennett, who was the warden of the Home of Healing at Crowhurst, and went there to visit him occasionally, to drink in the atmosphere and watch George as he ministered healing and the Holy Spirit to searching people.

It was during this time of greater peace but continuous searching that Nicholas met a man called David Green. His shock of ginger hair stood out even in the murky atmosphere of night-time London. But David often became violent and abusive and had no home. It fell to Nicholas on many occasions to try and get him into a hostel for the night. Very often the phone rang the next morning: the hostel was very sorry but as David had stolen something or been disruptive, they were going to have to ask Nicholas to take him somewhere else. Chucked out again, thought Nicholas in desperation one day. Where on earth could he take him now? There simply was nowhere. Then he remembered Vic had a hostel in Bromley and when he rang, Vic agreed to take David in. Next morning the phone rang as Nicholas had been sure it would.

'Look,' said the tired voice of Vic at the other end, 'I'm sorry but I'm at the end of my tether. I've got to get away on holiday and we just can't cope with David being here while I'm away. I've only got a few young helpers and I don't think they could deal with him at all. It wouldn't be right.'

Nicholas thought quickly. There was no doubt that Vic needed a rest. 'If I come and stay with David, would that do?'

'Well, yes, that would be fine, but . . .'

'I'm on holiday from today, you see, Vic, and I don't need to go to the conference I'd booked myself into. I'll come and stay at Bromley instead.'

'Oh, that would be fine. Solve all the problems.'

So Nicholas went to the hostel in Bromley and when he arrived David was waiting for him in the hall. As the two of them stood awkwardly together a young woman helper strode up. She stopped dead, stared at David and said clearly, 'You're involved with black magic, aren't you!'

David immediately went still. His eyes nearly popped out of his head. He said, 'How did you know that?'

'Well, I just had this discernment about you.'

Nicholas watched the two of them, deeply fascinated. He had never come across this kind of thing before and it impressed him.

Then she said to David, 'Look, are you willing to be delivered?'

'OK,' said David very quickly.

Does he really mean it, thought Nicholas, but he did not say anything.

The young woman turned to him and said, 'You're the clergyman. You lead us in prayer!'

Nicholas was taken aback, but said yes all the same. They went to a side room and he went through the motions of casting out the devil from David in the name of Jesus. Nothing happened. The room was deadly quiet. Nicholas hung his head and stared at his useless hands. What was it all about? Here he was, a clergyman, meant to have the power and authority to cast out demons – and he could do nothing.

Then he made a decision. He stood up and said to the young woman, 'Look, you carry on. I'm going to go upstairs and pray until I do receive the power of the Holy Spirit.' And as he climbed the austere stairs he made up his mind. He was not going to leave the hostel until he had met God in a new way.

Somehow three or four days of his cancelled holiday went by. He took part in the activities of the hostel, moved furniture and helped generally. But when it came to mealtimes he could not eat. Nor did he drink. It was as if he were caught up in a supernatural desire to meet the Lord and be given that power and authority to do the work he felt called to do. Days seemed to pass as he prayed. It was an experience that had never happened to him before and, with a flash of insight, he knew it would possibly never happen again. There was no sense of wrestling with God, simply the longing to meet him and be filled with the Spirit, to be equipped to minister for him. He knew it was amazing as the days went by, and as the more or less sleepless nights passed too. He was completely taken up with his asking. Then, quite quietly, he knew it was time to go downstairs again and meet the others.

'Will you pray for me?' he asked simply and they smiled and said yes and laid hands on him and prayed.

It was all over in a few moments but Nicholas felt as if

something had burst within him, a torrent of feelings and longings all poured out in that one, single-syllabled cry in another tongue. For over an hour he cried out in this way. All his stiff-upper-lip reserve melted in the joy and peace that flooded through him. It was like coming home, like the end of a long journey.

When Vic came back the next day he took a long look at him and said, 'You're on fire!'

And Nicholas knew he really was. The long search was over. The confusion, darkness, doubt and despair were put to flight. Again they prayed for David and he seemed to come through and be set free. But again Nicholas had the same slight feeling of unease about him.

Ever since then Nicholas has been involved in the healing ministry. From those several days in Bromley he made a commitment both to healing and to helping the ex-prisoner, the drug addict and the drop-out. But David did not stick to his new-found freedom and ended up in prison. Nicholas still tried to help him from time to time, but he never seemed to turn fully to Christ.

Shortly after this Nicholas received further prayer and was released into praying fluently in tongues. Then George Bennett invited him to come and preach at one of the services at Holy Trinity, Brompton, where he was leading a divine healing mission. 'Then you can meet Pat Gilliat the vicar there,' he said.

Part II

Your Kingdom Come

The Lord loves the poor. And the rich. But you don't usually find this concept in books about the class struggle: they often seem to have paragraphs about the hatred or distrust between one side or other of the great divide.

Here it is different. For the Lord's is a different kingdom.

He loves the down-and-outs. And the up-and-outs!

Jenny Cooke
Diary

6

Holy Trinity Church, Brompton

St Francis' deep sense of brotherhood under God
embraced his fellow-men for, 'he considered himself
no friend of Christ if he did not cherish those for
whom Christ died'.

Encyclopaedia Britannica

Nicholas stood in the nave of Holy Trinity, Brompton.
He felt still and stilled, throughout his whole being.
Then a door banged and a great laugh rolled around the
dark and heavy pews. It was Pat Gilliat the vicar
striding towards him, his black cloak flung wide as he
clapped Nicholas on the back.

'Lovely sermon you gave at the Divine Healing
Mission service. I'm so glad George Bennett invited
you.'

Nicholas smiled and bowed his head. Somehow he
and the genial, big-hearted Pat got on so well, as if they
had known each other all their lives.

'You know,' said Pat, 'George and I have been talking
and, well, we were wondering what your vision for your
life was?'

The stillness held Nicholas. He said calmly, 'After my
Orange Street experience – you know I was baptised in
the Spirit then – I just feel the Lord wants me to be
totally and completely identified with the drop-outs and
the drug addicts and people like that. And I believe in
healing too and . . .'

Pat laughed again. 'You see George and I have had a good idea! Look, would you like to come to Brompton as a curate? We were already planning to share a curate with the Divine Healing Mission and George would like it to be you. So you could come here, be the London chaplain for them, and have a day off a week to help Vic Ramsey with the drug addicts.'

Nicholas stood quite still for a few seconds. It was more than he could have asked for. He looked up. 'You mean a sort of threefold commission?'

'Yes. I feel we have got so much at Brompton and we're too privileged and we'd like to be helping in this way. So, how about it?'

Nicholas took a deep breath. 'Absolutely marvellous. Yes. Yes, indeed I'd like to come very much.'

And so it was arranged.

Nicholas soon (miraculously some said) found accommodation at Roy Calvocoressi's house in Green Street. He loved to run the twenty minutes from there, past Marble Arch, through Hyde Park to Holy Trinity, Brompton. It gave him time to think and the exercise kept him feeling well. There were very few days when he was rained off and had to wait for the bus. Often as he jogged briskly to the church he found himself thinking about Bermondsey. How all his time there – the searching, all the darkness and confusion that had been pain in his mind – was now set firmly behind him, sloughed off for ever. Now it was like springtime after a long hard winter. He ran on and turned into the narrow road leading down to the church. Snowdrops were bursting out all along the pathway. It was an oasis from the noise of the Brompton Road, the sophistication of Harrods and the fine living of Beauchamp Place and Lennox Gardens.

He slowed down, enjoying as he always did the grassy area around the back of the church and the almost park-like surroundings of Church House. He went quickly to his room in the new building and tried to begin thinking and preparing for a sermon. But for once he could not concentrate. His mind filled with the image of the drop-outs he knew from his Rotherhithe days. He sighed deeply. He had to be identified with them, he knew that. It was almost as if his concern for them was supernatural, over and above that English 'thing' of concern for the underdog. He had been in the probation service, he realised now, not of his own choosing but really out of deference to godly advice. God had allowed it, and through it his awareness of people and their needs had sharpened. God had caused him to read *The Cross and the Switchblade*, and had taken him to Orange Street when he went forward to give his life to Christ. There the Holy Spirit had given him that supernatural identification, so that he felt completely identified with the drop-out people, thrust into it, almost beyond himself.

He stared unseeingly across the early spring grass. His calling, he was so sure, was to follow the Lord in this complete and utter identification. It was as if he had taken a private vow of poverty, chastity and obedience. And yet, tiny and unseen like a seed hidden under-ground awaiting a further spring, there was going to be another calling.

Nicholas soon settled down at Brompton. With the full encouragement of staff and parish he decided to open the crypt on Saturday evenings. 'I want it to be open house for *anyone* who wants to come. So any homeless people can come!' he cried.

It was easy enough to find them. He met them all the time on the London streets and he guessed other big cities had their share too. Sometimes late at night he saw them sleeping under bridges or in cardboard boxes near the stations, or propped up by the warm pavement vents and grids of hotels. He went into this work with these people with his eyes open. The probation services had taught him that. Such people were usually difficult, in rebellion against society and their families, often mentally ill, unable to form relationships, disturbed and alcoholic. But somehow he loved them and wanted to show the love of Christ to them.

On the first evening he went out and bought a loaf of bread, some cheese and some soup. Then he walked into the Brompton Road and invited the first three he met. 'Would you like to come and have a meal and some fellowship over the Bible?' They came. As he struggled with heating the soup he wondered how the meeting would go. But he need not have worried. When the men were warmed with soup they seemed happy enough to let him open the Bible and share a passage from its pages.

'What do you think God is saying here?' he asked at the end, expecting an awkward silence to follow.

Someone cleared his throat. Someone shuffled. And then, like a tiny miracle, each man opened up and talked. And it did not happen just the one week. It happened every week. The passages came alive. Nicholas was thrilled. Yet at the end each man pulled himself up, wiped his nose and trudged out. Out to where? Nicholas did not know but he had a very good idea. It troubled him that he could do nothing about it.

The following Sunday morning as he stood gazing at the congregation dressed in furs and pearls and well-cut overcoats, he wondered what would happen if any of the crypt people were to stray upstairs into the warm rose-dark and ornate building. He wondered what would happen if Jim and Shaun stumbled up the stairs and in among the well-heeled upper-class parishioners, who were sitting so calmly below the white-painted galleries in the pinkish light filtering through the stained-glass windows. Jim could not read. And Shaun would probably smell like a distillery.

It happened sooner than he thought when a broken-down man in need of a bath came and sat next to a lady in a fur coat. A silent tremor seemed to run like a shock round the congregation. One or two heads turned. Later Nicholas waited in the church porch and wondered.

And yes, the congregation was shocked. But to Nicholas's delight it was a good shock. The majority of people were pleased – pleased to share and pleased to help. Some ladies heard about it and began to help on the Saturday evenings. A prayer group run by Dorothy Kerr was formed to pray about the work. And to these groups came Helen Clark, Mary Bird, Peggy Thompson and others.

Nicholas felt the Holy Spirit was moving in all this and was deeply glad. He decided to begin a series of meetings in the crypt library where people could receive teaching on the Holy Spirit. Again he got the full backing of Pat Gilliat.

But before he could get the series under way he began to face up to the problem of what to do with the drop-outs at the end of the crypt meeting. He decided that if they did not have anywhere to stay he would take them to a hostel. He knew of several: Salvation Army, Church Army, doss houses and cheap hotels that took in social security people. It was to be the cry of his heart for many years: *where* could they go for the night? The law was, then and now, adamant: if you could pay for the first night you could reclaim the money from the social security afterwards. But before you could get any social security money you had to give an address. And you could not give an address until you had actually paid for the night. It was a vicious circle. More often than not Nicholas found his hand dipping into his own pocket to pay for yet another down-and-out. For anything was better than leaving them on the streets. Occasionally he knew the men were not genuine and were just using him. Even so their need was so great he still helped them.

He found there was a need for discipline too. It was quite unloving to be undisciplined. He and his helpers learned it was a waste of time trying to help people who were drinking and had no intention of stopping. So all they could do was to show their concern and say, 'Come and join us for Bible study and a meal. And when you've stopped drinking we are available to you every week.

But it's no good us talking to you of other things until
you are ready to change your life.'

Peggy Thompson chuckled one evening and Nicholas's
eyes twinkled too.

'It's a good thing there are lighter moments,' she said,
'like this evening when I cooked toad-in-the-hole.'

He roared with laughter. 'Shaun couldn't take his
eyes off the oven! I've never known any of them be so
quiet before!'

'Well, I didn't realise it would take so long to cook in
such large quantities. I think every eye in the room was
glued to that oven!'

'Yes,' he said. 'Including mine! Fancy making them
wait until *after* the Bible study before they got their free
meal!'

After he had been at Brompton for eight months Pat
Gilliat left and Nicholas became the priest-in-charge.
He still jogged nearly every day across Hyde Park and in
his concern to run the church as the Lord wanted, used
the time to pray in tongues to himself. This continued
and strengthened a habit he had begun after he was
baptised in the Spirit. He decided to keep things exactly
as Pat had done but also seek to bring the power of the
Holy Spirit into the services. To that end he invited
visiting preachers whom he knew would speak on the
subject. And without his being aware of it many seeds
were sown there in 1968 that would continue to bear
fruit into the late 1980s and beyond. Now the church is
over a thousand strong, full of young people; and two
other churches have been planted.

'It's like a football crowd on a Sunday evening!' said
the caretaker.

Nicholas felt the effects of the prayers being poured
out in the weekly ladies' prayer meetings and in the half
nights of prayer for revival were incalculable. He
continued the monthly teach-ins on the Holy Spirit and
these were very popular. He also felt that the church was
greatly influenced by George Bennett and the weekly
healing services. Nicholas always went to these and

loved to watch George as he laid hands on the sick and prayed for them. Nicholas learned from him as he watched and believed for their healing. George had such a ministry and such grace that he knew whenever he prayed the Lord would answer, would touch and would do something. His set prayer held great meaning for Nicholas: 'The healing mercies of the risen living Lord Jesus Christ present here with us now, enter into your spirit, your soul and your body. Heal you from all that harms you and give you God's peace.'

7

A Single Woman

It's difficult for the single woman. I had a very loving family and friends around me. My sister and brother were both married with three children each and they couldn't have done more for me. But I still longed to be married and have children of my own. It's very difficult for the single girl. It's very frustrating and it seems there's nothing you can do about it.

In the end the Lord had to get through to me and show me it was only He who could satisfy me completely and that He had called me to be single for Him. He wanted to fulfil his best plan and purpose for my life and the lives of those around me.

Marigold Copeland

One evening a woman in her early thirties drove to Holy Trinity Church, Brompton. Her name was Marigold Copeland. As she negotiated the London traffic she found herself thinking of the evening ahead. Supposing they had changed the night of the Brompton Choral Society and it no longer met on Tuesday evenings? Supposing Robert Munns had stopped being organist at Brompton? Supposing she did not know anyone when she got there? Marigold glanced out of the car window at the crowded streets, glaring lights and tattered posters. Well anyway, she was determined to try and join in with her old choral society again if she could. They had had such pleasure singing the *Messiah* and the *St Matthew Passion* and it was fun being with friends.

Perhaps this evening would turn out well and she could forget the loneliness of a new job at a big London hospital. When she left England over a couple of years before she had had a wide circle of friends. But two and a half years as an occupational therapist in Africa – friendly, hot, vibrant Africa – seemed to have changed her for good. She had left so many wonderful new friends behind there, many thousands of miles away. Part of her heart itself seemed to have been left behind in Africa. Now back in London most of her English friends had moved on or married and only she was still single. She gazed bleakly at the traffic lights and then changed gear. There was James of course, who had been such a good friend at her church in Cape Town. It had been a satisfying brother and sister relationship, but now she was back in London she missed him.

Suddenly she sat up very straight. I am not starting on that line of thought again, she said to herself very firmly. She parked the car and with head held high and shoulders very square she set off in search of the choir rehearsal at Brompton.

When she arrived at the door of the crypt her first feeling was one of relief. People were milling about. But as she looked more closely her heart sank a little. Robert Munns was not there and neither were any of the old faithfuls. In fact a man with a dog collar was standing up at the front obviously having just begun to lead a meeting. All at once she chuckled to herself. Of course, that was what it was! She had stumbled into an entirely different meeting. She glanced at her watch and looked round. One or two people smiled back, so she found an empty seat and settled down to listen. I might as well stay, she thought. It is a pity about the choral society, but there it is.

She watched the man in the dog collar in a detached way. He appeared to be in his forties, pale and tired, but his eyes were very bright and his smile glowed from him to all the people present. She found herself thinking, he needs someone to look after him. His shirt cuffs are all frayed. He must be one of these clergymen who go in for second-hand shirts. But then her attention was taken up by the speaker, Fred Elgar. Quite soon she was on the edge on her seat for here was a man talking about the gifts of the Spirit. This was something she had heard about in Africa; something that had become dramatically personal to her alone in her cabin in the boat coming home from Cape Town. But no one in stiff-upper-lip England seemed to have heard about the Holy Spirit, let alone talk about him. And as for speaking in tongues, well!

At the end of the talk she found Fred and said, 'I thought I was the only person in England speaking in tongues! I haven't known what to do. This amazing experience happened to me on the ship coming back from Africa.' She paused. 'Does anyone here know anything about it?'

Fred threw his head back and roared with laughter. 'We all do,' he said at last. He gestured to the curate with the frayed shirt cuffs. 'And Nicholas Rivett-Carnac here has begun this monthly series of teach-ins. Why don't you come along?'

Why not indeed, she thought and made it a priority in her diary. After all she was hungry to know more about the spiritual life.

In the months that followed Marigold enjoyed going regularly to the teach-ins. There she met a crowd of new friends and acquaintances, Peggy, Helen, Annette, Mary Bird, Sandy Millar and Dorothy Kerr among them.

One day Sandy said, 'You know I've just been reading a book called, *The Cross and the Switchblade*, and I wish we could do something like that here.'

Nicholas, who had come up quietly and joined their group, said, 'I know that book. It's good, isn't it. And yes, I agree. But what can we do and where?'

'Well, can we count on each other?' asked Sandy. He darted a look around the small circle of faces. All were nodding, bright with dedication. 'OK. In that case I shall go round every place I can think of one by one until I find a hall somewhere. And then we'll begin something for the down-and-outs!'

Annette gave Sandy a special smile. 'Yes,' she said. 'Oh, let's do it.'

Someone laughed. 'Trust a barrister to organise the whole thing so methodically!'

Sandy raised his eyebrows and then smiled broadly.

Peggy said, 'I'll get the prayer group to pray about it.'

At first nowhere could be found. Then Peggy came along one day and said, 'You know Jean Darnall gave a prophecy at the prayer group the other day. She said that the Lord promised us we would have found a hall within the year and begun the work.'

The group went quiet. But they all believed. And before the year was out Lionel Ball of the London City Mission invited them to bring a team each week to the hall in Shorts Gardens near the old Covent Garden. He was happy for them to open it up, give out sandwiches and have talk and fellowship with the down-and-outs and anyone else who came, young and old.

Right from the beginning the informal team gave it all they had got. Some often rushed there straight from work, going without their supper. The women got busy in the kitchen preparing sandwiches, soup and coffee. Then the doors were opened and yet another busy exhausting evening began as the queue of tramps shuffled in. Other people came too. There were young northerners who had thought the streets of London were paved with gold. There were meths drinkers, drop-outs caught in a vicious downward spiral, the homeless and people without jobs. A few women wandered in as well. And they all seemed to enjoy the caring, the food and the singing.

At other times, in a rare moment of quiet in her flat Marigold would have a sudden memory of herself as a girl home for the holidays from boarding school. Often there would be an evening dinner and dance to look forward to. She would get dressed in her ball-gown and go down the stairs of their lovely and happy country house. Her mother would be in the background full of fun and excitement, while she hovered in those last few expectant minutes before the doorbell rang and the invited guests spilled into the hall, their laughter tinkling in the evening air. She contrasted that with her memory of the night before when she had looked round the London City Mission hall and seen the men, hair unwashed, hands trembling, some of them still quite young and wearing the cast-off trousers and jackets that she and the others were able to dole out from time to time. The world of velvet cloaks and long evening gloves and the Christmas holiday dances was so far removed from her present reality that it was as if it belonged to a different person's life altogether. But I am so glad, she thought fiercely, I'm glad I'm here now. This is right for me. I'm glad. And the loneliness she had felt on her return from Africa was receding now she was getting to know the group at Shorts Gardens.

However such moments for reflection were rare. Most nights she and the other women were rushed off their feet in a seemingly non-stop call for soups and coffees. She noticed that on many an evening she got involved with talking to someone and it would be her turn to finish the washing-up, so that somehow she always seemed to be one of the last to leave. But Nicholas was always still there, often as not leaning on a mop in the middle of the floor. She watched him for a few moments one evening as he cleaned up behind some benches. Why, she thought, he really is the most saintly man I have ever come across. He is always putting himself into the background, gently encouraging other people to come forward and develop their gifts and talents and grow in confidence and grace. He really is extremely nice, she thought. Perhaps apparently shy and retiring, but full of hidden strengths.

'Would you like a lift home?' she said, glancing at her watch. 'It's late.'

'Well, thank you. I would.'

So quite regularly he and any other helpers climbed into her car, often with a homeless man as well huddled in the back. Together they toured the streets of South London searching for a hotel with a room. And when finally the homeless man was settled and the others dropped off at their homes it was so late that Marigold gave Nicholas a lift back to Green Street. In the car they talked about the people they had met and perhaps prayed with during the evening. When they arrived in Green Street he climbed out of the car, said goodnight and went slowly in through the front door.

She watched him go, very slightly stooped as if he carried a burden on his back. It is a burden for the poor, she thought with a sudden flash of insight. And then, as the car slid into gear, she said to herself, 'He really is the most St Francis-like-man I've ever met. He's just like St Francis of Assisi.'

So she drove home in the small hours. She bowled down the deserted streets and thoughts of the evening at Shorts Gardens completely filled her mind. She knew she was beginning to feel happier and more fulfilled. But she did not get to bed until the small hours and was late for work next morning. Little did she realise that the most difficult year of her life was looming around the next corner.

8

The Vision

We are to be his body, sharing the heart of Jesus and
being his hands and feet.

Christ Incarnate at St Marks
(a booklet, 1986)

When Nicholas had been at Holy Trinity for about a
year his father suddenly felt unwell. Cancer was
diagnosed. George Bennett came to see him and said
afterwards to Nicholas, 'You can thank God for giving
you a father of such honesty and integrity.' But
Nicholas, still troubled by thoughts of the great divide in
society, wondered in his heart of hearts where his father
would spend eternity.

Later, after the funeral, Mary Bird, who had helped
to nurse his father, had a dream. She dreamed that
Nicholas was preaching the gospel to a crowd of people.
His father joined the crowd. At the end Nicholas
appealed to those who wanted to trust Christ to put up
their hands. In the dream Mary's hand shot up
immediately. But his father stood still, hesitating.
Eventually, and slowly, he put up his hand. The telling
of this dream meant a great deal to Nicholas. He
believed in the truth of it. And he was also comforted by
the knowledge that even before his father had died his
mother had offered this relationship to God. 'Please take
him to yourself, dear God,' she had prayed. He knew she
had offered to God her most treasured relationship, and

she wrote on the card she put with the flowers on the coffin, 'Till we meet again'. Nicholas was deeply moved to see the reality of her faith.

Life, however, still had to be lived day by day. It continued for Nicholas in the round of weekly meetings, teaching people about the lordship of Christ, the word of God and the love of the Holy Spirit. Deeply rooted among all this was what he called the 'mercy ministry': the caring for the down-and-outs. At times it was so demanding and gruelling that he felt tired. But his army training in fitness had given his body strength and resilience and he drew deeply on his own reserves. He watched with love and thankfulness as Sandy Millar and the others gave themselves unstintingly in the work.

And yet he did not feel quite as settled as before. There were stirrings and rumblings going on under the surface. Then John Morris, the new vicar of Brompton, and the Bishop of Kensington began to suggest it was time he began thinking of moving on and running his own parish. Yes, thought Nicholas, and he knew he was ready to face this. But he could not settle with the idea. He tried running in the park and praying in tongues as he did nearly every day, but even that did not help much this time.

The problem was, if he was honest, he did not *want* to be a vicar. The Anglican Church was a vehicle and means of ministry, he agreed with that. But to be a vicar of a local institution that most people in society regarded as irrelevant and never went near – oh, no! He had no vision of himself as a vicar, and no vision for the Church either. He put more energy into his jogging and began to spurt away. But after a moment his footsteps slowed and he drooped ever so slightly. He'd have to do something of course. He sighed. Then a thought occurred to him. Maybe when Michael Harper came to visit Brompton the following week, Nicholas could ask his advice.

Later the same week after one of the half nights of prayer for revival, a parishioner called Marjorie Milne rushed up to him. 'Oh, Nicholas,' she cried, 'I'd love to

link you up with John Pearce. He's a vicar in the East
End and he's doing marvellous things there. He's a
conservative evangelical and I know you are charismatic but I'd love you both to get together.'

Nicholas smiled. He knew all about Marjorie's
passion for unity. 'All right,' he said.

After a visit to John Pearce, Nicholas was deeply
inspired and impressed. John seemed to be one of the
few clergymen in the East End who had made any
impact in the area. And when he invited Nicholas to join
a community he was forming, Nicholas did not hesitate.
'I'd love to!' he cried.

'It's to be called the Community of the Word of God,'
said John, 'because I want it to be founded upon and run
by the word of God.'

Nicholas agreed wholeheartedly. Ever since the Billy
Graham organisation had sent him Jim Packer's book,
Fundamentalism and the Word of God, he had known and
believed the Bible to be of fundamental importance.
You could never search out its riches and wisdom. It was
a treasury of knowledge and insight. You could never go
beyond it. It was quite simply God's word, and so he
expounded it faithfully in the services Sunday by
Sunday.

Now as he contemplated the idea of joining John's
community he had a sense of joy. So many things that
were important to him were coming together. If only he
could get his job sorted out too, then his peace would be
complete. In a quiet hour he began to meditate upon
why the idea of community was so dear to him. Was it
simply that he wanted a home where he could invite
drop-outs and try to rehabilitate them? Was it so that he
could be on a level with ordinary folk in a group and not
set apart, dog-collared and pedestalled? Was it so that
he could share with others and pour back on them all the
blessings God had poured on him?

Unbidden, a memory came back to him of his
younger brother Miles first coming to Lambrook
Preparatory School at the beginning of Nicholas's last

term. Miles was five years younger than he was and Nicholas knew now that he had been jealous of his brother. Miles seemed to be so good at everything. And then his parents had taken Nicholas on one side, treating him as a grown-up almost, and asked him to look after Miles. 'He's so young,' his mother said. Now Nicholas knelt, a mature man remembering himself at the crossroads age of thirteen. That very simple request had somehow released him. He had half-recognised it at the time. It was strange, but as he watched over his brother and saw him developing and coming top in work and games, Nicholas knew he was pleased and delighted and proud of him and for him. His former jealousy simply withered away. It was the same now when he met people, all of whom had talents and gifts of one kind or another; he was pleased and delighted to encourage them, and to stand back and help them release their talents.

He buried his head in his hands. He did not want to start getting too proud of himself. Yet the thoughts about his parents and his young life persisted. Indeed he found himself often thinking of them since his father's death. Even the remembrance of his father's naval shoes half-hovered in his mind. Why, Lord, he began to wonder. Why, when I had to turn my back on all that former life and it was so bitterly hard and . . . But don't you see, said another part of his mind, that the need to follow in your earthly father's footsteps was not simply to copy his success at being a fine man with a naval career. In fact it was not really that at all. Nicholas suddenly sighed deeply and a tremor passed fleetingly over his hand. Don't you see? It was to do all that as a means to an end. Your own happy, loving family meant so much to you that you wanted to emulate it and in your turn have a happy home and family. You wanted to be like your father, even walking like him and having your hair brushed in the same style because he and your mother had given you such happiness and peace in your home. You wanted the same. You even wanted to go

into the navy as a means to provide for a happy family
life. You did not realise it of course, but that was your
vision, veiled though it was at the time.

Nicholas clambered off his knees and sat for a long
time in the quietness. Finally he raised his head. His face
was completely at peace. Then he nodded slightly. Yes,
it was true. And the Lord was now speaking to him,
intimating that, flawed and worldly though it had been,
his parents had granted him a great treasure. It was
almost like a tiny copy of the pearl of great price,
because he, the Lord, was calling out for his Church to
be like a happy, close-knit family, where all the
members truly cared for one another. The Lord had a
great and glorious plan for his Church to be like a deeply
happy family, filled with many small and happy
families. Nicholas let these thoughts wash over him. It
came to him that in his own earthly family there was
absolutely no *question* but that each member cared for
the others. Everything was shared: food, house, money,
concern, everything. So it should be and could be in the
Church; an atmosphere in which drop-outs could be
helped and people healed. Suddenly his heart started
beating a little faster. He raised his head and stared
straight ahead. Of course! This was the way to heal the
divided kingdom! The Church like a home, where all
were equal and no one had greater rank.

He found he did not want to get up, his thoughts were
so deep and joyous and new. So he let himself remain in
the seat. He remembered his own pain and trauma
about his family when he was so shocked by Bermondsey.
They had all been so close. But now, as the gentle light of
the Holy Spirit came seeping and then flooding into
him, he knew he was being finally released from all that
pain. Without knowing his own family as he had, he
could never now have appreciated this vision for God's
family. Without the strength his own family had given
him, there would be no foundation in his own life for
God to build on. Everything fitted. Indeed he realised
now why he had such a concern for the drop-outs. It was

because he longed for them to be settled back into families. Thank you, Lord, he managed to say at last. He looked down at his knees. He knew he had been granted a vision for life.

Yet somehow in the next few days, thrilled though he was by his new vision, he did not see how it could possibly fit in with being a vicar of an Anglican church. He went along to the Michael Harper teach-in in the church hall, still very unsure in the middle-area of his mind about what he was supposed to do next. Michael Harper got up and did not mince words.

'I have just come back from the States where I have been visiting the Church of the Redeemer in Houston. Graham Pulkingham is the vicar there – and I want to share that this is the nearest thing I've ever come to finding the body of Christ on earth! Warts and all! It was absolutely marvellous. Local people, drop-outs and highly-educated, all kinds of people, were being helped, changed and healed at every level!' He stopped and laughed. 'I'm sponsoring Graham coming over here and I hope you'll all come and hear him.'

By now Nicholas was sitting bolt upright on the edge of his seat. At last he was hearing about a church that was relevant. Would he go and hear Graham? Yes, he would!

When Nicholas finally heard Graham he felt like a parched plant suddenly being given a massive drink of water. Everything fitted.

Graham said, 'What we must learn is to see Christ in one another and expect to hear Christ through each other. The body of Christ is a covenant community. Christ has covenanted himself to us. He has said "All that I have is yours". So yes, Lord. All that we are and have is yours – in covenant, abiding promise with him and with each other. So a church is a church where people are in that covenant relationship with each other.'

Nicholas felt challenged from the top of his head to the tip of his feet. That is what I want, he cried to

himself. It would be like a family! Because we all have
the same Father.

Graham said in a great voice, 'Together we reach out
for the lost with all that we are and all that we have. We
need to be able to say to people, "Come in and share
what we have."' He paused. Then he said, 'But you
can't do any of this without the grace of God and a
reliance on the Holy Spirit.'

I want this, cried Nicholas silently. If only I could go
and visit that church, Lord. But he knew it was
ridiculous. He had not got the time or the money.

Yet within a few weeks he was in Houston, enabled
both by the generosity of his aunt Mona who paid his
fare, and by John Morris who gave him leave of absence.
On the plane coming home he knew himself to be
changed. Being a vicar he could now accept, if his
church was like Graham's church with households and a
covenant community, and the family atmosphere and
the caring and the ever-open door. His vision was
expanding so rapidly he could hardly keep up with it.

Back at Brompton he found that five or six church
members wanted to join him in the John Pearce
Community of the Word of God. But before any
arrangements could be made, and literally one week
after he returned from America, he received a letter
from the Bishop of Southwark. Nicholas stared at it so
long that he finally realised he was waiting for his heart
to sink and for his old complaint about vicars to surface.
They did not. Instead a warmth and expectancy spread
through his chest.

Would you like, said the letter, to consider coming to
St Mark's, Kennington as vicar? In an instant, even as
he read, Nicholas believed the Lord was saying yes. And
he was saying yes too.

There were formalities to be gone through. Nicholas
visited the PCC and the wardens and boldly shared with
them his new vision for the church to be renewed in the
Holy Spirit, for him to be living in a Community of the
Word of God household and for the whole atmosphere

to be like the family of Christ, 'the family of St Mark's'. Naturally they wondered if the Lord was saying all this to them, so they asked Mervyn Stockwood, Bishop of Southwark, to see Nicholas. At that meeting the Bishop was enthusiastic, but asked him to see Hugh Montefiore, Bishop of Kingston. After this further meeting Nicholas wondered what was going to happen. But he did not have to wait long. The very next day he received a phone message from the Bishop of Southwark saying, 'We do invite you to come to St Mark's as vicar.'

So with great peace of heart Nicholas accepted, rejoicing that he could move forward there in integrity because everyone concerned knew his vision and his stance on the Holy Spirit. And they still welcomed him.

There remained a night of prayer at Brompton, where he and a few others called on God to show them how belonging to the Community of the Word of God fitted in with St Mark's. By morning it was all sorted out. Some remained at Brompton, some went and lived in John's vicarage and some came with Nicholas to St Mark's vicarage where he had decided to form a household. Peggy Thompson came and was the housekeeper. Mary Bird came, along with Mary Stokes, a doctor friend. Helen Clark helped out as parish secretary. It was, as the tram drivers used to call out opposite St Mark's church, 'Kennington! All change!'

In November 1972 Nicholas was inducted as vicar of St Mark's, Kennington. And one of the people who had been invited to the service, as a past member of Holy Trinity, Brompton and the Shorts Gardens team, arrived late. She sat down at the back, slightly out of breath, looking a little drawn and older because of the hard year she was going through. Her name was Marigold.

Part III
For Yours is the Kingdom

What would happen, I thought, if Christ came to
Britain? Few would doubt that our nation needs
healing, but how would it happen? Where would he
begin?

The idea of national celebration caught my
imagination! It is a long time since we last saw
dancing in the streets of Britain and it is now very
difficult to imagine.

But if Christ came... what then?

Nigel Swinford on Movement Three
of his composition *Symphony of Nations*
(concert programme)

9

Living in Community

> If anyone has material possessions and sees his
> brother in need but has no pity on him, how can the
> love of God be in him? Dear children, let us not love
> with words or tongue but with actions and in truth.
>
> John 3:17–18 NIV

Peggy Thompson and Nicholas stood together in St
Mark's vicarage garden and stared out across the
November lawn. A few last leaves clung to the trees and
a damp wind blew across the drive from the direction of
the Montgomery Hall. Peggy shivered and pulled her
coat closer about her body for warmth. But Nicholas
seemed oblivious of the raw air.

'This is it, Peggy,' he said eventually and his eyes
shone. 'This is it! At last we're going to live in
community! Those of us called to it are going to form a
household. We seem to have waited so long!'

She smiled and nodded. It was exciting, that was true.
Exciting to think that in a few days they would all have
moved into the vicarage and started a Community of
the Word of God household there. But there were one or
two things at the back of her mind that niggled. Mostly
she had managed not to think about them while in fact
expecting Nicholas to mention them first, but somehow
he had not and she knew that now was as good a time as
any to ask him. She took a deep breath.

'Nicholas,' she began quietly.

He did not hear. 'Peggy,' he cried, 'you know I've always said that since my Orange Street experience I've realised that what people like that need above all else is a home.'

'Oh, yes, yes, I agree. But...'

'And if we can give them a home here and love and serve them, well, who knows. Perhaps they will be healed by the Lord's love in us.'

'Yes,' said Peggy. 'Oh, yes, I do agree.'

Suddenly she was fired again with the vision and her doubts were temporarily forgotten. She lifted her head and smiled confidently. Even retiring at the early age of fifty from her job as a Higher Executive Officer at the Ministry of Defence seemed as nothing to the joy of coming here. There was such a sense of purpose for her in knowing she was going to be the housekeeper for Nicholas and the other members of the community and of course for the needy people they were going to help. It filled her with happiness.

'Come on,' said Nicholas. 'Let's go inside.'

And the two of them almost ran to the front door. Inside the hall struck chill and there was a slightly musty, damp smell. The uncarpeted floor echoed as they walked down to the kitchen. After a moment's hesitation she stopped dead in the middle of the heart of the home and took a good look round. For a minute or two she stood in complete silence and her eyes took it all in. She sighed. It was no good. All her niggling doubts suddenly sprang again into Technicolor.

'Nicholas,' she called, 'look, could you come back in here.'

But he had wandered into the dining-room. 'Peggy,' he called, 'what lovely meals we can have in here. What a marvellous sight with that beautiful lawn and the mulberry tree casting its shade outside the window. It will really be like home. We can all sit round the table and chat and relax. It seems so very right.'

Peggy drew herself up to her full height and blocked the doorway.

'Nicholas,' she said, 'there *isn't* a table!'

He was gazing out of the window. 'Er, I beg your pardon?'

'We haven't got a table! We can't have any cosy meals if we haven't even got a table!'

There was a slight pause.

'Oh, no. Mmm. Yes. I'll have to see about that.'

Peggy stood her ground. 'Well, when? Mary Stokes and Mary Bird are due here soon. There's no food in the cupboards and I don't know what we'll eat for supper!'

Nicholas said, 'I know you'll rise to it, Peggy. I know you will.'

She smiled suddenly. Yes, she knew she would too and had bought a few extra tins just in case, and had them stored in her flat.

'And, Nicholas,' she said.

'Yes?'

'Come in the kitchen.'

Together they went and looked round the empty room.

'It's not quite as it should be,' she said.

'Er, no. But it seems a very nice room.'

'Yes, it is. But Nicholas, there's *no* stove. If I'm going to cook for you all I'll need a stove.'

He was silent as they contemplated the empty square of floor where the previous vicar's oven had stood.

'And Nicholas, follow me.'

He followed her up the cold stairs. She opened door after door of empty rooms, their floors neatly brushed and scrubbed, all waiting to welcome new occupants.

'Nicholas, there are no beds!'

There was another pause. He thought and then said, 'Oh, well, that's no problem. I'll bring mine from home. My mother won't mind. And, Peggy . . .'

'Yes all right. I'll bring mine from the flat.' And sheets and blankets too, she thought. There was obviously going to be more to this setting up of a community than she had realised. Dear Nicholas, now he was talking about who was to have which bedroom, and of course choosing the smallest one for himself when by rights any vicar in a vicarage should have the master bedroom. All he really wanted to do was to go away and pray about the setting up of this household.

She said, 'Nicholas, what about the stove?'

'Oh, I've had a good idea about that,' he said quickly. 'I'll give you the money Holy Trinity, Brompton gave me as a leaving gift and you can go and buy one. And I'll bring a sort of table-cum-dresser from home too. That'll do for our meals.'

'Oh, that's wonderful!' she cried. And for a few moments it seemed as if community life was going to be easy, with all the problems being ironed out so smoothly.

But somehow in their general rush of enthusiasm a lot of details had been forgotten. There were no towels. And no tumblers to drink from. There was no cutlery. And so it went on. Gradually Peggy and the others brought many of their own things across from their flats. One day Helen Clark, parish secretary on her day off from a similar job at Brompton, offered to help Peggy. They collected some things from Peggy's Earls Court flat and brought them over to the vicarage in Helen's car.

'How are you getting on?' asked Helen.

'Well,' said Peggy, 'I'm not sure. So far, so good, I think.' She glanced at the pile of bulging cardboard boxes on the back seat. 'Anyway those matching sets of towels and the cut-glass tumblers mother gave me for Christmas should be useful and look nice too. I'm pleased to do it, Helen.'

And she was even more pleased when she hung all the towels up in the bathroom, which along with all the other rooms Mary Bird was keeping spotlessly clean. It was really beginning to feel like home at last. And not a moment too soon as Nicholas was bringing Alan to live with them. Alan, whom he had met at Shorts Gardens, really seemed to have got over his alcoholism and only needed the experience of a good family home to set him on his feet again. As Peggy's hands lingered over the quality towels she had brought with her, she thought to herself, 'Why, all my things belong to the Lord. I am merely a steward of all my possessions. And I am really glad to let people like Alan, who don't seem to have anything much of their own, use them.' And humming a little tune, she ran downstairs to her kitchen.

Slowly she and Mary Stokes, Mary Bird and Nicholas and the others began to settle down. But not for long. Soon it was noised abroad in the parish that help was to be had at the vicarage. Sometimes the phone rang in the early hours of the morning with a desperate caller, whom Nicholas spent time in calming down. Tramps called at all hours for sandwiches. In no time at all several needy men were living at the vicarage and swamping the dedicated little band of Christians who were running it. The men did not always appear for meals on time and Peggy found she was constantly serving sandwiches and preparing meals and snacks, sometimes without even getting the chance to eat her own.

Nicholas noticed she was becoming exhausted and suggested she had one day off in the week. At first this seemed a wonderful idea and she relaxed completely and enjoyed some peace and quiet. But when she returned in the evening she stood transfixed in the kitchen. She opened her cupboards and stared horrified at the empty shelves. All the food she had left prepared for the household had been eaten. And all her carefully hoarded stock of extra tins and packets, which she had somehow managed to buy out of her shoestring budget, was gone as well. The needy men must have eaten the lot behind Nicholas's back. For a moment she felt defeated. She found a chair and sat down heavily. It just wasn't fair. Then she gave herself a mental shake. It was fair. She had accepted the job as housekeeper with her eyes open and Nicholas, with his probation officer experience, had tried to explain what it might be like. She stared dully across the floor and half saw a filthy floorcloth near the stove. Someone had obviously

heated some milk and it had boiled over, but, well, at
least they had tried to mop it up. With a sigh she heaved
herself off the chair and went to finish clearing up the
mess. She bent to pick up the floorcloth and then
stopped. Surely not! It couldn't be! She looked closer at
the cloth. Yes, it was. Someone has used a matching
bath towel from her favourite set as a floorcloth to mop
up a disgusting pool of milk. She sniffed. It smelt sour
too. Disheartened and defeated she began to rinse it out
in the sink. Being a steward was all very well and she did
want to share her things. Only it had never occurred to
her that people might spoil them, might not even care if
they did. Her hands, reddened now, trailed in the greasy
grey water. This whole business of community was a lot
harder than she had bargained for.

  She decided to tackle Nicholas after their evening
meeting. Yet as the evening wore on and all the men
joined in the Bible study and seemed so relaxed and
happy sitting round the fire, she found she had not got
the heart. Nicholas was tired out and she had heard he
had been up half the night with Alan. She glanced
sharply at Alan as he lolled back on the sofa. It had
appeared such a good idea to have him at the beginning,
his probation officer was so sure he had kicked the
alcohol habit, and Nicholas had wanted to believe in
him. But now she wasn't so sure. It was one thing to meet
Alan once a week at Shorts Gardens and hear about his
commitment to the Lord. It was very different living
with him. It was quite obvious to them all that he was
drinking heavily in secret and trying to conceal it. She
was sure Alan had meant it when he said he wanted to
become a Christian, but he just did not seem able to help
himself. She sighed. Nicholas was talking and despite his
tiredness his face shone. He really loves them, she
thought. He's pouring himself out for them day and
night. No regular sleep and up early for prayers in the
church. How he did it she simply did not know. Yet as
the old well-loved words from John's Epistle rolled
round the room she found her anger about the bath

towel evaporating. When she stood up at the end to go and make them all a cup of tea she knew herself to feel quite differently. After all, in the final analysis what did a bath towel matter compared to someone's immortal soul?

As her understanding of stewardship increased so did her ability to cope, to take knocks. But even she had to grit her teeth as one by one her expensive cut-glass tumblers were smashed. And no one said they were sorry.

One night, very late, there was a tap at her bedroom door. Outside was Nicholas and a sort of human bundle behind him.

'Peggy,' he whispered, 'look I'm sorry, but I found this poor woman at Waterloo Station.'

Peggy blinked and crawled out of her warm bed. 'You'd like me to put her in the spare bed in here,' she said, with no hint of a question in her voice.

'Yes, please. I'm so sorry. Only I couldn't leave her.'

No, thought Peggy rather grimly as she hauled the pathetic woman on to the bed. How could you leave her? Of course ninety-nine per cent of people did and had. But not Nicholas. She sighed heavily. The woman soon began to snore and Peggy prepared herself for a sleepless night. Surprisingly enough, she slept. Next morning, before the woman awoke and they faced the problem of what to do with her, Peggy crept slowly downstairs and made herself a cup of tea. It was a bright spring morning and out of the window she caught sight of a drift of bluebells. Her heart lifted, she smiled, drank her tea and felt at peace.

It was strange, but despite all the problems – and by now they all knew they had made a mistake in being outnumbered by the needy – she was glad to be here. She opened one of the cupboards and began to chuckle. All the cake tins had disappeared. She shook her head and wiped the tears of laughter from her eyes. Only *she* knew where they were, safely hidden under her bed, away from a certain needy gentleman they were looking

after, who prowled nightly on the hunt for food. At least
she had kept her three dozen buns safe for tea that
afternoon. Her practised eye assessed the contents of the
cupboard. Not much left, but they could manage until
she went shopping on Monday. There would be just
enough left until then.

They had now decided not to invite all and sundry to
the vicarage on Sunday evenings after church. 'We'll
establish a rule,' Nicholas had said only that week.
'We'll have a quiet family time on Sunday evenings. No
guests at all then.' Peggy breathed a sigh of relief. It
would be so nice to be quiet and she might even be able
to have some peace and relaxation later on that evening.

She went to the evening service and enjoyed it. There
were only about fifty in the congregation and Nicholas
had decided to experiment with some open prayer. The
choir sang the hymns rather quietly. The curate Roy
Smith preached, and the parish worker Joan Impey
read the lesson. The Youth Group was attending in full
force and Veronica Elen was in the choir there ... Peggy
relaxed. There was no big supper to think about and a
pleasant evening round the fire to look forward to.

Once back at the vicarage she rescued the final bun
tin from under her bed and began setting out a few cups
and saucers on a tray. She heard Nicholas come in and
placidly walked over to the sink and began filling the
kettle. Suddenly the kitchen door flew open. He rushed
in.

'Oh, Peggy!'

She glanced up and smiled. Then her smile faded
slowly. There seemed to be rather a lot of people milling
round in the hall behind him. She opened her mouth
but he rushed in first.

'I know I *said* we'd have no more guests on a Sunday
evening. But this is very important. Have you *anything* to
give them?'

'Who are they?' she managed to ask.

'Oh, well, it's the whole choir, actually!'

'The *whole* choir!'

She swallowed the words that immediately sprang to mind. She took a deep breath. Then suddenly she realised the tap was still running and water was spilling out of the overfull kettle. He turned it off for her and said hopelessly, 'I'm so sorry, only you see...'

'Don't worry,' she interrupted. 'I've got a few eggs I was saving for breakfast tomorrow. But we can do without them. I'll cook those now and I'll try to make some cheese sauce to go with them.'

As she hard-boiled the eggs and stirred some remnants of Cheshire cheese into a roux mixture, she found she did not really mind after all. The supper was served, the choir loved it, Nicholas was delighted, and everyone said it was the best supper they had ever had. And she, well, she was learning to be a steward.

It was not *her* kitchen, she now realised, but the Lord's. They were not her shelves and tins, but the Lord's. Time, talents, money, possessions, rights, none belonged to her. All were her Lord's. And she knew she had to learn how to love; not just to love in word and tongue but in deed and truth.

Many years later she looked back on those hectic days and saw how marvellous and freeing they had been. Oh, yes, it had nearly killed her at the time but it was an excellent training ground for the work the Lord was to call her to do.

10

An Open Church

You've seen the needy lives around you: diseased,
bound, suffering and tormented by sin; you've asked
me to open their blind eyes and deaf ears, and to
soften their hardened hearts. I'll do it, all of it – at
your hands. I'm offering you grace enough for that.
But grace of this kind is costly, not free like the grace I
give for yourself. It's free for them, but if you
continue to serve me in the needs of these people, in
one way or another I'll require your life at their
hands.'

How can these things be? My heart pleaded with
earnestness.

'By my Spirit.'

The Lord speaks to Graham Pulkingham
in his book, *They Left their Nets:
a vision for community ministry*
(Hodder and Stoughton, 1974)

The community had been running for over a year.
Nicholas tried to review it in his mind one morning. He
and the Christian group who ran it were outnumbered
and swamped by the needy and that was a mistake, but
they had decided not to ask anyone to leave. He sighed.
Alan had stumped out of his own accord. Homeless Alan
with his ever-smiling face and blue eyes, a big nose and
thinning hair; he was slightly built but it had taken two
of them to hold him down when he was drunk and
crossed in any way. Poor Alan, so proud of his

commitment to Christ, and able to hold up a pleasant mask when Nicholas used to meet him once a week at Shorts Gardens. But all that had been stripped away in community living. Alan could not take the closeness and the necessary openness. Concealment was impossible. Perhaps Alan did not really want family life. Certainly he was unwilling or unable to kick the drink habit. It was as well he left, Nicholas knew that. But an aching sorrow for Alan swept over him. He stared down at his hands. It was one thing having a vision for a Christian dimension of family life with its enormous healing potential. It was quite another thing to actually cope with people like Alan, and to know afterwards you were a failure because nothing you said or did changed anything.

There was a knock at his door. 'Come in,' he called, unaware of the tiredness that coloured his voice.

It was Mary Stokes. 'May I?' she said, 'just for a moment. I'm due at the hospital any minute.'

'Yes, of course. Do come in.' He offered her a seat.

She said, 'Now the thing is that the hospital says they are having difficulty in reaching me here when I'm on emergency call.'

He nodded. It was a problem. With thirty or forty different people in and out of the vicarage all the time the members of the community often didn't receive their telephone messages. It was yet another part of the cross to bear; but emergency calls with patients at the end of the line were vital responsibilities.

'I'll see what I can do to tighten things up,' he said and made a note in his diary.

'I've got an obstetrics clinic this morning,' she said, 'and then the gynaecological operating list this afternoon.' She smiled. 'I'm beginning to realise that living in the parish and the hospital being so local means I'm probably delivering about a third of the St Mark's babies! I am really getting to know the local mothers too. It is good.'

He said, 'It all fits in with my vision of a local parish

church, even in inner-city London.' Then he said, 'Will
you be too tired for this evening's spell of duty in the
church?'

'Oh, no. That'll be fine.'

When she was gone he sat on and his thoughts
reverted to Alan. He hoped Alan's leaving would not
send any of the others off too. But living in community
was not how he had imagined it would be after hearing
Graham Pulkingham speak. In a way it was a bit
traumatic, having the edges rubbed off you and your
pretensions exposed. It was like having the layers of the
onion peeled off. He guessed that the Spirit was leading
them into the truth as they were able to bear it. They
had started reading together *The Calvary Road* by Roy
Hession (Christian Literature Crusade, 1950) and
trying to live out its principles of walking in the light
with one another. This was hard. But there was no
doubt that they were beginning to see the importance of
the lessons they were all learning. And if they could not
learn to be committed to a small family-style group, how
could they ever develop a similar commitment to the
larger body in the parish? How could they ever be a
covenant community in the local area?

He got up and looked out of his window across to the
Montgomery Hall. Everywhere was quiet and he began
to relax. It was interesting to think the hall had been
dedicated by Field Marshal Montgomery and named in
his honour because his father had been a St Mark's vicar
in Victorian times. He wondered briefly what the parish
had been like in those far off days. He knew St Mark's
had been built in 1824, along with three other churches
named after the other gospel writers. The four churches
were popularly thought to have been built in thanksgiving for the victory at the battle of Waterloo. But in
fact the previous vicar, Colin Scott, had once told him
that the government of the day had been so worried
about hordes of hungry people wandering about in
dangerous crowds searching for food and shelter, that it
had paid to have the four churches built. Obviously they

must have thought a dose of religion might calm the people down. It was only in discussion in Parliament that one of the MPs had hit on the idea that the churches were a form of thanksgiving – which in a way no doubt they were.

Nicholas let his thoughts wander to Colin and his wife Margaret. They had been so kind and helpful to him when he came after the interregnum. Colin's vision for work in the parish was so very much his own. Colin had begun house groups in the days when such things were unusual, and had fought to have black children's parents feel free to enrol them at St Mark's Church School. Colin had believed passionately in St Mark's being a parish church. Wallace Bird too, the vicar before Colin, had had the same vision, rebuilding this very vicarage and the hall and... Nicholas shook himself. He was sleepy after a long session with one of the men during the early hours. What was it Colin had said, something about – his brow furrowed and he took off his glasses and polished them – yes, that was it. There were hordes of people aimlessly wandering about in 1824. Ready to fight and gang up. Ready to do anything. It seemed as if Kennington had had its problems for a long time.

In his mind's eye he pictured the present-day street scene near the church. By midnight there would be many drunks and addicts and problem people in the area. They would be slumped at street corners, hanging about on benches, lolling around on the pavements, wild-haired and glassy-eyed. Some would be vomiting. Some drugging. Many were homeless. For a while he and the others in the community had felt unsure what God was saying about it all. But they could not ignore it. Gradually they all began to realise that the Lord was calling them to be available. Yet what did that mean in practice? Anyway he had decided to start keeping the church open all day and all night. This meant keeping it manned and tonight it was Mary Stokes's turn on the rota. He thought of her, and Peggy Thompson, Mary

Bird and the others. How faithful they were to the Lord;
how reliable and how committed to the vision. He
bowed his head and gave thanks for them all, and after a
pause, also gave thanks for the drop-outs in the vicarage.
Then he smiled a little tiredly to himself. No doubt none
of the latter would be up and out of bed yet!

Much later that evening Mary Stokes walked the
short distance from the vicarage, down Harleyford
Road to the big crossroads at the traffic lights. As she
crossed the road she saw men and women milling on the
pavement outside the Surrey Tavern, with the light
spilling out behind them in a pool of radiance. It was a
vision of gaiety. But she very much wondered whether
most of them faced happy lives as they wandered away
down the inner-city streets. She was aware of the
echoing voice of the announcer in the Oval Tube
Station. Trains here and trains there: but what was the
eternal destination of so many of these town people? She
was used to seeing blank-faced young people lurking in
shop doorways, waiting as it seemed endlessly. Waiting
for what? She walked towards St Mark's, her face set in
its direction and her head held high. She knew, without
actually turning her head and seeing them, that men
were slouching over the few park benches in the church
grounds and that one or two others with a forlorn stance
were gazing at the church steps.

She strode quickly across the pavement and up the
steps to the front entrance and the open church door. It
was no use feeling scared, although if she was honest she
had to admit she had a few nerves. You never knew what
might face you inside or who might come creeping in
after you. But as she marched defiantly into the body of
the darkened church, she knew the Lord was in control.
She trusted him in this situation.

The previous person on the rota had left the lights on
at the back. Mary settled down in one of the pews, said a
brief prayer and then got up to stroll round the building
It never did any harm to look round and be seen
wandering up and down, before settling down to a

longer prayer vigil. Only last week one of the others had found a sobbing woman and had been able to help her. Of course fairly frequently a drunk wandered in and it had been known for them to vomit in a corner or use the pulpit as a lavatory. She bit her lip.

She began to walk towards the east end of the church when all at once she stopped dead. She stiffened and leaned her head forward slightly. Had she heard something? No, surely not. It must be her imagination. But – yes! There it was again. A slight rustling noise, almost imperceptible. Then it came again, only this time louder. Suddenly Mary was very glad she was wearing soft-soled shoes. She crept forward in the direction of the noise. The rustling was getting louder now, and once something, almost like a twig, snapped. Please help me, Lord, she breathed and made slowly but unerringly for the Emmaus side-chapel. If only she could see better, she thought. She peered into the shadowy area, through its tracery of oak carving and panelling. She saw or thought she saw a human shape bending down near the altar.

Without having time to think she sent up another arrow-prayer. Then, frightened but determined, she marched into the chapel. A man was bending down over what seemed to be a pile of crumpled newspapers and some wood shavings and on the floor was a box of matches. She opened her mouth to speak.

'Can you tell me what you are about to do?' she said, her voice sounding fiercely loud in the hushed church.

He spun round and leaped up. The papers and wood chippings scattered wildly. He seemed to fill the tiny chapel, towering over her. He said absolutely nothing, but simply stared at her from bloodshot eyes. In an instant she took in his wild appearance, his unkempt clothes and scrubby beard. She made a small movement towards him with her hand.

'Would you like to come and sit down and talk to me?'

Still he stood there, hesitating.

She knew she was vulnerable and became aware that

her breath was coming in sharp bursts.

Then he half shook his head as if to clear it and stumbled a few paces towards her, inadvertently kicking the matches away with his foot as he came. He pushed past and then slumped in one of the seats. Mary took a deep breath and came and sat next to him. Resolutely she put out of mind the item she had read in the local paper that the police had unsuccessfully tried to catch an arsonist in the past few days, who had burnt down a neighbouring church. She made herself shelve the knowledge that no one would be coming over to the church to relieve her for ages. She looked straight at him and smiled slightly.

'Are you in trouble?' she asked quietly.

He sat on, still slumped, and bowed as if all the fight had gone out of him. Slowly he nodded.

'Expect you'll tell the police,' he said, a flat, hopeless statement and not a question.

She thought for a moment. Then she took what seemed to be the wisest course of action.

'Well, there wouldn't be any point in telling them if you haven't actually done anything, would there?' She looked in the direction of the altar. 'And I don't think a little pile of rubbish on the step amounts to much, do you?'

He looked straight into her eyes and then turned his head away. He shrugged.

'Why do you talk to me and help me?' he demanded suddenly, his voice stronger and aggressive. 'I'm not worth it. I seem to get – driven – to do things. I don't really want to do them. Why?'

She tried to talk to him. She tried to tell him about the love of Christ and the forgiveness of sins: of the Holy Spirit and the evil bondage of the enemy of God. He listened. He tried very hard to listen. But after ten minutes his concentration lapsed, so she sat with him in silence.

Then she said, 'Shall we say some prayers together?'

He grunted and she began. There was no feeling of

resistance from him, only a weariness and perhaps, she dared to hope, a tiny flowering of hope.

He said, 'I promise to go straight home now to the wife and kids.'

'Would you trust me enough to tell me your address? Our vicar will visit you and we can help you.'

He got up as if he had not heard and lurched away down the aisle. She watched him go rather sadly.

'Goodbye then,' she called.

But at the door he stopped and half turned round. She just managed to hear as he muttered a number and a street name and she realised she knew the road well. Then he turned and banged out into the night.

After he'd gone Mary found herself sitting down rather suddenly. Her lips moved for a moment in silent thankfulness. Then she pulled herself up and walked shakily back to the Emmaus chapel. She bent down and picked up the newspaper and the wood shavings. There was so much that it took her two journeys to clear it all away into a black plastic sack she found in the vestry. Then she went back and searched on her knees until she found the matches. She turned them over in her hands before hastily thrusting them into her pocket.

As she turned to go back to the vicarage she wondered what would have happened if she had come in later. Would the man have lit the fire? And if so could she have put out the blaze? Or would the church have been badly damaged? The timing of her arrival was miraculous really ... But of course it wouldn't have happened if the church was kept locked, said a different part of her mind. Yet which was better, she answered herself, to follow what they all thought of as a prompting of the Spirit and keep it open; a visible sign to the neighbourhood that they cared? Or keep the church cold and locked, its marble from a past age secure; and its façade forbidding and unwelcoming? Which would Christ do? She shook her head. She thought she knew the answer to that.

As she crossed the church grounds again she felt a

sense of sadness as she so often did. The night-time
people were all around on the streets. The pavement
people, aimless, hopeless, lost. It was like a vast sea of
human need. So vast that whatever you did and
however much you helped someone, there was still
another person with a problem looming in the wings
and waiting to take their place. But no. Perhaps that
wasn't the way to think about it. She should be thankful
for what had happened tonight, and see God's hand in
that.

11

'Kennington! All Change!'

In the 1974 *Jubilee* magazine, written to celebrate the
150th anniversary of St Mark's, Wallace Bird
remembered his first Sunday service which took
place in the bombed and ruined shell of the church.
He wrote: 'The tram drivers still call out, "All
change" at Kennington and the work of change that
began the day we stood in the ruins still marches on.
Changed lives are the key to the kingdom. Changed
lives are the evidence of the indwelling power of the
Spirit.'

Jubilee
ed. Hilda Jones
(June 1974)

In 1974 St Mark's celebrated its 150th anniversary. It
was decided to publish a magazine called *Jubilee* to
mark the event. This delighted Nicholas and he was
pleased to contribute to it. Hadn't he said to the parish
only recently that his vision for the church was for an
open Bible, an open door, an open table and an open
mouth in witness? So he decided to write an article to
that effect.

He smiled to himself. Keeping an open door at the
church and having all night prayer vigils had been
intensely costly, frightening and marvellous. The
previous vicar Colin Scott had opened the church on
Sunday evenings for a youth service. Some of the youths
came back week after week to cause disturbances and

fights. And yet Colin and John Calvert, the youth
leader, persisted. People prayed a great deal. Eventually the same unruly group settled down and joined
the Youth Group led by Roy Smith, the curate.
Nicholas smiled again as he thought of the open table at
the vicarage. There was never a dull moment there,
especially at meal times; and there was plenty of
housekeeping work in the background too.

He looked down at his desk and saw the unfinished
piece of writing he was trying to contribute to the *Jubilee*
magazine. The editor had passed on to him another
article about the history of the church, and because his
own article would not come together smoothly, he
began reading it.

Of course he knew the story of St Mark's and was
thrilled by it, but it was fascinating all the same to read it
again. No doubt the late-Victorian vicar Dr Darlington
would be amazed to see the church building as it stood
today. For although the outer shell remained exactly the
same, inside it was not the same. It was as if the church
had died and risen again. Colin Scott had said on more
than one occasion that what had happened to the St
Mark's building mirrored the spiritual life of the
church.

During the blitz in the Second World War Kennington and many other parts of London were bombed.
Once or twice St Mark's took a direct hit. But not only
the church; the surrounding area was bombed too.
People were evacuated or called up or killed. A main
air-raid shelter near the church was bombed one night
and many people lost their lives. The church was largely
destroyed and part of its roof was gone. Only the
Grecian façade and pillars remained with the delicate
cupola soaring above, topped by a slender cross.

It occurred to Nicholas that the cross standing out
above all the rubble and mess must have given hope to
the remnants of Dr Darlington's congregation. Dr
Darlington, who had been faithful for fifty years as
vicar, had been in the habit of coming to church in his

top hat and morning coat. He had seen a congregation that packed the pews and galleries dwindle from two thousand to about fifty stalwarts. But he had been a pioneer in his day. He encouraged the Tramworkers' Brotherhood to meet in the original church hall, which became known as the Tramway Hall. And the Transport and General Workers' Union had their origins in the Tramworkers' Brotherhood. It was sad that he died in 1947 while the church was a ruin, declared unsafe for the few who gathered among the fallen masonry to try and hold outdoor services. The gracious Georgian vicarage in Harleyford Road where he had lived and worked was bombed too. It looked very much as if St Mark's was finished.

But God had not forgotten them. Wallace Bird happened to read about Dr Darlington's death in the paper. As he did so a strange thing happened to him. He seemed to hear a clear voice within him cry, 'You must go to St Mark's! Go to Kennington!' Without a moment's hesitation Wallace Bird decided there and then to become the new vicar of Kennington. He met his first and massive obstacle when he went to ask the Bishop about it. The Bishop was kindly but firm. 'That place is finished,' he said. 'St Mark's is finished! We're going to pull it down. It's very sad, but we simply cannot afford to rebuild it.'

Wallace Bird was adamant. He refused to hear the words 'St Mark's is finished!' He believed he had heard God's call and he would not be put off. He knew the living of St Mark's was in the gift of the Archbishop of Canterbury. So he followed this up and eventually got permission from the Archbishop himself to go there as vicar and rebuild both the buildings and the congregation. There was only one condition. Wallace Bird had to be responsible for everything including the finances. It was a staggering vision and an out-facing task. But Wallace Bird was absolutely convinced that God was 'in' it. He wrote in the *Jubilee* magazine about his first visit to the church:

St Mark's had been closed for seven years, the blown-out front door nailed up and secured with corrugated iron. I managed to find a way in and what a scene! Dirt, desolation and destruction everywhere. The beautiful old ceiling was torn in ribbons, the windows were shattered and the pews splintered. But Miss Ethel Lewis, the parish worker, was there!

He called a meeting to see who would volunteer to help. And only twelve people came. But twelve, the number of the original disciples, was enough. Soon the word spread, others joined in and money was raised over a period of years. Much of the money came in as a direct result of prayer and quite amazed the parishioners. Wallace Bird's vision included taking down the galleries and building offices and a big hall upstairs in their place. The black and white marble floor was polished and the pews cleaned and restored. In 1960 the church and new vicarage were finished. It was as if the church itself had died and risen again out of its ruins.

But Wallace Bird did not only have a vision for buildings. He had a vision for people too, for preaching the word and for the church to become a place of healing. He was himself a chaplain to the Guild of Health. At his first evening sermon he cried out, 'Whenever I come to the Oval Station and arrive at Kennington, I hear a loud voice from the trams cry out, "Kennington! All Change!" That's the programme. We are all going to change!'

It was strange, thought Nicholas now, as he put down the typewritten sheet his predecessor had sent, how God often seemed to work when things were at their lowest ebb. All there had been in 1947 was a ruined church, a handful of laity and no money. Yet God and his people had risen magnificently to the challenge. The cross above the cupola still stood proudly over the church today. And it would stand for ever over a lost world until Jesus Christ came again.

Prayer had played such a part in that restoration. So

many people had prayed faithfully. One loyal member of Wallace Bird's early group was Veronica Elen, elderly now, who had prayed steadfastly in the church every morning and every evening for years. When Nicholas arrived she asked to be able to continue. Indeed he had given her a key so she could let herself into the church for her prayer vigils. Without prayer, he thought, everything would be a poor shadow of what it should be.

Wallace had built things up. Colin had consolidated them with his vision for a local church for local people. Nicholas let his chin rest on his hands. He believed firmly and deeply in what he had said only recently in a sermon: 'In everything we do at St Mark's we are standing on the shoulders of our predecessors.' Even the offices that Wallace had put in upstairs were invaluable now. The church had been able to let them out to the Ruanda Mission and the Christian Life College, run by Elmer and Jean Darnall. This helped on a financial level and also on a spiritual level. Wallace's vision for the building was spot-on for the 1970s. And perhaps one day, thought Nicholas, the work at St Mark's would become so big they might even need all the offices for themselves!

Now as he meditated on the vision and work of the men and women of the past, he felt both proud and humbled. Proud to be called by God to the work. And humbled because how could he or any of them, for that matter, do anything for the King of Glory? And in the light of that, whatever could be their vision for the future?

It was in the quietness of his room that his own article seemed to whisper back the answer: 'An open Bible, an open door, an open table and an open mouth.' Then the phone rang. The busyness was starting again and he knew it. But before he left the room he half caught another whisper on the edge of his mind, almost imperceptible, almost a still small voice. 'An open heart,' it seemed to say. 'Have an open heart.' But it was hard, he thought as he ran to answer the phone, to always have an open heart to God. Especially as so many of them in the church and in the community were unmarried; single in the service of the Lord. After the phone call he trailed slowly back upstairs. It was hard that the Lord appeared to ask for so much, everything really, from the single person, calling for a heart opened to him, even if it were breaking inside with loneliness. Nicholas was aware that underneath some of the bright single faces he knew, beat such hearts.

Yet perhaps it wasn't too much for God to ask when you considered what he had done. And if only, thought Nicholas, the church could catch his vision for being the family of God, then those solitary single ones, even like himself, could be welcomed and made to feel at home after all. Whatever it cost him, he decided, he would work for this. So with redoubled zeal and energy he committed himself yet again to the work of the church and the community household.

12

The Most Difficult Year of her Life

Jesus said:

'I tell you the truth, unless a grain of wheat falls to the
ground and dies, it remains only a single seed. But if
it dies, it produces many seeds.'

John 12:24 NIV

Marigold Copeland let herself in through the front door
of the bungalow she was renting near Chobham in
Surrey. She went quickly into the kitchen and put the
kettle on. A cup of tea was what she needed after a
gruelling day at work. She bustled about making a
homely noise with a cup and saucer and spoon. But
soon, in spite of the cheering drink and pleasant room,
the sense of silence and aloneness that was always
waiting for her when she returned home troubled her. If
only there was someone she could talk to, she thought
suddenly. That was the trouble with being single. It was
fine during the day in the occupational therapy
department she was setting up at the Beechcroft
Hospital in Woking. It was fine there with all the clatter
and activity and the knowledge that she was really
helping the geriatric patients in her care. Being single
never troubled her then.

Now, in the delightful but silent bungalow rooms, the
separateness of her single life seemed to wrap itself round
her like a cloak, cutting her off. All at once she stopped
dead, put down the cup of tea half drunk, turned and

ran to the telephone. She dialled a number. After a happy and animated conversation with one of her Brompton friends, she felt a lot better. The aloneness was put aside for a while. She hummed to herself as she started to prepare her supper; but gradually the humming faded. Eventually it stopped altogether. It was no use. She *had* to get to grips with the fact that she was single. And solitary in the bungalow. It was good and right to phone her friends, but in a moment of self-knowledge she realised she was doing this more and more, simply to stave off loneliness. To stave off facing the fact that she was in her mid-thirties and still unmarried. If only she could somehow come to terms with it. But I do in a way, she thought. It's just living on my own that is so difficult. Sometimes it felt so peculiar to wander from room to room, with no one there to speak to her.

She sighed. She had so *wanted* to be alone – that was the irony of it all. She had found herself unhappy and claustrophobic in London the year before. The comparison of that with the two years of wide open spaces in Africa had made her eventually change jobs and seek some quietness in the countryside. Even though she had loved going to Holy Trinity, Brompton and had drunk in all the teaching and worship at the meetings on the Holy Spirit, and had enjoyed helping out at Shorts Gardens, her need for the space and peace of the country had become paramount. In a time together in the church office the curate, Nicholas Rivett-Carnac, and Dorothy Kerr had listened carefully. 'The pressure, pressure, pressure of London is too much for me,' Marigold said, 'All the rush and noise is getting on my nerves.' After prayer they were all agreed that it was a good idea for her to move to the country. She had found the bungalow through an advertisement in *Renewal* magazine. And now she was here. And missing London! Was she never to be satisfied, she thought to herself, and grinned wryly. But the grin did not last. For underneath it lay her isolation.

She trailed back to the kitchen. It was getting dusky outside but she did not bother to put the light on. She opened the fridge door. There was some mince that needed cooking with onions. In the vegetable rack were some potatoes to peel and a cabbage to prepare. Suddenly she knew it was too much effort to spend up to forty minutes cooking. What was the point when there was no one else to cook for? She gave herself a mental shake and squashed that thought immediately. But it did not entirely go away. So, for the third time that week, she reached for a couple of eggs. She broke them and beat them and then scrambled them. Along with a piece of toast they made a small but adequate supper. I'll lose weight, she thought jokingly. And few would notice if she did.

On Sundays she went to Chobham village church in the mornings and Woking Baptist Church in the evenings. She enjoyed them both. Yet she did not seem to get to know many single people of her own age there. Mostly they were either married or older. The weeks went by and she made herself cope, somehow. She found she half managed to get used to the lonely evenings. Then she was invited to help with a group of ten- to thirteen-year-old girls from the church in Chobham, and one of them stayed with her for some weeks while her mother was in hospital. Marigold learned the importance of throwing herself into the Lord's work in this way. She learned that loneliness was not so bad when she was giving of herself to others. It was a lesson she never forgot.

Sometimes she found herself reflecting upon her life and its meaning. As a young woman of twenty-three she had worked for a year as an occupational therapist in Montreal. After that she had toured Canada and the United States by car with a girl friend. It was just outside the little town of Fort Collins in Colorado that the accident had happened. Marigold woke up to find herself with a broken back and a head injury. Happily her friend was all right and staying with her doctor's

family. Marigold was in hospital for four weeks in a
plaster cast from her armpits to her hips; and slowly
recovering. The doctor and nurses were kind but that
could never be the same as family and friends visiting.
She was able to have long telephone conversations with
her mother in England and that helped. And the kindly
doctor and his wife invited her to their home on
afternoons out from the hospital. But something else,
eternally precious, began in that hospital ward too. An
elderly Christian lady in her ward used to come over
and say she was praying for Marigold and give her
verses from the Bible. Marigold was touched at first and
then intrigued and then, as she grew stronger,
challenged to think about what Christianity meant. It
was the beginning of her spiritual pilgrimage: a time
when she finally handed her life over to God.

She longed to be home. But when she arrived back in
England in a leather spinal jacket Marigold realised she
was no longer the outgoing person her mother had seen
off in the *Queen Mary* at Southampton. Delayed shock
made her depressed and nervous, too nervous at first
even to face a gathering of people. She could not talk
properly because of the head injury and even now still
had a very soft voice and hated noise. People who teased
her or said 'Speak up!' had no idea that inside her head a
whisper sounded like a shout. So there she was, with a
loving family doing all they could to support her. Yet
her depression was such that she became convinced she
would stay single all her life.

Now, as she faced up to herself in these reflections she
saw how the accident had changed and altered the
course of her life. She had become a Christian through
it, but also very sensitive because of it. Although she had
received a considerable amount of healing at the
Brompton healing services she still felt she needed more,
and from time to time asked for prayer for this.
Sometimes she felt the healing power of the Holy Spirit
coming upon her head and moving right down her spine
to that part of her back that had been damaged,

especially when praying on her own in the bungalow.

On this particular evening she found herself putting all these thoughts into the form of a prayer. As she poured it all out and prayed earnestly, slowly the atmosphere in the room changed. Gradually the presence of the Lord gently enveloped her. She knew she was being listened to. And afterwards, with joy, she realised in her heart of hearts and not just in her head, that she was no longer alone. The cottage was not empty. She was not and never had been truly single. Her heavenly Father was there. Always. Only she had to learn to come to him and talk to him in a new way. But of course! So this must be why he had allowed her to be on her own: to learn that he could and would be everything she needed. All she had to do was to give him the time. If she really let him fill her with the Holy Spirit then all would be well. Slowly as she tried to develop this beautiful relationship she found herself being healed from the emotional scars of the accident. Part of the healing was in spending time alone with the Lord.

Yet there were times when she wanted a human being to talk to, a person in the flesh, and so she cried out to the Lord to fill her loneliness. Then, when she was thirty-seven, a miracle seemed to happen. She met a man of her own age. He was a Christian, committed to helping needy people and down-and-outs in London, seemed interested in her and was called Martin. Life looked up. The loneliness lifted. He phoned her at six o'clock every evening in her office, took her out to meetings and conferences, visited her in the bungalow and invited her to meet his parents. Early on in their relationship he had proposed. With a fast-beating heart she agreed that it was a good idea, but suggested they needed more time to get to know each other. It was almost an unofficial engagement and her mother was delighted. Marigold knew she was happy to marry this man and that she loved him with the Lord's love. All that remained was for her to have a ring and for the engagement to be officially announced.

But then as the months slipped by she noticed that the phone calls were not as regular as they had been. And soon she would be thirty-eight and if they were going to marry and have a family it was getting a bit late. Tentatively she broached the subject with him. He shied away from it. 'I need to wait on the Lord and see,' he said more than once. Still she hoped. She hoped so very much. She braced herself too and it was a good thing she did, because one day he phoned up and explained he felt the Lord was saying that they should gradually separate. She knew he had been badly hurt by a girl in the past and that was probably the reason why he was unable in the end to be committed to her. That helped to explain things, but it did not ease her hurt. It was awful too, to break the news to her mother, who had been so pleased Marigold was settling down at last. In fact, this was to be the most devastating year of her life.

Her eighty-nine-year-old father, who had been in hospital for two years unable to walk or talk properly, now had his life ebbing away. He died at last. Marigold was relieved he did not have to suffer any more. She relived the happy memories she had of him as a child, recalling their times together as they sat in companionable silence in the garden, and how often he had come and sat by her bed when she was ill.

Then one day in late summer in her office at the hospital, she received a shocking phone call. Her mother, hale and hearty the last time Marigold had visited her, had collapsed in the garden over the lawnmower. Marigold rushed to Orpington intensive care unit and sat with her beloved mother to whom she had been so close. But she never regained consciousness and in the early hours she died. Marigold wept and was deeply shocked and distraught. There was so much to do. Her brother and sister came and were equally shocked and sad. In moments of quietness Marigold cried out to the Lord in her inner pain and desolation. For the loneliness that surrounded her now was so much more acute than before. Martin was gone. That relationship was dead and buried. Her father had died. Her mother was dead.

Somehow she clung on to the Lord. She moved to another cottage in Blackheath village with a friend called Jean. She attended Millmead Baptist Church in Guildford and was deeply grateful for her friends there. But her heart was bruised and broken. Her days of mourning seemed without end, and her grief unabated, her joy gone.

By 1975 she was still not eating properly and friends began to notice how thin she was. It was suggested that she had a complete break. So after an encouraging pastoral consultation at Millmead she left her job and accepted a wonderful and unexpected invitation to go to South Africa again for a three months' holiday with friends.

13

A Community Church

For several months in 1964 the enormous weight of
sin and suffering in the lives of a great number of
Houston's East-Enders had become mine. During a
Lenten despair God broke me under the burden of it.

Then during Eastertide I caught a new vision of
His Church... because while sharing with me the
secrets of His earthly kingdom, He filled me with an
enormous love for Himself.

During 1965... there was added a dimension of
radical faith and the postulate of life lived wholly in
worship and praise.

Graham Pulkingham
Gathered for Power
(Hodder & Stoughton, 1972)

Helen Clark was now appointed full-time parish
secretary at St Mark's. At first she worked in one of the
downstairs rooms at the vicarage, in the thick of things
at the community household. She used her wallpaper-
pasting table with a cover as a desk. Then she moved
over to a downstairs office in the church building. Once
she was settled in her new job she bought a house in
Offley Road and formed a St Mark's household there.
Six others lived with her and they called it 'The Lord's
house'. They worked closely with the vicarage household. Right from the beginning Helen felt it was right to
have more stable than needy people in her household, so
that the stable folk did not become swamped by the

needy. It was a different emphasis from the vicarage and worked well.

One day she was typing in the office, sitting as she always did with her back to the door. Nicholas had been out for nearly two hours. Helen glanced at her watch, stretched her legs and flexed her fingers. There was just time to finish the report, if she really put her back into it. Her hands began to fly across the typewriter keys, when all at once she heard a noise. That'll be him, she thought, back from his visiting. The door opened and she did not turn round, subconsciously waiting for him to speak first.

After several moments she became aware that he had not spoken. Nor had the door closed behind him. Her hands slowed down. The silence grew. In the end she swivelled round and stared open-mouthed. There was Nicholas standing rather helplessly in the doorway and at his feet was a bedraggled rust-coloured puppy. Helen took in the puppy at a glance. It was too long in the body and its legs were thin and spindly. No doubt it was one of nature's fifty-seven varieties. She opened her mouth to speak, but Nicholas rushed in first.

'She's followed me from every door. From doorstep to doorstep. I've tried shaking her off but nothing works. She seemed to pick me up from the very first go.' He shrugged and stared at the hopeful bundle, who was by now trying to thump a rather straggly looking tail. 'In the end I stopped at a lamp-post and prayed and said, should I be involved with this animal? Then I decided that if she followed me into the church I would be involved. And, well,' he raised his hands in the air, 'she followed me in!'

Helen found her voice at last. 'Poor little thing! Do you think she's hungry?'

'Er – I'm not sure.'

Suddenly they both started to laugh. They laughed and laughed and the stray mongrel puppy's nose began to quiver. Then she started sniffing rather determinedly in a corner behind a chair.

'Quick!' cried Nicholas.

'I'll take her out,' cried Helen, and gathered up the pup in her arms and rushed outside.

They decided to take Hannah, as they called her, to the police and then to the Battersea Dogs Home and see if anyone claimed her. The kindly man on duty shook his head and sighed, 'I expect she's been dumped. But you never know. If she's still here in two weeks and you want her, you can have her.'

Helen and Nicholas were silent in the car on the way home. Then Helen said, 'I'll put it to the members of my household. If they are agreed, and no one claims her, I'd like to have her!'

'Oh, Helen, that's wonderful!'

And so it was that Hannah became an intimate member of St Mark's – and a friend for life for Helen.

Meanwhile Peggy was still working as the house-keeper at the vicarage, Mary Stokes was still at the hospital as an obstetrician and gynaecologist and Mary Bird carried on with her role of keeping the vicarage spick and span. Nicholas continued with his calling as vicar and leader in the household. But something was wrong there and they all knew it. They were swamped by the needy and their undisciplined ways. Nicholas sighed. He had begun to accept that his 'experiment' in community living had not really worked. The family atmosphere in which he had longed and hoped to achieve so much had not been enough. Simply running a home for those with special needs was not enough on its own. It needed people to run that home with tremendous discernment, strength and discipline. This was a calling in itself and, as he now realised, required people to do it full-time. It was too much to expect someone who was working hard all day at a responsible job to come straight back and work with the needy men most of the night as well. People at work all day needed to relax in the evenings and recharge their batteries for the next day.

He frowned. He was beginning to have a new and

exciting vision for the role of the laity in the church. And all this began with his perceiving their own needs for rest and relaxation.

It was sad though, that his high hopes of giving lonely and lost people a home were being swamped; sucked down by the vast and never-ending sea of human need. As he faced the facts he saw that organisations like the Church Army and the Salvation Army had more experience in dealing with the sort of experiment in which he had longed to succeed. But would there ever be a way for people in a parish to care for their own needy people in the context of homes and care, without being unbearably dominated? It took several stable people to cope properly with one unstable person. If only he could somehow enthuse more of his local congregation, and then provide them with the opportunities and training to help. Perhaps that would be the answer.

He sank into his armchair and stared hard at his knees in their very elderly trousers. Someone had given him a cheque to go and buy a new suit. Well, if he went to the Oxfam shop he could get fixed up nicely and the remainder would then come in useful. There were always plenty of men at the vicarage who needed some spare cash and another suit of second-hand clothes. He stood up in his room, its austere simplicity in striking contrast to the sparkling life of Lennox Gardens. But he never thought of his early life now, so used had he become to a life of simplicity and austerity. It was not quite poverty. But the less he owned the more he was like most other people. And that was where he wanted most to be; with the poor and the simple. So rather grimly he set off with an unsmiling face to walk the few hundred yards to the church. Once there he was going to take his turn praying in the empty building, keeping it manned and open all night.

He tried to pray but his prayers were rather leaden tonight. He buried his head in his hands and then raised it again. The great pillars on either side of the east-end stained-glass window stared back at him. He shook his head slightly. It was no use getting upset. He had to accept the inevitable. In any case he had a sense of peace from the Lord about his decision. For not only had the household failed in a way, he now knew he would be unable to keep the church open all night, seven nights a week either. It was getting too dangerous. It was too much for his gallant band of helpers to keep cleaning up vomit inside the church. The alcoholics who wandered in and then were ill in the pews and even in the pulpit, were becoming too much for them all to cope with. It would not matter if it was only occasionally. But frequently, almost nightly, was too much. Nicholas raised his head and gazed straight at the altar. The Lord had kept things remarkably in the church during the past year, even to preserving it from arson. But now it was time, and it was right, to close the doors during the night.

So with sadness, and a strange peace as well, he walked with heavy steps to the great church doors. He opened them and glanced at the street people briefly. Then he shut the doors firmly behind him. He took the keys out of his pocket and locked up decisively. Without a backward glance or pause he pocketed the keys and strode down the midnight streets. I'm sorry, Lord, he said as he stood on the threshold of the vicarage. We were too few in number and too stretched. And there were so many needy. What could we do? He paused and looked up at the night sky. Some familiar words ran through his mind and comforted him a little. 'When I look at the sky, which you have made, at the moon and the stars, which you set in their places – what is man, that you think of him; mere man, that you care for him?' (Psalm 8:3–4 NIV). He sighed deeply. Perhaps, a hint of a thought seemed to whisper to him, one day you will be able to open the doors again? He shrugged his shoulders sadly and closed the front door behind him. Slowly he made his way upstairs. The vision for family life at the heart of the parish was still with him: a covenant community; the family of St Mark's. But the open door had to be truncated; shut firm, locked and bolted.

It was some weeks later that Graham Pulkingham came to visit Nicholas, and as a result of his suggestion Nicholas decided to sever the formal links with John Pearce's Community of the Word of God. Instead the vicarage community household would be simply a St Mark's household. But he knew he was still going to value and retain the informal help and friendship of John Pearce.

'Let the church become your community,' said Graham. 'Let that be your vision.'

As a result some of the ladies from the vicarage household went to join Helen Clark. Mary Stokes shared a house with Ethel Lewis, the former St Mark's parish worker. Nicholas then ran an all-male household with Bob Bruce, Nick Jewitt and Trevor Stuart for a while longer. Although these changes and restrictions could be seen as a failure, and although Nicholas felt at times the whole thing was a failure, there were moments when he caught a glimpse of what the Lord had been doing through it. For seeds had been sown in those eighteen months of community life. Eighteen months, it had to be said, of much sacrifice for them all. But the seeds would bear fruit in later life at St Mark's. So much of what they had done had apparently ended in the desert of failure. Or so it seemed. But as seeds fall into the ground and die, so they spring up the following year and bear fruit.

He remembered when he was in America meeting a man at a community in Denver. In a rush of enthusiasm Nicholas had said, 'I long to run a vicarage for the homeless!'

The man was quiet and then he said gently, 'That won't work. What's needed is prayer. Pray for such people, so that they'll change inside.'

Nicholas was surprised but listened all the same.

The man said, 'You can't help someone till the Lord says so. What I mean is, until the Spirit says yes, you can't really do much.'

Now as he thought back Nicholas recognised the
wisdom of that man's words. In the household they had
learned discernment the hard way. They had learned
when to say yes and when to say no. And if he was
ruthlessly honest, it had not all been failure. He thought
of Jack, an alcoholic who had died recently after a heart
attack. He had become a Christian in the vicarage and
Nicholas knew that the day before he died he had
prayed all night with a down-and-out Welshman; a
Welshman who had finally understood the gospel and
received its strong and sure hope with joy.

No, there was far more to it than his immediate
feelings of failure. If only he had known then that many
of the St Mark's people were to learn from the vicarage
example. Over the next few years several households
sprang up in the parish. Many people in the church
gained a vision for shared living. Many opened up their
homes and took in friends in need. And many young
people who were so welcomed went on to become
mature members of the church. Some went into the
ministry of the Church of England. And several went
abroad as missionaries to difficult places. The fruit grew
slowly. But it ripened and was good. At the time
however, Nicholas was not to know all this. He simply
had to carry on in faith.

Fruit was far from his mind though, later at a meeting
in the vicarage. People began saying that his policy of an
open table at lunch-time on Sundays was not right.
They needed time to relax on the day of rest. Yes, he
nodded without saying anything. Yes, of course they
were right. There were very good reasons for resting on
Sundays. But something, he knew, was being lost
forever. When you were a servant, he thought, and had
no rights, your dedication was all-out. That had given a
quality of life to the vicarage in the early days. Yet now
in fairness, he had to admit, if he pressed the point and
swayed the meeting, it would only end in a rigid
legalism. It was all very well for him to rule his own life
with an iron will. But if he persuaded people to be more

dedicated because they had to and not because they wanted to, it would be wrong. He knew enough to know that love had to be spontaneous. Households and all the personal sacrifice involved must spring up from the Lord's leading. People had to have freedom to choose. Now they were choosing and saying it was time for the household to have more rules. They were free to do that.

'Yes,' he said at last. 'Yes, of course you must rest on Sundays.'

'And I caught head-lice from one of those tramps!' said a young member and shuddered.

Nicholas said nothing. Running a church and a household for St Mark's was fraught with problems. And even as he nodded in agreement to all these suggestions something inside him was breaking. For he was having to face up to what in overall terms seemed like another failure. The open table was breaking down. Its welcoming seats were being closed to the outsider. He stared hard at his knees and said nothing. The open table was coming to an end.

Some weeks later Nicholas caught the Tube to Liverpool Street and met his mother off the train. As ever she was delighted to see him and held out her arms to embrace him.

'I'm so looking forward to our time together and our lunch out,' she cried. 'It seems ages since we last met.'

'Er, yes.'

'And what about some shopping first in Knightsbridge? I'd like to get you some shirts and a mackintosh.'

Nicholas was grateful and as they walked and shopped and talked he found himself relaxing. When they had finished their shopping they realised they were close to a hotel which was a favourite with the family, but expensive.

She said, 'I know you don't like lunching at expensive places. Shall we walk over to the Victoria League and get lunch there?'

He nodded in agreement. But the walk was longer than either had realised. By the time they got there she

was tired and he was tense. Inside the club was very
crowded but the food was cheap. They waited for a table
and sat down. The noise was terrific and his mother
found it difficult to hear him as she was partially deaf.
He kept having to raise his voice and then looked round
in embarrassment to see if anyone was watching.

'Are you happy, darling?' she asked at last.

'Yes. Of course.'

'And is the community going well?'

He looked across the table at her and saw her properly
as if for the first time that day. She was wearing a hat
and it seemed to cast a shadow over her face. Or was it
simply that she was tired? Tired after such a long walk,
said a tiny voice in his heart. But irritably he pushed the
thought away at once. It flashed through his mind now
how much she had tried to understand him and enter
into his feelings about the community. She had even
invited the whole community to stay at Fornham
House. She had tried to follow his argument when he
explained about holding all possessions and everything
in common.

She said suddenly, 'I've enjoyed reading Graham
Pulkingham's book on community living, but I felt sorry
for the families in that community. I felt sorry for his
own family. The families seemed to have to be so much
in the background.'

'Oh, no!' cried Nicholas vehemently.

But before they knew it they were having a row.

Finally she said, 'I'm awfully sorry, but I've got to go
and catch my train now.'

They stared at each other helplessly. He knew he had
been intolerant and rude. But he could not bring himself
to apologise for his anger.

'I'll get a taxi for you,' he said.

He saw her into the taxi. And so they parted.

The next week was shocking with news. His mother
had had a heart attack. He was never to see her
conscious again. He and his brother and sister managed
to drive over to be with her before she died. But they

were not able to communicate with her.

It was afterwards that the shock hit Nicholas. He cried once, briefly in the local vicar's study, but after that the stiff upper lip took over. He could not shake off the terrible feeling of remorse. He had loved his mother all his life and it seemed wrong of him to have left her on that strained and angry note. Why, he asked himself over and over again, why when his whole life was dedicated to love and concern for others, hadn't that love and concern flowed out to his mother?

His head fell forward on to his chest. He did not want to listen to his inner thoughts but they commanded attention and he knew the Lord was speaking to him through them. Here you are, they seemed to say, giving up everything for God, but you don't begin to understand the love of God. Do you? Do you? Ever so slowly he shook his head. All at once he saw the truth. It hurt him. For it was not so much that the community-changing was a failure; nor that his mother had not fully understood; nor the church closing its doors at night; it was not so much the failure of the open door and the open table: it was he that was the failure. He had failed even his own mother. It was he whose proud and stubborn heart was shot through with failure.

The trauma lived with him and crushed him for some days. It hemmed him in and hedged him about. He remembered George Bennett saying about his father, 'He is a man of tremendous integrity. You should be proud of him.' As Nicholas recalled this he realised with shame how he had criticised his parents in the past for their Establishment views. If he had spent more time loving them and less time being critical and extreme, he might have been a better witness. And a better son. For now he saw only too clearly that the Lord accepted people where they were, whatever their views.

But there were two things that helped him. One was that when he and Isla and Miles had to go through their mother's things they found she had kept one letter from each of them, which they had written after their father

had died. Nicholas held his own letter in his hand and
swallowed the lump in his throat. He had written and
told his mother 'I love you so much . . .' and she had kept
it. So she knew I loved her really, he thought, in spite of
that last meeting when I was so awful. She knew and she
accepted me, warts and all. And a tiny bit of his burden
was lifted.

Then one day when this dark night of the soul
wrapped itself round his joyless austerity until life
seemed bleak and harsh, the Lord spoke to him.

'Nicholas.'

He raised his head.

'Nicholas.'

He parted his lips.

'Nicholas, if your relationship with your mother had
been perfect . . .'

He sat quite still and listened without moving, hardly
breathing. He was stilled and he waited.

'. . . there would have been no need for me to have
died.'

He sat in total silence as he contemplated these words.
In their truth and simplicity lay peace. A peace that
understood and forgave. An acceptance that was
boundless.

At last he knew himself to be forgiven in time and
eternity. His lips moved in thankfulness. What did being
a failure matter now anyway? Everyone was a failure
without Christ. In his failure and sin at that last meeting
with his mother lay the whole glory of the gospel. The
Christ who had died and taken his sins upon himself,
understood. The Jesus who had agonised on the cross
rose again on Easter day, and with that rising had shed
light into the world, and peace and joy in the face of
hopeless failure. Thank you, Lord, he suddenly cried
out in his heart. Thank you for all those hard and
difficult days, and even for breaking me in the furnace of
failure. For I have been big in doing much for you, Lord.
I've been big in my own strength – and short on love. I
never realised that without you and your love I can do

nothing. Absolutely nothing. He rested quietly for a while after his prayer. He felt spent, as if a great storm had passed. But now everything was calm. He was at peace.

In this brokenness and new humility he felt the Lord was close to him. At his mother's funeral, which he attended with members of the household, he felt a sense of assurance in his heart that she was with the Lord. After the service they all drove back in time for a renewal service at St Mark's. Nicholas was able to join in with a grateful, thankful heart. A friend watched him praising God with his hands held high above his head, and said to him after the service, 'Only by the grace of God could you be filled with such joy at such a time.'

In the future Nicholas was able to comfort many others at funeral services with the comfort he had himself received.

'Rest assured,' he often said, 'that Christ will not reject anybody who is willing to come to him for forgiveness. Try to picture the risen Christ standing behind the cross saying, "I have accepted responsibility for all that was wrong in your relationship with your deceased loved one. Put it down to my account. Leave it at the cross and remember only the good times and the happy memories. And become a part of my forgiven and forgiving family."'

14

Into Africa

There is often a sort of unspoken expectancy that
society puts on a woman to be married and have
children. And a single woman often longs and yearns
for just that. She sees all her friends and relatives
getting married around her. It can be very
frustrating for her until she realises and accepts there
is nothing she can do about it except pray and pour
out her longing to God. If she can allow him to fill her
with his Holy Spirit and show her *He* is her eternal
bridegroom and husband, as in Isaiah 54, then she
can let Him give her satisfying and fulfilling
Christian brother and sister relationships. For He
promises in Psalm 68 to 'set the lonely in families'.

Marigold Copeland

Some weeks later Nicholas found himself at a Wholeness
Through Christ Counselling Conference, which was on
this occasion to do with the healing of the memories.
Sometimes he was himself a counsellor but on this
particular evening he was the one who was going to be
counselled. The session was proceeding well when all at
once the man counselling him went very still. Then he
said quietly, 'I think I may have a word of knowledge
about you.'

Nicholas swallowed. 'Er, yes?' he said rather hesitantly.

'Well, it is this. Are you open to marriage?'

There was a very long pause. After his initial surprise
Nicholas said at last, 'Yes, I think I am.'

But the man persisted. 'Are you *really* open to marriage?'

Nicholas thought. It was so long since he had thought of women in this way that he could hardly remember what it was like to have a girlfriend. He had subconsciously schooled himself for years in the three virtues of poverty, chastity and obedience so that the idea of a happy marriage relationship with a woman never really entered his head. The man waited quietly as Nicholas continued to think back. He remembered his girlfriends of the army days and the drinking parties. It seemed so long ago as to be part of a different person's life. He recalled with a slight shudder being pursued by a girl at college who was convinced God had told her Nicholas was to be her husband. He remembered his fear of perpetuating the class system and his old decision never to marry and have children. He looked up and found the counsellor's eyes on him.

'I think you are being challenged,' said the counsellor gently.

'Well,' said Nicholas resignedly, 'if the Lord wants me to be married then I will.'

The counsellor paused, as if weighing up something. Then all he said was, 'No, that's not what I believe the Lord is saying. You need to be really open to co-operate actively with the Lord. He's going, I think, to bring you to marriage. But this must be something that *you* really *want*.'

Nicholas was deeply challenged, but the counsellor took it further. Was Nicholas willing to believe the Lord could give him a really happy marriage in the midst of all his fears about it?

Slowly Nicholas nodded. He believed the Lord could do that. But whether he would was quite a different matter. So he bowed his head and asked the Lord for a new and godly attitude; and for the grace to accept whatever he was being called to in the future.

'You need,' said the counsellor calmly, 'to be really open to co-operate actively with the Lord.'

Not just passive, thought Nicholas with a flash of

intuition. That was the problem. He felt quite passive and unsure about this new development.

'I'll pray it through,' he said to the counsellor before he left. 'And, er, thank you.'

Some time later Nicholas went to a Fountain Trust International Conference, which was run by Michael Harper and took place in the Westminster Central Hall. He took Alan with him. He put his hand under Alan's arm and guided him up the great flight of steps. Alan was still fighting his alcoholism – while no longer living at the vicarage.

It seemed as if the whole population of London was crowding up the stairs. Noise and excitement crackled in the air. All at once Nicholas saw a familiar figure and seconds later they were laughing and smiling in greeting each other.

'Why, Marigold,' he cried, 'how lovely to see you after all this time!'

Her blue eyes danced brightly and her burnished hair swung round her face.

'Oh, yes,' she cried. 'It's so good to see you too. How are you!'

'How amazing to bump into you here among all these hundreds of people!' he said.

'Yes!'

They talked a little as they were hustled up the stairs and into the auditorium. It seemed to be the most natural thing in the world to sit together, with Alan next to Nicholas on the one side and Marigold on the other. Some music was floating through the air and people began to sing.

'Er, I don't seem to have a song sheet.'

'Oh, that's all right. Share mine.'

So they sang together. Together they prayed and then listened to the speaker. Nicholas found himself stealing a glance in Marigold's direction. She was so slender and delightful really; so full of praise to God. Wouldn't it be lovely to be married to her, he thought suddenly. Then just as suddenly, he blushed at the surprising thought and stared very hard at the song sheet. But the thought persisted. Perhaps I'll test it out, he thought, in a flurry of decision. Obviously his mind-set had been changed after that session with the counsellor. So he prayed: Lord, if you are in this, please give me confirmation it is you, because I don't want to be side-tracked and out of your will. He sat on the edge of his seat until the meeting was over. He followed her closely down the stairs, with Alan following behind.

'Oh, Marigold,' he finally managed to get out, 'would you like to come back to the vicarage and join in a group discussion with Frank Lake?' He waited, his breath held for a moment.

But she was already setting off in the direction of the exit. 'Oh, no,' she said over her shoulder. 'I'm awfully sorry but I've promised to go swimming at Hurlingham with my friends Denise and David.'

'Oh yes,' he murmured, squashing instantly his feeling of disappointment.

She stopped and turned to face him. 'Do you know,' she said, 'they've just got engaged! And both in their forties, too!'

Immediately Nicholas was interested. Here were people he knew well, of a similar age to himself and in the Anglican ministry too.

'Well, good-bye,' she said and smiled, quite unaware of anything more on his behalf than friendly interest. 'I'm going back to Africa soon,' she said finally, 'for a three months' holiday.'

When she was gone Nicholas began wondering why he had so suddenly started thinking of marriage. To Marigold. He shook his head. He simply did not know. But she was such a lovely person. He sighed. His prayer for confirmation had not been answered. Obviously the whole thing was some sort of mistake. Or was it? But more than likely he was to remain a bachelor for yet more austere and simple years. But as he walked down the road back to the vicarage he found himself humming. It was the tune he and Marigold had sung together in

Westminster Central Hall.

The South African experience was marvellous in contrast
with all that Marigold had left behind in England. The
three months were soon up and still she was in Africa, one
invitation to stay following hard on the heels of another.
She met an elderly Norwegian lady everyone called
Tante Signe. This lady had a ministry of healing and
speaking and required a younger person to drive her in a
borrowed car all around Africa as she visited missionaries
and Christian friends everywhere. Somehow Marigold
found herself in the driving seat and they were off. It was
to become the sort of life she had only ever dreamed of in
the past.

It was an adventure of living by faith, as the only
money she had left was for her ticket home. All her
carefully laid plans were turned upside down as she
learned to become totally available to God every day. She
found herself getting alongside many single women
missionaries and able to talk to them and pray for them in
ways she could never have done if she had been married.
It was a Spirit-filled ministry and she loved it. The
loneliness receded and was finally sloughed off. Even her
grief for her mother lessened naturally as she drove,
worked with and looked after Tante Signe; an elderly
woman who became for a while a mother figure to
Marigold.

After some months Marigold felt the time had come to
think of returning to England. She decided to travel home
via Israel. Eventually one day, through a chain of friends
and acquaintances, she was due to speak at the
evangelical home for orphan Arab girls in Ramallah,
outside Jerusalem, which was run by three Sisters. Sister
Mary welcomed Marigold and gave her a room
overlooking the Judaean hills, which Marigold saw to her
delight were covered with grey-green olive trees.

'We're glad you've come,' said Sister Mary. 'We get
lonely here and need some fellowship. Just share yourself.'

Marigold was encouraged by these words. During her stay she watched the women who had given themselves in singleness to the work of caring for the orphans. She saw how free and joyous they were, even the older ones who had obviously given up all thoughts of marriage. So when Sister Mary said she was tired and invited Marigold to come on a week's retreat at El Qubeibeh, one of the two supposed sites of Emmaus, Marigold agreed. The two of them stayed at the convent retreat house, next door to the Emmaus chapel with its window depicting Jesus sitting down and breaking bread with the two disciples he met on the Emmaus Road. Marigold sat for some time in the chapel and drank in the sparkling picture of stained glass. Later she threw open the window of her room and gazed out across the fragrant pine trees beyond to the Judaean hills. The room was full of birdsong and she watched the birds darting in and out of the conifers. She sighed with happiness and, opening her heart and mind to the Creator of all things, picked up from the bed a book Sister Mary had lent her. It was called *My All for Him* and was written by Basilea Schlink (Lakeland Publishers, 1975).

After the first few chapters Marigold put it down and stared unseeingly through the open window. Her heart was deeply warmed, moved to her depths. She stood up and crossed the room, unaware now of the beautiful view. So this was it. At last, her Lord had spoken to her at the depth of her being. And she was able finally to respond. She had known him as Lord, Saviour, Brother, Friend and Father. But never until now had she fully realised Jesus was her eternal bridegroom and husband, the only one who could satisfy her completely. She saw afresh that no human being, however lovely, could do that. For some minutes she basked in the eternal love offered from the heavenly bridegroom to her, his bride. I'm not single, she thought. I'll never think of myself as being single again. But I'll be single-minded for him. He is my bridegroom. She reached out her arms as if to embrace this new way of seeing life and clasp it to herself. And it satisfied her. I'll never be truly lonely again, she thought.

Deep down in her heart and without quite putting it into words, she found herself thinking, this obviously means I won't be getting married. The Lord has called me entirely to himself. I'm ready now to go and do whatever and wherever he calls. Then she turned and picked up her Bible. She stood motionless by the window for a long time, before turning to Isaiah 54 and pondering the ancient and beautiful words. Something so deep in her had opened up that she knew she would never again be the same. A slow peace washed through her and she felt as if she had come home. She knew at last she had accepted her singleness.

But next morning when she and Sister Mary went back to Jerusalem she suddenly saw a cloud of white lace and tulle in a shop window. She took a step or two nearer to look. And then she stopped dead. It was a wedding dress on display. She gulped and then held her head up bravely. Well, I'll just think of wearing that for my Lord, she said to herself firmly. In a few minutes the wrench was past and she was at peace again.

The peace was still with her when it was time for her to return home. She came via Geneva, where she rang her flat-mate Jean in the new flat in Shere.

'I'm coming home at last!' she cried. 'Expect me in two days and please can you try and find someone to meet me at the airport? I'm really looking forward to seeing you again!'

She put the phone down and smiled. The peace had lasted. She was looking forward to getting back to England and longing with single-mindedness to do the new work God would surely call her to in her own country. Perhaps it was to be missionary work among expatriated Chinese. Or as a parish worker in England. She did not know. But suddenly the future was full and exciting, filled with possibility. All she needed to achieve it was her single-mindedness and dedication to the Lord. She would find out what it was she was meant to be doing. And then she would do it!

15

Dreams for the Future

'No eye has seen,
   no ear has heard,
no mind has conceived
   what God has prepared for those who love him' —
but God has revealed it to us by his Spirit.

1 Cor. 2:9-10a NIV,
quoting Isa. 64:4

For nine years Christian Life College, run by Elmer and
Jean Darnall, rented its offices upstairs at St Mark's. Each
year Nicholas taught Genesis to the students. Early in
1976 he got to know one of them, a young man called
David Lamb. After a lecture one evening they settled
down on a couple of chairs in the upstairs hall of the
church and had a chat.

'Have you been a Christian long?' asked Nicholas.

Dave's face broke into a happy grin. 'Three years. And
three good years too.'

'Well, that's wonderful. Tell me, how did you first get
interested in Christianity?'

Dave resettled his large frame into the small chair and
laughed. 'I think we'd better have a cup of coffee, because
it's quite a long story!'

Nicholas smiled. 'All right then. Let's have a cup of
coffee together.'

Dave collected their drinks from the coffee bar and put
them on a small table between them. He took a sip and
then seemed to be searching for words – the right words.

He rested his chin on his hands for a moment.

At last he said, 'My family were Geordies originally. Dad came to London years ago to find work. He's a skilled worker, a precision lathe turner, and eventually the family settled on a nice housing estate in Watford.' He grinned and ran his hand through his mop of fair curly hair. 'You could tell we'd come up in the world, see! Because when I was a kid and we were in London we only had one bath a week and that was in a tin bath in front of the fire. I was always the last one in and the old water had to be topped up with a kettle full of hot. Anyway by the time we got to Watford there was more money around and we could have a bath every day if we wanted to. Things weren't always easy for Mum and Dad though. My grandfather was a coal merchant and he took part in the Jarrow march.' Dave's face set into a frown. 'Marching down to London in the depression of the thirties can't have been funny. It's easy for people in the south to forget the north, I suppose.'

Yes, thought Nicholas sadly.

'Anyway I grew up in Watford and,' he shrugged. 'I got into a drug-taking crowd. Whatever I did I threw myself into. First it was football, and then it was drinking and then it was drugs. I was working in a window cleaning business and living at home at the time and in spite of the drugs, somehow I managed to keep working and paying my way. You see, what happened was that we'd go to these parties and experiment with amphetamines at first. Then we gradually got into the heavier stuff: cocaine and heroin. How I concealed it from Mum and Dad I don't know. But my weekends were getting longer and longer and I was slipping into it all deeper and deeper. Then one day I accidentally gave myself an overdose and Mum found me on the bedroom floor. I'd gone quite thin as well. Not like now!' He laughed and then went serious again. 'She called the doctor and he was quite friendly and gave me a lecture. But none of it was enough to change me. It was funny though. My brother had got hold of a Bible from somewhere and he tried to tell me about Jesus, but I thought he was crazy. I didn't believe in God. It just wasn't on.'

Dave paused and drank some coffee. Nicholas watched him and his heart warmed to the younger man.

Dave said, 'Then I had this dream. It was quite something. I don't ever remember having such a vivid dream before nor remembering it like I did either.' He shook his head almost in wonder at the memory. 'In the dream I was sitting in a big crowd of people, but it was like in Bible times. Everyone was wearing those kind of flowing garments and I had a big cloth wrapped round me. I looked across and there was Jesus teaching that crowd. He just looked like any wiry Jew. But it wasn't what he looked like that mattered though.' Dave's voice dropped low and Nicholas leant forward slightly to catch his words. 'Everyone was listening and then he turned and looked across at me. And it was in his eyes.' Dave sighed. 'I'd never seen any look like that before. It was deep in his eyes. He seemed to look right into my soul, pierce me through and through. Yet it was gentle. He looked at me and I knew he loved me. And I also knew that he knew everything about me. All my sins and failures. Those eyes knew.' Dave shook his head. 'I can't describe the impact it made on me. I've never forgotten it. It's as fresh to me now as it was then.

'When I woke up it was vivid in my mind. I got up immediately and took down my Sunday school Bible. My father had forced me to go to Sunday school, you see, as a kid. Well, I found the part about the feeding of the five thousand and began reading it. It was like as if I'd been there. But, I kept saying, what does it all mean? And then, in the quietness of that bedroom, I seemed to "hear" like a voice speaking to me. I don't know whether it was inside my mind or outside in the room – but the words sank in deep. "If you go on the way you are going, you know where you'll go to," it seemed to say. "But there's another way to lead you home." Then there was a sort of silence. And after that the voice said, "I'll bring you home. If you choose it."'

There was silence between the two men at the table.

'What happened then?' asked Nicholas eventually. 'Did you decide to become a follower of Christ straight away?'

Dave shook his head. 'No. Not for about two or three years after. I spent a lot of time searching in my mind, you see. But,' and he stopped. He stared straight at Nicholas and his eyes were completely serious. 'From about one week after that dream I came off drugs. That dream was so powerful. It buried itself in my heart and soul. And I've never taken drugs again. Not even wanted to. Really that dream saved my life.

'And the word "home" meant something to me as well. I'd been searching and, it's a long story, but I decided to become a Christian two or three years later. I went into nursing and met Joyce there. She helped me. She comes from Malaysia and was doing her SEN. We've known each other for about six years now.'

For some reason Dave blushed. Nicholas smiled kindly and said nothing but there was a twinkle in his eyes.

'Well, actually,' said Dave, 'she's going to come and study at Christian Life College as well!'

'Oh, that's wonderful,' said Nicholas. Then he said, 'Dave, there's something I'd like to share with you about my vision for St Mark's. I don't know why, but it seems right.'

'Yes?'

'Yes. You've shared so much with me and I've appreciated it.' Nicholas stopped for a moment and then he said, 'At St Mark's our vision is for four things. We want to see these established.'

Dave leaned forward in concentration. 'What are they?'

'First to get the balance right of biblical teaching; so that it can release people.'

'Yes.'

'And secondly our vision is for fellowship and deep friendship in the church family. You know, where you can speak the truth in love.'

Dave sighed. 'That won't be easy.'

'No. And then of course there are worship and intercessory prayer. These four areas are important to me. Like four big pillars to hold up the life of the church.'

Dave said, 'But what about missionaries? And being a local parish church? And what about community. Someone said you were involved in one as well! And if you count all that up it makes seven aims! Not just four!'

Nicholas laughed in delight. Seven was the perfect number. 'Yes,' he said. 'I am involved in a household. And I suppose my umbrella vision, if you like to call it that, is for a church to be a local community church. A real parish church in the inner city. A real family relationship between all the members. And where people can feel joyful and released into their own unique gifts and ministries. An every-member ministry.'

Dave watched Nicholas as he said all this and his respect for the older man glowed on his face. He thought for a while and said, 'I've never given much thought to the Church of England before. When I tried out a few different churches back home it was all dark ties and hush and rows of pews. It just reinforced my impression that the Church of England wasn't for the likes of me.' He sat upright, his voice crisp with enthusiasm. 'But what you've said really makes sense. I'd like to be part of it.' Then he slumped back in his chair. 'But I come from a Pentecostal church. They don't worry there if you've got no training and no ties! They accept you as you are. I'd never be able to help in the Church of England. I've got no ties and no training and I don't speak proper!' He grinned wickedly at Nicholas, who had to chuckle. Then Dave said, 'I'll be off, then. I promised to meet Joyce. But I'll see you next week. It's been great talking to you.'

He bounced up from his chair and the empty cups rattled. Nicholas Rivett-Carnac's a real decent bloke, he thought as he thumped his way down the stairs, even if he is a baronet or whatever you call it.

As Nicholas watched him go a new and exciting possibility teased at the corner of his mind. Surely St

Mark's could use a young man like that. What did it matter if he had no so-called training? He knew the Lord and had a powerful testimony too. Nicholas had a feeling that David Lamb and St Mark's church were somehow going to be working together in the future.

It was while his mind was still full of his conversation with Dave Lamb that Nicholas bumped into an old friend downstairs at St Mark's. The friend stopped him and began to talk. They seemed to be making conversation rather, and Nicholas began to wonder what if anything it was all leading up to. He stood first on one foot and then on the other. After a few more moments of bright chatter there was a pause. The pause continued. Then the friend looked Nicholas in the eye, glanced away, coughed and said hesitantly, 'Nicholas, I believe I've been given a word for you about marriage.'

Nicholas felt himself go cold. To gain time he said, 'Oh?'

The friend continued rather more firmly. 'Yes. I believe I've been given the name of the person whom God is wanting you to marry.'

The pause reappeared and this time it was prolonged. Nicholas's heart was sinking. All at once his unhappy experience at college, of being pursued when he had not chosen to be, sprang into his mind. The college principal had helped him then and calmed him down and released him from a bondage to another's will. Was the same problem, but now in a different guise, to reassert itself?

He looked intently at his friend. This was someone he had known and trusted for years. It was obviously not undertaken lightly, to come and tell him a thing like this. To take such an enormous risk could not have been at all easy. But he knew he trusted and valued his friend's judgement. So, even though his heart had sunk to his boots, he smiled and inclined his head to hear the rest of it. Yet even as he did so, he sighed inwardly. His sigh was ever so slight, but it was there all the same as he braced himself for what was coming.

The friend said, 'The name of the person I have been

given by the Lord is Marigold Copeland!'

For a second Nicholas could not believe his ears and shot a glance at his friend's face. But no! He had heard aright. Marigold! His heart suddenly leaped, right from his shoes, through his chest and up into his face. His eyes lit up and he could not stop his mouth from breaking into a momentary smile of delight: the lovely burnished-haired Marigold, whose face shone at the mention of the Lord's name. Then he rearranged his face. 'Oh?' he said quietly.

The friend nodded and smiled and slipped away.

As the days passed Nicholas grew more and more excited, thrilled and pleased. So eventually he went back to Peter Walker, his old college principal, and asked his advice again. Peter was quite adamant in his response.

'Nicholas, the proof that this is a word from the Lord is that first of all you had that desire in your own heart to marry her. You felt it for yourself at the Fountain Trust meeting when you shared the song sheet with her. If you hadn't had your own feelings, your own choice, first, I'd be very suspicious. But this word comes simply as a confirmation of what you felt yourself.'

Nicholas clasped his hands together. 'Yes, that's true,' he said slowly.

On his way home he remembered how disappointed he had been when Marigold had been unable to come back to the vicarage with him after the meeting in Westminster Central Hall. He had wanted a confirmation then – and so wasn't this word from the Lord a more than remarkable confirmation? He really couldn't ask for more.

He prayed continually about the matter. Marigold, as he remembered her saying, was not even in England, but had gone to Africa again. It was supposed to be for three months, her flat-mate had said, but somehow that holiday was stretching out to nearly a year. He wanted to know very badly when she would be coming back.

He said in his prayers one day, 'Well, Lord, I am open to the idea of marriage. If you want it, I want it.'

He was quite taken aback, shocked almost, by an instantaneous reply deep in his soul. What do you want, Nicholas?

'Well, I want what you want, Lord, and...

What do *you* want?

'Well, Thy will be done...

That's pride, said a tiny voice in his heart of hearts. Pride and a proud detachment. You think you can live alone, continued the small voice, and have no needs and rule your life with your iron will, living a poor, simple, chaste and obedient life. So be it. But the true question is, what do *you* want?

He knelt down slowly. He thought and thought. Yes. It was true. So much of his life was bound by that iron will. It was all pride really. And the slow knowledge dawned on him, that he was being humbled by his Master. After some time and some readjustment of entrenched attitudes in the light of what he had just heard, he said, 'Yes. Yes, Lord. I want it, Lord. I do want to marry Marigold.'

Very slowly something inside him changed. A tiny warmth grew in his chest. And peace, like the sun reflected on still water, gradually seeped and then flooded into his heart. It was to be a decision he never went back on. It stood for life.

It crossed his mind to wonder what she was going to make of all this. She knew nothing about it. When he got back to the vicarage after his time of contemplation and prayer in the church there was a phone call for him. It was the friend who had had the word about Marigold.

'She's coming home from Africa in two days,' said the voice on the end of the phone. 'She's returned via Israel and Geneva. Her flat-mate has just been in touch with me.' There was a pause. Then the friend said, 'Shall I arrange a casual meeting for both of you next Monday?'

Nicholas swallowed. He was forty-nine years old but felt like a teenager about to embark on his first date.

'Er, yes, all right then,' he said. 'Next Monday it is.

16

Marriages are Made in Heaven

See! The winter is past;
    the rains are over and gone.
Flowers appear on the earth;
    the season of singing has come,
the cooing of doves
    is heard in our land.
The fig-tree forms its early fruit;
    the blossoming vines spread their fragrance.
Arise, come, my darling;
    my beautiful one, come with me.

                                        S. of S. 2:11–13 NIV

After her long journey Marigold was surprised to be
immediately invited out for the following Monday to
meet some friends from St Mark's. She felt tired and was
reluctant to go. But after some persuading, she agreed.
This was partly because she was interested in perhaps
becoming a student at Christian Life College, and
partly because she had become interested in the mission
field and wondered if the vicar, Nicholas Rivett-
Carnac, might give her some advice on which course of
action she ought to take.

So it was that she arrived. She looked round the
lounge for the friends from St Mark's, but only Nicholas
was there.

He said, 'Tell me about Africa.'

And she did. She talked and shared and talked again
to his wonderful listening ear. All her experiences and

longings to serve the Lord poured out. At last it was nearly midnight and still she was talking, half aware as she did so that she was loving every minute of it.

He said, 'I'd love to come back tomorrow morning and pray with you about your future.'

She hesitated. She had planned to rest tomorrow, but - well, he was so nice, she found she could not say no.

Next morning Nicholas arrived promptly and over a tray of coffee began again asking her about her future. She put down her coffee and stared at him in slight astonishment. The wonderful listening ear of the evening before was now replaced by 'ums' and 'buts' and 'ers'. He seemed to be able to say nothing without a stutter. She glanced at her watch. Time was pressing on.

'The thing is,' she said, 'I'm not sure what I'm supposed to be doing. I wondered about mission work for OMF, and then there's Elmer Darnall and the Christian Life College. What do you think, Nicholas?' She leaned forward, her eyes dancing.

He cleared his throat. 'Well, er, um, you see...'

'I wondered if you wanted a parish worker at St Mark's?' she interrupted crisply.

'Er, er...'

She looked at her watch again and said firmly, 'It's so nice of you to offer to come and pray with me about my future but don't you think we ought to start actually praying? It's nearly midday!'

Nicholas took a deep breath and forced his lips apart. 'I think we'd better come to the point,' he said. 'You see, it seems to me that, you see, I think that, er, well, I think God is calling us into marriage!'

If he had said bombs were dropping again on London she could not have been more startled. Utterly amazed, her eyes flew to his face. She saw he was deadly serious.

He said in a rush, 'Well this is what I believe, that we are being called to marriage. But it's up to you to hear the Lord for yourself. And if you don't,' he shrugged slightly, 'well that's that!'

She finally managed to get out the words, 'Well, this is

a shock!'

She stared at him for a few more moments and then looked at her hands. A tangle of thoughts raced through her mind: he's proposed to me right out of the blue. I've never even had a letter from him when I was in Africa. He's never taken me out to dinner or bought me any boxes of chocolates or any bunches of flowers. He could have prepared me better. But I must be very careful and I don't want to hurt his feelings because I do have a deep Christian love and respect for him and his ministry. But what a shock! He's a minister. At least I thought I could trust him! She found herself sinking to her knees on the carpet.

'This is such a shock. Perhaps we ought to pray.' And her voice sounded faint even in her own ears.

He leaned forward anxiously. 'I wouldn't have proposed like this,' he said. 'I know it's far too quick and I know what a shock it can be. Quite traumatic, really. Only I was so worried you were getting hold of the wrong end of the stick. I wasn't in any way thinking of you as the St Mark's parish worker. I had to be really honest with you. I felt it would be wrong to conceal my feelings. It was the only way. I am truly sorry.'

She said, 'Well, perhaps the best thing is for us to get to know each other.'

Even as she said it, it brought back a painful echo in her mind. Hadn't she said almost exactly the same thing to Martin a few years back and look what happened in the end. She moved away from Nicholas fractionally.

He caught her feeling of indecision and said kindly, 'There's no pressure. I'll give you two or three weeks to pray about it first on your own. I may have it wrong even, and you must have the opportunity to hear the Lord for yourself. Please believe me, I don't want you to be worried or pressurised at all.'

And so they parted, he promising to phone her in a few weeks.

She was left in the room, her mind in a whirl. Uppermost now in her thoughts was the memory of her time in the convent overlooking the Judaean hills; and the feeling she had had of being called at the age of thirty-nine to be single. She had known then that she had finally accepted it. Peace had come then. Peace and a knowledge that a whole new area of work would open up to her when she came home. She accepted it still and had had peace about it until a few minutes previously. How could this proposal of Nicholas's be in God's will, then? Wasn't the distraction of a wrong romance what held back so many from becoming all out for the Lord? Even if she did go along with it, hadn't she done that before – and been bitterly hurt and disappointed? She shook her head. This was the last thing she had expected to happen to her when she returned to England. It was the very last thing in her thoughts.

When the two to three week period was nearly complete she received the telephone call from Nicholas as she knew she would.

He said, 'Can I come down and see you on my day off next Monday?'

'Er, yes, all right,' she replied. She was not eager. She certainly had not fallen in love. She was still confused and very unsure. But yes, she had to admit it. She was pleased he had phoned. And pleased he was coming. She was actually looking forward to seeing him. She put the phone down and thought for a moment. Would she be able to cope with him? Would she be able to make him relax? He was so serious, repressed almost. He never laughed. He needs to relax, she found herself thinking. And he really ought to have shirts without frayed collars and cuffs!

For their first date Nicholas came over to Shere in a borrowed car and took Marigold to a Capel Bible Week meeting. As the day went on he seemed to expand, glow almost. He kept introducing her to what seemed like hundreds of his friends. Marigold found herself becoming rather tense as smiling face after smiling face said hallo. But Nicholas appeared to enjoy it all, almost as if it were an adventure to him. By the end of the day she was tired. Yet she had to admit he was charming.

As the months slipped by the two of them slowly got to know each other, meeting on the Monday that was his day off. The countryside around Shere was beautiful and Marigold wanted to share it with him. One Monday they walked in Albury Park next door to the old rectory. There was a stream by the little old church in the park.

'Oh, it's so warm, let's sit by the stream,' cried Marigold and flung herself on to the grass.

Rather gingerly Nicholas followed her, lowering himself down. Suddenly she was pulling at her shoes and slipping off her stockings. She thrust her bare feet into the water and they made a tiny splash.

'Oh, Nicholas, it's lovely feeling the water running over my toes!' She chuckled and splashed her feet up and down. 'Come on, Nicholas, why don't you paddle too!'

There was a silence.

Then he said, 'I beg your pardon?'

'Paddle! It's lovely!'

'You mean take off my shoes and socks and dangle my feet in that stream?'

She looked at him and laughed. 'Yes. Why not?'

'Well – it's not something I'd do normally.'

'Oh.' She was surprised. It was so natural to her. She stole a quick glance at him and saw his face had a rather granite and resigned look about it.

'I've never heard of anyone except children paddling,' he said.

'Oh.'

There were a few moments of silence. Then she watched, fascinated, as he leaned forward and slowly untied first one shoe lace and then the other. Then he put his shoes in a precise pair on the grassy bank. He peeled off his socks one by one and placed them neatly inside the shoes. His face was a study. It's quite a shock to him, she thought suddenly. He's obviously thinking, whatever will I have to do next to marry this girl! As

slowly as a snail his feet inched towards the water. Then
his toe tickled the surface of the dancing stream. And
plop, his heel followed after. The other foot reluctantly
joined the first and she watched, without breathing a
word, as the beautiful white feet wriggled on the bed of
the stream. All at once came a sound she'd very rarely
heard. It began as a chuckle and ended as a great big
laugh. Nicholas was standing in the stream, shaking
with laughter.

Back at the flat later he changed into his dog collar
and dried his feet so as to be ready for a meeting he had
to address that evening. She brought him a cup of tea
and he drank it on the sofa, where they sat in silence for
some time. Then he put down his cup and saucer on a
sidetable and reached across to where she was sitting.
He took her hand in his and kissed it gently. The
delicacy and kindness of his action shook Marigold. She
accepted his kiss and knew it to have been a precious
moment. The gentlemanliness of his behaviour was so
unlike any way she had been treated before. It was – well
– it was lovely.

But as the months continued to go by Nicholas began
to worry. Suppose she did not love him enough to marry
him? Supposing she had been too hurt before to learn to
trust a man again? Supposing he was to be for ever a sort
of kindly elder-brother figure to her, and not the
husband he longed to be? He spent some anxious nights
at the vicarage tossing and turning until the small hours
wondering how to make her love him. In his
imagination he strove to work it out. And he became
quite tense and anxious again in the process. The old
strained, burdened look was replacing the relaxed and
happy laughter of recent weeks. At last he poured it all
out to the Lord and waited patiently for his answer.

In the meantime he decided to persevere with
Marigold and began to take her for a day at a time to his
Aunt Mona's. She still lived at Fornham St Martin in
Nicholas's parents' old house. Marigold loved it there.
She loved the beautiful rooms and the gracious

furniture, the huge grounds and the air of peace. Aunt Mona was kindness itself. And as Marigold relaxed in their lovely old home so Nicholas grew in understanding of how she felt.

'It seemed so right in Israel,' she said, 'that call to be single. It took me years to get to that point and then at last I finally accepted it and was at peace about it. Now I just can't,' and she twisted her hands together. 'I can't quite see how getting married fits into all that.' She saw a shadow slip almost imperceptibly across his face. Impulsively she reached out a hand. 'It's not that I don't like the idea – and I do certainly like you – it's just that I need to hear it from the Lord himself.'

He said, 'Well, maybe what happened in Israel wasn't so much of a call to be single as a call to be willing to be single. And that's a different thing.'

'Yes. I know.' She hung her head. 'But I need to hear it for myself.'

Later as Nicholas thought about this he felt the Lord draw close to him and intimate in a very still and very small voice: Nicholas, you can't do this. You cannot bring this to pass. You can't make her love you. You have to trust me in the matter.

He bowed his head. Yes, it was true. His heart was in accord with what he had just heard. He had to trust the Lord in this exceedingly difficult and delicate matter. He had to trust the Lord to win Marigold for him.

Events however took a far quicker turn than expected. One day Nicholas heard that Sister Mary was coming over to England. This was the same Sister Mary with whom Marigold had stayed in the convent and who had lent her the book that had so challenged her singleness.

'Marigold,' he said, 'I'm going to believe that the Lord will speak through Sister Mary to you about us. When you go to that prayer meeting with her tomorrow I believe she who is committed to being single will speak. One way or the other!'

Marigold was startled. Then she nodded. 'All right,'

she said.

By the time Marigold came back to Shere the next evening her face was radiant.

'She did,' cried Marigold. 'She gave a word!'

Nicholas suddenly went very still. 'What . . . ?'

'She said, "Marigold, the Lord says to you, Go forward!"' And, eyes shining Marigold clapped her hands together.

Nicholas was thrilled.

But by the following evening Marigold was again full of doubt. He took her hand and said jokingly, 'How much more evidence do we need?'

She shook her head.

So after a moment he said, 'If it's a nice day tomorrow, let's go down to the beach and bathe.'

She brightened up at once. 'Oh, yes. Lovely.'

Next day as they sat together on the beach, hair wet and wrapped in towels, she suddenly turned to him and clung to him tightly. He waited, his heart in his mouth.

'Nicholas,' she said in a muffled voice, 'don't ever leave me, will you?'

'No, of course not, darling,' he said. He put his arm round her. 'I'll never leave you. I've never wanted to.'

She looked up at him, her face a little red. 'You won't be like the others? I know they couldn't help it, only I was always the one who was left.'

He shook his head and clasped her so hard that his knuckles were taut. 'I will never leave you,' he repeated.

Their relationship slowly matured throughout that autumn until one day in Advent she said when he least expected it, 'I feel quite happy and at peace now, Nicholas. It's well, it's going to be all right.'

'You mean?'

She smiled shyly, 'I mean I'd like to get engaged.'

'I'm so thrilled to hear you say it now,' he cried.

She said, 'I saw my brother and sister-in-law and family the other day. I began to tell them about you, Nicholas, and I told them I still wasn't sure about this engagement. They knew all about my past of course and how sensitive I was about plunging into another relationship.'

'Go on,' he said intently.

'Well, it was just so helpful to be able to talk about it to them. And then the most amazing thing happened. It was on my way back. I stopped in Tunbridge Wells and went into a church that was open so that I could be quiet. I knelt down and poured out my heart to God again. I told him everything. I prayed that if our marriage was the "right" thing, then he would go on confirming that to me. No sooner had I prayed this when I felt a tap on my shoulder. I looked up and saw a man I didn't know. He must have been a member of the church. Anyway he opened his mouth and said simply. "The Lord tells me I must tell you that whatever it is you are praying about and are burdened about, he wants you to know it is all right. He wants you to go forward!" Then quietly he drifted away and slipped outside.'

Nicholas stared at her, his thoughts racing.

'An absolute joy and peace flooded through me then,' she said. 'I felt I'd had a complete confirmation. A perfect answer to prayer. So, yes, I'd like to get engaged!'

'Oh, that's wonderful,' he cried and every fibre of his being thrilled with wonder and joy. 'I tell you what,' he said. 'I'd like to buy you a ring from a shop my parents used sometimes at Bury St Edmunds. You can find a ring and choose it there. I don't know a thing about jewellery!'

She lifted her face to his. 'That's lovely,' she whispered.

He laughed suddenly, a deep, clear ringing laugh. 'Here we are,' he said. 'I'm nearly fifty!'

'And I'm nearly forty!'

'And we're dancing about like a pair of teenagers!'

'Better than teenagers,' she said.

'And let's get engaged at Christmas!'

'We could announce it at the Christmas Eve midnight communion service,' she said, 'and have a party first.'

'Right,' he said. 'What a wonderful idea.'

When the day came for choosing the ring, they came rather shyly into the shop. Marigold examined tray after tray of rings. But somehow none of them seemed quite right. She tried on one after another. Several stuck on her finger and the assistant rushed to the back of the shop to find some soap. Marigold saw Nicholas glance at his watch.

'Have we got time?' she asked.

'Yes, just, beloved,' he said.

She stared rather hopelessly at the counter, knowing that if she did not hurry up they would miss the train to London and Nicholas would be late for his Christian Life College lecture on Genesis. If only she could find a sapphire or a turquoise that seemed just right.

His hand was fingering yet another glittering tray when all at once he said, 'That's a nice one.'

The assistant lifted it up and placed it before them. It was an oval garnet surrounded by diamonds.

'It's beautiful,' she said breathlessly, as it glowed and gleamed red as life in her palm.

'It reminds me of the blood of Christ,' he said in a whisper.

'Oh, I like it,' she said. 'Please can I have it?'

And so the choice was made. A choice that reminded them whenever they looked at it, that Christ had shed his blood for them, and that the same Christ had brought them together.

They raced for the train and just missed it. They flew back to Fornham House, and the gardener George very kindly got the car out and drove them as fast as he dared to Cambridge. There they tore on to the platform, only to miss that train as well. Nicholas shrugged and rang Elmer Darnall, who promised to cover the first half of his lecture for him.

Nicholas said, 'I told him we had been buying a ring and he seemed rather pleased!'

Eventually Nicholas and Marigold arrived at the lecture and were greeted by an enormous uproar from the students. Everyone was delighted. In the end Nicholas gave up trying to teach Genesis 2 in the second half of his lecture that night. The students simply found the whole subject too relevant to be able to settle down!

Soon it was Christmas Eve and time for the engagement to be announced to a hushed but twinkle-eyed congregation, who were sitting formally in the pews. Hugh Wakeling the curate did it for them and said afterwards that the most nerve-racking thing he had ever had to do was to announce his vicar's engagement! All was now set for their wedding on June 11th 1977. David Pawson from Marigold's church at Millmead gave them a pre-wedding talk, which included a breathtaking vision for what Christian marriage could mean. Colin Urquhart was to take the service. Sandy Millar was to be the best man. The whole choir from Millmead, of which Marigold had been a member, and the Millmead Music Group were to lead the singing, praise and worship. The St Mark's family did everything else; ushering, catering, flowers, everything under the supervision of Anthony Cordle. And Marigold and Nicholas gave a party for all the helpers beforehand.

They planned for the hundreds of guests to go to a reception in the vicarage garden, as Nicholas decided it was not right to spend a lot of money on a marquee. 'We'll trust for a fine day,' he said confidently.

Marigold's head was crammed with details. 'The guests will have to file through the Montgomery Hall, take a plate of food and drink and sit at some little tables under sun umbrellas in the garden,' she said.

Six hundred fruit jellies were being made by some girls in their flat. 'They've got jelly in cartons everywhere in that flat!' she cried.

Nicholas hardly heard her. He was busy looking up at the sky and wondering if the weather would hold for the next day.

On the day it was raining. Marigold got ready in a fumble of excitement and a tremble of billowing white.

She watched the rain scoring down the windows of the car as she was driven sedately to the church with her uncle. She felt anything but sedate. Her stomach was a knot of butterflies. But as she was handed out of the car and walked up the flight of steps to St Mark's doorway a miracle seemed to happen. The rain began to stop and photos were taken outside. As she entered the church on her uncle's arm, followed by six bridesmaids and a pageboy, her nervousness seemed to melt away for she was met with a great burst of praise and joy from the Music Group and was able to join in the singing from Psalm 100: 'I will enter his gates with thanksgiving in my heart. I will enter his courts with praise.' During the service the African New Testament Church girls' choir sang two songs unaccompanied and in African style. This reminded Marigold of her deep links with the African Church. She and Nicholas were filled with joy at the blessing of it all. But during the service everyone could hear the rain drumming on the roof of the church.

For the bride and groom there was no time to think about the weather as they swept smiling delightedly down the aisle past rows and rows of equally smiling guests. They moved on and out into a gradual miracle of June sunshine and white scudding clouds in a vibrant blue sky. As they drove to the vicarage garden for the photos they saw the wind blowing all the table cloths on the little tables dry. Helpers were scurrying here, there and everywhere putting the jellies out. Nicholas clasped Marigold's hand very tightly in the garden and they gazed for a quick moment into each other's eyes. It was to be the start of a wonderfully happy marriage; a marriage that matured and bloomed over the years with richness and joy.

Part IV
Thy Will be Done

Jesus said: 'I will build my church.'

Matt. 16:18 NIV

One of the greatest needs today is for the Church to be a listening people, responsive to God. The dangers confronting us in the world make it essential that the nations should be receiving the word of God for our times. They can only do this through the Church, whose task it is as the body of Christ, to carry out the work of Christ in the world and to proclaim faithfully the word of God in the hearing of the nations.

The Church is to be the watchman to the nations... And every believer has a part – a vital part – to play in this prophetic task.

Clifford Hill
A Prophetic People
(Fount, 1986), ch.13

17

Passers By

Jesus said:

A man was going down from Jerusalem to Jericho,
when he fell into the hands of robbers... A priest
happened to be going down the same road, and when
he saw the man, he passed by on the other side. So
too, a Levite, when he came to the place and saw
him, passed by on the other side. But a Samaritan, as
he travelled, came where the man was; and when he
saw him, he took pity on him. He went to him and
bandaged his wounds, pouring on oil and wine...
and took care of him.

And Jesus said:

Go and do likewise.

Luke 10:30–37 NIV

Nicholas left St Mark's Church School with the glad
shouts of excited children ringing in his ears. He smiled
to himself. They loved their class Christmas plays so
much. It was a pity he had this late afternoon meeting to
discuss ways of grouping the gradual influx of new
people into the church. He hurried forward, his feet
slipping occasionally on the icy pavement. He glanced
back at the squat, single-storey building. All the lights
were on and shone out into the December gloom. Jean
Parker the headmistress did such a marvellous job. The

children were really happy this afternoon and it was
good that Marigold had been there and was now about
to have tea, and simply lovely that his sister Isla had
come along as well and ...

His feet suddenly shot from under him. He gave an
enormous jerk and somehow managed to steady himself
in time. That was a near thing, he thought, and
buttoned up his coat tightly against the icy wind. He
must be more careful. The pavements were like a sheet
of glass and he slowed down.

But seconds later he was hurrying again, his mind
focusing on the meeting ahead with Roger Bagge, the
London City Missioner from Vauxhall, who was also an
elder of St Mark's and in charge of the evangelism. Since
Roger had joined the church in 1975 the links between
St Mark's and the City Mission work at Caine Hall were
strengthening all the time. He and Roger got on really
well and their respective gifts complemented one
another. They had both noticed how the numbers of
people coming to church, particularly in the evening,
were steadily creeping up now. They had been around
the fifty mark but now, sometimes, it was nearly a
hundred. Yet he and Roger had had no particular
outreach or evangelistic drive. Roger said people
somehow were sensing God and ...

Nicholas never quite knew what happened nex' One
moment he was scurrying along, head bowed into the
wind, his mind busy with his thoughts. The next his feet
slid violently away from under him. He clawed wildly at
the air. But in a second the pavement seemed to come up
and bang him with such a force that for a moment
everything went dark.

He found himself lying on his back on the black ice
with the cold smarting through him. After a minute he
got his breath back and attempted to get up. But
however hard he tried, the pain in his chest was so severe
that he could not draw his legs up and get to his feet. The
simple action of standing upright, done normally
without a second thought, eluded him. He was just

beginning to wonder what to do when he breathed easier. He saw some feet and legs coming towards him. It was a passer-by and just at the right moment. He made a movement with his hand and called out, 'Please. Could you help me?' The feet never wavered. The legs did not falter. They passed by as if they had not seen him. Nicholas bit his lip. Then he thought, well, never mind. Perhaps they were in a hurry. There will be someone else.

And there was. There were in fact many people who passed him by as he lay on the ice that afternoon near the Oval Cricket Ground entrance. After a while he realised that not one of them was going to help him. So he lay face down on the pavement and tried to pray. He had been there some little while with the pain increasing in his side, before the thought struck him. Do you see, said the thought, how people pass you by on the other side? As if they don't see you. Or don't want to see you. And you see how much it hurts you in mind and in body - be so ignored. Now you know what it feels like – to be the one who is passed by.

Nicholas closed his eyes. Yes, he knew now. The pain. The feelings of helplessness, uselessness, anger, misery even. But wasn't that what the inner city people must feel so much of the time? They were the passed-by; passed by on the other side so often by the Establishment, by the Church, by the middle classes, by ignorance. It wasn't that people were actively evil, but more that they had blinkered vision, tunnel hearts, so that they hardly saw the person crushed and collapsed under the load of life.

He sighed. He had absorbed the lesson. Oh yes, and in what a dramatic way. But as he tried yet again to get up, he did begin to wonder how much longer he was going to have to lie there. He raised his head and stared back at the school. If only he could manage to pull himself up and somehow get back to it, someone would help him.

After some time and considerable pain in his numb limbs he managed to drag himself up and stagger to the

school entrance. Then at last a voice, warm with
concern, seemed to speak to his ear, 'Are you all right?'
and a couple of strong hands guided him inside.
Everyone was horrified to see him so badly shaken. Jean
Parker called an ambulance and he was taken to
Casualty at St Thomas' hospital. After waiting hours
there surrounded by other victims of the black ice, he
was sent home and told to rest. He had broken ribs, was
concussed and was very sick.

Next day Nicholas was better and able to relax in bed.
But the lesson he had learned so painfully the previous
afternoon was not, he knew, ever going to pass him by.
He remembered how in the days of the work with the
down-and-outs at Shorts Gardens he had thought that
his ministry was to bring Jesus to the poor. And it was
true that he still felt this call deeply and believed in it
passionately. But now he realised even more fully this
was not simply a call to the poor. It was even bigger and
wider than that. It was nothing short of a call to the lost.
And that included everyone. Some of the feet, he
remembered, that had passed him by that afternoon
were not the feet and legs of poor people. They had been
well-shod and warmly and fashionably clothed. His call
was as much to such people as to the poor. He bowed his
head and warmed his hands round his cup of tea. As he
did so he remembered the words of Christ, 'I have come
to seek and to save the lost' (Luke 19:10). Nicholas
thought further. Somehow the Church had to get out
and find folk, bring more people in, and be good
Samaritans in the neighbourhood. But how?

Winter moved slowly to spring that year. Soon
Nicholas and Marigold's first wedding anniversary was
looming. They had had a good year living in the small
two-storey flat which they rented from the Bible and
Medical Missionary Fellowship (BMMF). They often
joked about having to live near the gas works on the one
hand, the gin and vodka factory on the other and the
Oval cricket ground nearby. Yet when they had a
moment to spare and looked out of their windows down

Kennington Road they could see not only traffic, flats, roads, shops and people, but also the tops of trees. And across the main road and just out of sight was Kennington Park.

Sometimes Marigold and Helen Clark took Hannah the dog for a walk there. The space, greenery and approximation of countryside meant a lot to Marigold, as did the grass and trees around the church itself. In fact the park and the church grounds were the only spacious bits of green for anyone to walk in anywhere in Kennington, as far as she could see. In the summer Jean Parker and other teachers brought the children down from the school to play organised team games on the grass in the park. And once they held a summer sports day on the grass outside the church. Marigold joined in the fun and took photos for her album and the church magazine. It was good to see the children racing round on the grass beneath the trees. It was lovely to hear them laughing and joking, as they ran races, danced and had a tug of war.

Kennington was a very mixed place. There were the huge curves of the council flats, red-bricked and in 1930s style, often in poor repair. There was decaying property, broken windows, graffiti and rubbish. And then there were the little squares hidden away with gracious Georgian houses, all spruce and sparkling. Vandals were at work here. And MPs lived here. It was a jumble of South-East London properties. Often the council blocks had flats that were 'hard-to-let', while professional people were beginning to move into the area and see parts of it as 'up and coming'. The local people too were a complete mixture: black, white, Asian, professional and working class. This was reflected in the congregation. Some of the St Mark's people lived in Brixton and some came from the area that stretched into Clapham, 'Muggers' Mile' as it came to be known. Marigold knew they lived in a dangerous area and wondered what would happen if violence spilled out more obviously into the streets of Kennington. She was

very thankful that God had given her his peace, a
freedom from fear and a deep love for the people living
there. Nevertheless she had found it quite a trauma to
have to come and live in the London flat after being in
the country, which she loved. It was a sacrifice for her,
and yet as she became knitted into the family of St
Mark's she and Nicholas knew themselves blessed in
their relationship and neither had ever felt so happy and
secure in their lives as they did now. Perhaps there were
many things they might have done together if they had
had the time. But in putting the Lord's work first they
found happiness and peace.

There were however adjustments to be made. As with
all other newly-married couples it was not always easy
for them. Nicholas found Marigold's habit of being late
on occasions difficult to cope with; especially after ten
years of punctuality drilled into him in his army days.
Yet after his fall on the ice he discovered himself
thinking more and more of the Good Samaritan; and of
Marigold with her more African concept of time.
Whereas Europeans were always on the dot, tensed up
and ready for action, Africans would wait and put
people first. It was part of their culture. He began to see
being late as not a negative thing, but the other way
round. If you were too worried about a time schedule
you might be neglecting to show love somewhere, too
busy to stop, always in haste, of necessity having to pass
by on the other side. He saw that Marigold had a heart
full of love and that she would not leave a person or a
situation until she had done and said all she could. And
if that meant she was going to be late, so be it. They were
going to have to learn to listen to each other and learn
how to keep the Lord's time.

For his part Nicholas began to see how, ever since his
Bermondsey days, he had begun bottling up his feelings.
For long years he had repressed his thoughts and he
realised now that he had only begun to get the vision of
how to walk in the light and share himself after he had
come to St Mark's, where household life in the vicarage

had so greatly helped him. But learning to share was to
be a gradual thing and it was Marigold who helped him
enormously and so patiently in this area.

Right from the beginning they decided never to go to
sleep until they had put right any wrong thought, word
or action between them. This was costly in one way but
freeing in another. In any case, he had to admit, she
would always sense if he was holding something back.
One particular evening he simply could not bring
himself to say 'sorry' for being impatient with her earlier
in the day. He turned over immediately in the bed and
went to sleep. But in the night he woke up and knew he
must say sorry to her. She had come to bed later than he
had, and it took quite a lot of grace on her part to accept
the first apology, and then hear the second apology for
waking her after a gruelling day!

The marriage was to bring a different vision for
money to him. In the community he had had nothing.
Then all his stipend had gone into the common purse for
the running of the household in the vicarage. Indeed his
brother Miles had helped them sort out the complexities
of a common purse. Then he had left the household
when he married and they had come to the flat. He
knew he had tried to follow a life of simplicity and
poverty in those community and household years and
did not regret them. But life then had had its legalistic
and austere side. Now with Marigold he found himself
relaxing; learning that in spite of the very real simplicity
of their lifestyle in the flat he was now a steward of his
possessions for the Lord. There were indeed to be foreign
holidays occasionally and even luxuries sometimes. He
had to learn to accept them all with joy and
thanksgiving. It was Marigold who helped him into this
new freedom and relaxation and gave him the gift of
happiness.

They also decided that they wanted their home to be
open. They had one spare single room and one sofa, and
with great willingness offered these to God and asked
him to send them people they could care for, as and

when it seemed right to do so.

Their first 'guest' was an elderly Nigerian who felt like committing suicide and had nowhere to go. He lived with them for a while. His father was a headmaster and he was himself intelligent but appeared to live in a fantasy world, unable to cope with reality. It was hard to 'reach' him and for a few months it was demanding on both of them. Eventually Nicholas realised it was not good for the situation to continue. So they found the man a room and paid the first week's rent. Sadly he never kept in touch with them. They felt keenly the pain of seeing something that had not worked out.

The Nigerian was only the first of several people who came to live with them over the years. There was a Zimbabwean girl from the Matabele tribe who came to study at the Christian Life College. Hers was the old story. Genuine Christian though she was she could not resist the advances made to her by an old boyfriend, just over from Zimbabwe. She became pregnant. He left her and she remained in London, desperate, submerged in guilt, suicidal and wondering about an abortion. Marigold and Nicholas took her in and really rescued her. She lived with them for several months, decided to keep the baby and after much prayer received the courage to go on living. There was for her a happy ending: she took the baby home to Zimbabwe, her own mother helped and now she is a happily married woman with a son growing up whose life was spared because Christians in England gave a desperate young woman the love and support she needed at a critical time in her life.

A second girl they were to have much to do with was Miranda, a young solicitor working in the City. She came along to a Welcoming Group at the church one evening. But at the end she simply slid to the floor and when they tried to bring her round with prayer and ministry, nothing happened. Eventually they carried her downstairs and took her to the hospital in their car. The hospital rang them next morning and asked them to take her home and look after her. Marigold said, 'It was as if the Lord himself spoke to us through this phone call. We decided to take her back to our own home.' As they got to know her they discovered she was brilliantly clever and had gained a First at Cambridge. About a year before she had realised how empty her life was and had given her heart to Jesus. But twenty-five years of living without God and the recent death of her father had taken their toll. She now had a severe psychiatric illness.

'There were difficult times,' said Marigold, 'but because Miranda loved Jesus so much she was able to respond to our love for her, and because deep down she believed he could heal her, we were able to spend many hours praying with her. She needed medical help too and she eventually became a patient of Stuart Checkley's, a consultant psychiatrist at the Maudsley Hospital and a member of St Mark's. Linda, Peggy and others at the church have also befriended and supported her over the years. Now eight years later she is a completely different person, able to live alone and hold down a worthwhile job. She remains a committed member of St Mark's, particularly gifted in hospitality and ministering to the elderly. And of course when she invites us to lunch and gives us one of those meals she is so good at cooking, we love it!'

There was another girl who lived with them who was anorexic. The only way Marigold could get her to eat was to let her prepare her own food before their meals and then eat it alone. Stuart Checkley again helped Nicholas and Marigold with advice, which included suggesting a year in hospital for the girl. After two years of support from many at St Mark's, much of the time passing in difficult days, this girl finally won the battle against anorexia, put on weight, stopped being suicidal, went home and managed to hold down a full-time job in the City. Again it was someone whose life had been restored, but only by much sacrifice and pouring out of Nicholas and Marigold to her.

Blessing came to Nicholas and Marigold because of all this. And also there was cost. It was almost like having a ready-made family, Marigold joked sometimes. And secretly in her heart of hearts, she thought to herself that perhaps one day they might just not be too old to have a child of their own. In the meantime they carried on with their task of re-parenting any young person who came to them in need. So many, they found had not had love and security in early childhood, and much time needed to be spent with them. Yes, the Lord could make it up to a person, but only step by step as deep emotional scars were slowly healed.

'Of course,' said Marigold, 'you can only point someone to the Father. You can never replace a human parent. That wouldn't be right. But our role is a complementary one, to help them to understand his love.'

As the years went by Marigold threw herself into her life as a vicar's wife, working alongside Nicholas, always ready to visit someone in need or take someone to a hospital appointment or drive them miles in the car, take them shopping, buy them clothes and gifts or pray with them. She often became very tired but soldiered on. Her whole life was devoted to caring for people in one way or another. Often she and Nicholas would get a phone call late at night and then have to make up the sofa for a bed; or they would race in the car over to St Thomas' hospital either to visit a parishioner or, more seriously, to see someone in Casualty. Only afterward in the late-night drive home could they enjoy the vista of the Houses of Parliament and Big Ben across the Thames.

There were lighter moments though, when on days off they could wander hand in hand in the setting sun along the Jubilee Walk down by the river. They would pass in front of the Festival Hall and the South Bank Centre and then go in for a snack supper and listen to music in the foyer of the National Theatre. Often they walked in one of the many parks in London enjoying the air and the flowers. Sometimes they sat on the terrace of a café and watched the river and the view of St Paul's. It was at such moments, when all the pressure slipped away and life was golden that romance blossomed in the air between them. They could look into each other's eyes or laugh at some shared memory or joke. Once or twice a year on days off they stayed with their families in their country homes or shared meals with them in London. Their families have always been encouraging and supportive and Nicholas and Marigold would return to work in Kennington refreshed.

By the end of 1978 Nicholas was able to write in *Crossroads*, the church magazine, that the congregation had increased to some two hundred regulars and that the giving was up by sixty-six per cent. The house groups were bulging at the seams and the crypt had been opened up and brought into use for the youth work and the crèche. The children stayed in the body of the church at the beginning and end of the morning service and trooped off in the middle to the crèche or for their own junior church upstairs. Once a month Roger Bagge led a family service when the children stayed throughout.

The mornings had a structured and timed approach, mainly for the needs of the children, and the congregation used the liturgy for communion. In contrast the evening service was freer. There was always room made for the Holy Spirit to prompt the use of spiritual gifts and they were used frequently, though less so in the mornings. There was no controversy about the Holy Spirit's work at St Mark's. The evening service at first only had about thirty people and so was small enough for the gifts to be used without giving offence. This thrilled Nicholas.

He saw how the same people began coming on a Wednesday evening to the prayer meeting, all longing for the work of the Spirit in their lives. It was decided to hold the AGM on a Wednesday evening as well, as folk were already used to coming out then. It was open to any and all who wanted to come. When it came to the time for electing church officers for the PCC they were all elected from among the people who had bothered to come to the meeting, people who loved God and who prayed. So with mounting excitement Nicholas realised that all the leaders were going to be spiritually-minded people. So it was, and is, that Nicholas is able to say how inspiring and wonderful his PCC meetings are. If the members get stuck or argue the whole meeting pauses and prays, before continuing with a quieter and rather different spirit. 'As far as I know,' said Nicholas, 'there's never been a meeting where anyone's gone away with bitterness.'

Mervyn Stockwood, Bishop of Southwark, did all he could to encourage the renewal he perceived to be happening in the diocese and at St Mark's. He appointed Nicholas an honorary canon of the cathedral. Nicholas was also voted Rural Dean of Lambeth for five years by his fellow clergy in Lambeth.

The present Rural Dean is Chris Guinness, a neighbouring vicar, who was recently asked what if anything the wider Church of England could learn from St Mark's. He answered spontaneously: 'In the context of an inner city environment with all its brokenness both within individual lives and in many structures that militate against the individual, St Mark's presents the gospel as Good News. They have responded to the Lord's call to proclaim Good News to the poor, to bind up the broken-hearted, to release the captives and to heal the sick. And they have waited on the Lord with prayer and fasting until they have received the power of the Holy Spirit to do this. I know that they consider prayer is the key. Prayer lies behind everything.'

In the early hours one morning Helen Clark woke up with a start to the sound of her phone ringing. As she fumbled for the receiver she noticed the time: it was two o'clock. She shuddered and tried to take in the call.

'It's Marigold,' said the well-known voice. 'I'm so sorry to wake you, but there's been a bomb scare at the

gas works. Everyone who lives nearby is being
evacuated by the police, including us! We're opening up
the church and taking people in. Can you come? It's so
cold and we're all shivering in our night clothes! And
can you bring some milk for the tea!'

Helen came, as did some of the other St Mark's
people. They discovered that the flats had been
evacuated by the police, and people, some quite shocked
and distressed, began pouring into the church. Some
carried budgies in their cages. Others led in dogs and
cats. For what seemed the whole night cups of tea and
coffee were made and passed round. It was a general
mêlée of children, animals and folks yawning and
talking. Some even bedded down on the pews. The noise
was tremendous. Many people leaned forward to thank
Helen and to ask about the church.

'This is *your* church,' she found herself saying for the
hundredth time that night. 'It's *your* church and we are
here to help you.'

'Yes,' said several people, 'and when the police tried
to take us to the pub, it was closed! There was no one
there! We found out that the landlord lives in
Kensington! But fancy the church being open *and* the
vicar living here in Kennington!'

It was the following year that the full fruit of the night
of the bomb scare became apparent. When St Mark's
people began nervously to visit in the parish they found
that once they said they were from *St Mark's* church
people remembered it from the night of the bomb scare.
Their faces cleared and many were happy to be visited
and receive the parish magazine. The good reputation
of the school helped during the visiting too. Parents of
children there also knew of the church and were happy
on the whole to receive a visit.

David Lamb and his wife Joyce had come to live in
the parish and eventually spent ten months in the
vicarage household, now run by Graham and Maureen
Ashdown. Nicholas believed in Dave and gave him the
opportunity to preach and help out at church. He

wanted Dave to have the opportunity to use his gifts of evangelism and preaching. Dave, who would have naturally gravitated towards a Pentecostal church, stayed on, being much encouraged by Nicholas and Marigold and by the other members of the leadership team.

'What a man Nicholas is,' Dave said to Joyce one day. 'He gives his pulpit over to me when I'm not even fully trained. He's always putting other people into the way of doing things. Releasing their talents he calls it. But he doesn't covet the limelight for himself. There's no personality cult at the church, unlike some places I've been to! He almost deliberately puts himself into the background. But not because he's weak. It's because he's strong and...' Here Dave ran out of words and his hands plunged through his unruly mop of hair. He drew breath and started again. 'And now he's encouraging us to go off and accept the invitation to preach in Malaysia.' He shook his head. 'And the church is sending us out and giving us this marvellous gift of £400 and...'

'It's for a one way ticket,' said Joyce, ever practical. 'We'll have to pray our way home again!'

Dave laughed. That was not a problem which worried him at the moment. 'Haven't you noticed how things have improved with Nicholas now Marigold's on the scene? It was tea in mugs with no saucers before. But now you get a cup, saucer and a spoon!'

Joyce giggled.

'And his clothes have improved too. Obviously marriage is suiting him in more ways than one! At last he's stopped wearing that old grey jacket with the enormous lapels he got from Oxfam! Out of date wasn't in it!'

Joyce said, 'I saw him yesterday jogging from their flat to the church.'

'Yes. I know. He likes to keep fit and he likes playing football in the park and talking to people there too.'

'Dave, do you know what?'

He looked at her with his eyes wide open and shook
his head.

'Well, I just remembered,' she said, 'a nursing friend
of mine told me she was working as an agency nurse at
one of the hospitals. About two years ago it was. Anyway
a porter there was using the lift to the operating theatre
and he noticed she had this Christian badge on her coat.
He asked her if she was a Christian and when she said
yes, he said, "Where do you go to church?" She said St
Mark's.

"Oh, you go to Nick's church do you?"

"Yes. Do you know Nicholas then?"

'The porter grinned. "Oh yes. He asked this really
poor old tramp I know to share his bedroom at the
vicarage."

"You mean his actual bedroom?"

"Well," said the porter, "I was standing there on the
street one day and a tramp I know came shuffling up to
me. Nick was passing by and the tramp just turned
round and asked him for some help."

'There was a momentary pause between the porter
and the agency nurse. Then he said incredulously,
"Nick said, 'Why not come back with me?' And he
walked off with the tramp alongside him!" The porter
rubbed his nose with his finger. "I've never heard
nothing like that in being a Christian before!"'

Dave had cause to remember this story just before he
and Joyce went to Malaysia. He heard Nicholas
preaching about the Good Samaritan. Dave settled
back in the pew and listened as Nicholas told the story of
falling on the ice. Dave watched him as he stood alone at
the front of the church, shoulders very slightly bowed,
using a clear and beautiful speaking voice. A man of
presence, thought Dave. A man of the people. A man, as
they say, with the common touch. A man who cared. A
man who had a message for the church about the Good
Samaritan.

'If only we as a church were more like Christ,' cried
Nicholas to the hushed congregation. 'If only we were

more like the Good Samaritan!' He looked around the
rows of faces in the church. 'It's one of my frustrations
that I and we are so unlike him. If only we here could be
the Good Samaritan to the neighbourhood. Having
time to stop and listen and help.' He paused. Then he
bowed his head. 'The Lord can help us,' he said quietly,
'if we really want him to and ask him to.'

And all round the church people's heads were
nodding.

18

The Wind of God

The building is going to be cleaned both inside and out and changed and renewed inside. This is exactly what God is doing to us who belong to him and have asked him to change us. In God's sight we have been washed clean from our sins and inside given new hearts of love.

From the middle of the summer you will notice the work on the building in progress. Remember as you watch, that your life can be cleaned up, just like the building, if you give yourself over to God.

Crossroads
(June 1979)

Dave Lamb leaned towards the aeroplane porthole window and stared out at his native land. Everywhere seemed grey. Grey marshes, grey mudflats, the shining grey ribbon of the Thames. As they circled lower the river appeared wider and he could make out the dull grey slabs of buildings on each side. Row after row of them, for miles. He stared at the sky. It was grey too and it looked like rain. He sighed and zipped up his jacket. The hot sunshine and brilliant colours of Asia, life and home to himself and Joyce for the past ten months, were now to become a memory. He tried to be cheerful for Joyce's sake, but she knew him too well. It was no good. Every time he looked outside it was as if there was a pall over London. And if he looked inside his own heart there was a growing pall there too, a dull pain of longing. The plane touched down and they were firmly back in England.

Dave tried very hard that October to be thankful now he and Joyce were back at St Mark's and Kennington. But 1979 did not seem to be a good year for England, economically or in any other way. Nor was it for him. Everywhere he looked the pall seemed to lie, except on St Mark's church, he had to admit that. Finally he voiced to himself what he had been thinking all along: that he did not like the British and the Empire very much, and all their grey reserved ways. He liked Asia and her people and the culture and the hospitality out there.

'You'd better give me back my love and respect for my own people, Lord,' he prayed one day, 'because the way I feel at the moment I don't want to work amongst them.'

Asia stood in his mind in vibrant contrast. His heart was filled with such vision of what they had done for God there and what he had done for them. Everywhere they had travelled in Malaysia they had seen healings, deliverances and conversions. It had been wonderful. The very atmosphere had been charged with the possibility of God's thinking. At Joyce's old Methodist school in Ipo they had found schoolgirls on their knees crying, fasting and praying for their friends. After Dave preached many came forward to find out more. It was like that everywhere they went. Everywhere people were talking, and he had even heard of Muslims becoming Christians. Everything they touched turned to gold.

'It was like the wind of God,' said Dave. 'There was such expectancy that God was going to do something. He can do anything.' Dave sighed. They had had vision, vision, vision for God then.

But once the plane was circling over South-East England the pall was there cutting him off from the golden East. Life seemed hard and charged with difficulty back at home. How he longed for it to be different. But it wasn't. Everything any Christian had ever longed for and dreamed of seeing he had seen daily in Asia. He stared at his hands. Would he, could he ever see the same things in materialistic and capitalistic London, in poverty-stricken and downtrodden London, in cynical westernised Britain? He did not know and the way he was feeling meant he did not expect to know.

Yet Dave, being Dave, could not be downcast for too long. The day came when he realised he did after all want to work with his own people, and more than that he increasingly had a sense of call from God to do so. The burden was small at first, yet gradually grew in intensity until its weight was with him day and night.

Tentatively he told Nicholas and discovered that Nicholas too felt exactly the same sense of call.

'We must do something,' said Dave. He thought of Kennington and thought of the council flats. 'We must do something for the people in those flats. Visit them. Invite them. Something.'

Nicholas leaned forward, his eyes filled with light. 'Yes,' he said. 'We must. We must.'

Could the wind of God blow on the streets of London as it had done in Malaysia, they wondered? They all wondered very much, but they were determined to put themselves into the way of God's wind. Nicholas then agreed to Dave's request that this evangelistic thrust should come through the main body of the church and not simply as a sideline. So it was agreed.

First they decided to divide the church membership into twelve discipleship groups and the parish area into twelve sections. Each group was allocated a section. Then over the weeks a monthly pattern emerged: the first week everyone met together; the second week the discipleship group met in a home for intercession and prayer; the third week was for direct outreach on the streets in pairs in the group's section; and the fourth week they met again as the discipleship group in a home for teaching and Bible study. This structure worked well.

Dave found out quickly that two things helped them
with the visiting programme. One was to take a new
copy of the bi-monthly *Crossroads* and deliver it
personally to the houses and flats. The other was to say
quite simply, 'We are from St Mark's church'. So many
people felt warmly towards the church or had children
at the church school, that they were not unhappy to
receive a visit. But it was not easy. Even though they
prayed as they went, knocking on doors was often very
hard. They were met with indifference and sometimes
verbal abuse. In some flats the smell was appalling.
Dave saw Nicholas stride in as if it was the most natural
thing in the world. Nothing ever stopped Nicholas from
relating to people.

Some church members were frightened of visiting.
There were stories in the local paper of muggings and
this naturally terrified some folk and the numbers
tended to dwindle on visiting nights.

Yet, as June Bailey recalls, 'It was tremendous
actually doing it. We met some rough characters, even
when we did a posh road. You'd knock on the door and
when it eventually opened the stairways up to the flats
were filthy. But I quite often said I was from the Sunday
school and that made a link with some families.'

In the end, at the height of the visiting campaign
Jeffrey Fewkes, the curate, noted that up to two
hundred and fifty church members would be out visiting
per month. The leaders all felt this was fantastic. The
church persevered with its visiting for over eighteen
months until by 1981 every home in the parish, over
three thousand of them, was being visited monthly.

During prayer they believed earnestly that God's
wind would blow over Kennington. Gradually they
came to a consensus that they should believe for ten new
converts a month. As the months went by the startling
thing was that, slowly but surely, that target was being
reached. And at least fifty per cent of the newcomers
lived in the parish. Every six weeks there was an
evangelistic service and people were able to bring along

those who had shown an interest during the visiting evenings.

In the middle of it all was Dave Lamb. He had a real vision and love for the people in the council flats. He used to walk over there often and visit and soon got to know a lot of the residents. He helped to get several groups started there and this helped in the mix of classes at church. Some church members even managed to put themselves down on the Lambeth Council waiting list for a flat. Bob and Shirley Bruce were one such couple. They had prayed for years to have an open home in the parish but the only way to qualify for one was to be made homeless first. Two days before they were due to move out of a borrowed flat into council bed and breakfast accommodation, a Kennington Park Estate flat became available to them. And a little girl from the church called Emma Sidwell saw a double rainbow over the estate and the church as if God himself was promising to bless the Bruce family there.

But for Dave this kind of constant outgoing activity and continual pouring himself out in public speaking had its shadowed side. Sometimes he would end up depressed, his emotions raw, and wish he could move on.

'I want to itinerate,' he said miserably one day in Jeffrey's office.

Jeffrey said nothing for a moment. Then he said, 'It's good for you to stay here. Itinerating is easier in one way. You don't have to see a thing through from start to finish. But it's good to get stuck into a situation for a few years.'

This was to be true for Dave, who now, several years on, works as a missionary and evangelist for Youth With a Mission (YWAM), based in England. The St Mark's experience helped him to mature and put down roots in his character. It bore fruit in Jeffrey's life too, who later became vicar of St John's, Bulwell near Nottingham, an inner-city overspill area with a big congregation mainly of miners and cleaners.

At the time though, neither man could foresee his own future. Jeffrey said without looking at Dave, 'You know, I don't feel I've got this sensational signs and wonders ministry like you. You're so public. And when you're on form your sermons are terrific! I'm just ordinary really.'

Dave leaned back in his chair and brought his hand down hard on his leg. 'You don't say! That's amazing! You really envy me?'

'Mmm.'

'Well, I envy you!'

It was Jeffrey's turn to look surprised.

Dave said, 'I wish I was the Number Two here like you. You're a Reverend and I'm nothing. I've got no qualifications. And I know I can get depressed, but you are so steady! Yes, I envy you!'

The two men looked at each other. Suddenly they were both laughing and shaking each other by the hand.

'It's ridiculous,' said Jeffrey. 'But I'm beginning to get it straight now. Everyone's ministry is different.'

Dave smiled a great big open smile. 'Yes, brother,' he said.

Later Jeffrey prayed about this conversation. It was good to be free of his feelings of envy, good and very freeing in spirit. Lord, he said, I know I'm not really a signs and wonders type of person like Dave and...

Instantly the Lord replied, for into Jeffrey's mind came unexpected and deep words that sank into his heart and stayed there for ever. 'Are you prepared,' said the inner voice, 'to have your emotions battered as much as Dave has his? For the two sides go together. If you are really going to be used in revival, you will suffer.'

Jeffrey was silenced. There was no answer to be made. But he never forgot those words.

It was not only in visiting and evangelism that St Mark's had vision. They had vision for, and formed, drama, sacred dance and music groups. These all flourished. Then there was the vision for restoring their church building. As Colin Scott, their former vicar, often says, 'What's happened to the building at St Mark's has always mirrored the spiritual life of the people there.'

After much discussion St Mark's church was closed for several months in June 1979 and all the services took place in the Montgomery Hall. The two church-wardens, John Harries and Raymond Hall, along with all the other leaders and the PCC, agreed that God was calling them to clean the church outside and to remodel it inside. Raymond, architect by profession, responded to this call 'to enable the building to catch up with where the people were at in design terms'. Later he wrote:

> When I first visited the church building there was a marked contrast between what was a neo-classical 'Temple of Zeus' built in the early nineteenth century – and the joy of the Lord in the life of the people that met within it. At that time the church building was depressing. Its poor decor, lighting and fixed pews fought against the freedom that was being experienced in the church as people. [He saw that] the radical and visionary work done on the church after the war with Wallace Bird and the then architect, Thomas Ford, had enclosed the balconies and created new offices and meeting spaces around three sides of the church in their place. (art. in *Church Building: magazine of ecclesiastical design*, Winter 1986, Project XXI)

Now it was Raymond's turn to catch a vision for the 1980s and beyond.

Helen Clark in the parish office was in the thick of all the plans, discussions and prayers. She and Jeffrey Fewkes did little else, apart from essential work, during those eight months, as they had the day to day oversight of all the building work in the church. The question of money and how they were going to pay for the refurbishment was uppermost in everyone's minds. A large brown Restoration Fund box was placed at the back of the church and the congregation was encouraged to give sacrificially into it. No one was pressurised. If you could give nothing that was fine. Or £5 or £500 was equally gratefully received. The total project was to cost £62,000 of which £29,000 was being provided via Lambeth Council grants and Community Industry. The rest of the money they had to find themselves. Anyone who wanted to help was welcome, only there was to be no coaxing of money from jumble sales, house to house collections or even bank loans. 'Every penny,' said Nicholas, 'must be given to God willingly.' On top of the £62,000 they also planned to give away a further £8,000 as their tithe offering. Helen was aware, as was everyone else, that tithing was being preached. Nicholas had always preached tithing, or the giving of a tenth of one's income, to be done in faith, to be drawn from the covenant community and not necessarily only from the struggling individual. At the same time he always taught the necessity of the individual to be free to seek the support of the church community, if in financial need. His aim was to teach the two aspects together: tithing and support.

Nicholas and the PCC felt the Lord was encouraging each person to start asking how much he wanted them to pray in. One pensioner who could only just make ends meet felt she was being told to pray in £50. That Christmas and birthday everyone gave her money gifts and she was soon able to give this amount. She was so encouraged that she began praying in her second fifty pounds – and sure enough this came to her as well. She was able to give £100 in all. So it was that, amazingly, within the eight months the church had got all the money. And this was in spite of the fact that the original costings rose to £75,000. Everyone was jubilant and the Bishop, Mervyn Stockwood, was particularly struck by this sacrificial giving from a poor inner-city church. Helen smiled to herself. Only that very Sunday morning someone had come up to her with a ten pound note in his hand.

'Where's the box gone?' he asked.

'Well we've got all the money we need now!' she said.

'There must be something else needed. Let's get the box back!'

Jeffrey knew that the giving had been £500 per week on average before the restoration. Yet during the eight months of the refurbishment the money poured in. And in the last three months before the work was completed the weekly sum averaged about £2,135. He wondered what would happen when the restoration was completed. But he need not have worried. To all their surprise and joy the giving, though dropping a little from its peak, remained on average about £1,800 to £2,000 a week. The weekly average had tripled.

So it was that the people of St Mark's became so used to sacrificial giving over and above their normal covenants to the church that over the years there was always enough extra money available to pay bursaries, salaries or part-salaries to the church's lay workers. Dave Lamb and Arthur Cunningham were the first to benefit, Dave becoming the official church evangelist and Arthur the lay pastor. Nicholas rejoiced at this development. All along he had felt that lay people with strenuous jobs were simply too tired and overstretched in the evenings to become burdened with constant church meetings, planning and advising. It was an excessive burden they should not be called upon to bear. Paying lay workers did two things: it released gifted laity to become themselves. And it gave opportunity for young people, unemployed, retired or indeed anyone else who felt called to work for the church, to accept responsibility and leadership. Nicholas did not believe there was any substitute for a tithe, thus freeing the church, among other things, to have full-time workers. It also enabled ministry to be released in the congregation.

This concept of 'releasing people for ministry' is one of Nicholas's gifts.

'I believe it's what God wants,' he said. 'We are all

called to be the body of Christ and each member has a
part to play. It's only sin that prevents us from releasing
others. It means that if we want the glory for ourselves
and men's good opinions we are acting out of insecurity,
hanging on to our own positions of power.

'As we lose our lives (in the worldly sense) so we find
reality. This links with receiving our inheritance in
Christ. But we can't do that if our hands are full of
something else, full of ourselves. I once heard Malcolm
Smith give a talk on the cry of Jesus from the cross, "It is
finished". Our old way of life is finished. The paradox is
that the way of the cross is a way not just of pain but of
rich fruitfulness. If only the churches could learn this –
to give away their life. To give away time, talented
people, money. Then the churches would find their life!'

So the work of restoration began. The pulpit and the
pews were removed, principally to clear a flexible space
inside the church. Even the eagle lectern went. There
was no bitterness among the older members, although
Veronica Elen wept. She mourned for the church of her
youth, the church that had been like home and family to
her, the church she had prayed for after the war when
Wallace Bird had had the vision and stamina for
rebuilding the ruins.

The outside stone and brickwork were repaired and
cleaned of their grey grime to the colour of 'clean balsa
wood'. Inside some pillars were removed. The floor was
largely levelled, new lights put in, and a colour scheme
of white, mushroom, gold and green chosen. There were
stackable chairs in green check and the whole main area
was carpeted in deep mottled green, giving a sense of
warmth. It was, as Raymond explained, done in the
colours of living things, like a tree green and pleasant
with light and shade.

The vision worked. The interior sparkled with
welcome and homeliness. The backcloth to any
gathering of people there was the magnificent stained-
glass East window, showing Christ the King of Glory.
The reredos and the altar were decorated with much

golden ornamentation and there was a cross painted gold. A lady called Sabra Curtis worked gold, white, red, green and purple altar frontal cloths over the years. On either side of the altar were four majestic soaring pillars, with a golden altar rail. The whole effect was wide, spacious and beautiful. In the space at the front Nicholas brought a circular table from his old home at Fornham House, which became the focus for the Holy Communion. People gathered around it with its flowers and candles, the bread and the wine, their faces radiant and rapt. The air throbbed with music, sometimes loud and rhythmic, other times soft and moving.

Raymond wrote, 'A sense of majesty enhanced the warmth and friendliness of the church, which encircled the essentially dignified, but nevertheless domestic table.'

The *Church Building* article shows photographs of the people in their renewed building, clapping or joyous or deeply quiet. Indeed this is the only article in this particular issue which shows any people at all in their buildings.

Truly the St Mark's building was the servant of the people, yet a majestic and homely servant at one and the same time, fit for a King of Glory in which to visit his people and wash their feet. The same photographs show Veronica Elen dressed in brilliant red, raising her hands aloft in a hymn of praise to God for the transformation. She was one of the first to step forward and offer praise and thanks to God. Her former tears were washed away with new joy.

So not only was the building cleansed inside and out, changed and renewed, but so too were its people. And the people in the flats, houses and streets of Kennington were part of it. After the intensive visiting campaign some were willing to hear the gospel and respond to Christ's offer of salvation.

In the course of her work as an obstetrician and

gynaecologist Mary Stokes had performed a hysterec-
tomy on a married woman called Linda who lived in the
council flats in Kennington. Linda and her husband
had two children. One evening Mary, who was the
leader of a discipleship group, was out on the church
visiting campaign calling at some of the flats. When the
door opened Mary recognised Linda immediately.

'Why, hello! How are you?'

Linda said, 'Well, I'm as fit as a fiddle now but I am
more worried about my little boy, Gary.'

Mary said gently, 'I'm visiting from the church this
evening, and not as your doctor at the moment. I've
brought you a copy of *Crossroads*. But I'll be very happy
to talk about Gary if you like.'

Linda stood back and Mary went in and listened as
the mother poured out her heart about her elder boy.

'He's been so upset because I've been in hospital that
he won't go to school. He won't leave the flat at all. He's
simply sat glued in here for weeks.'

A pale boy crept in just then and stared expression-
lessly at Mary.

Suddenly, without quite knowing why, Mary said,
'I'm going to fetch a puppy tomorrow in my car.' She
turned to Linda, 'I've been so worried about all these
burglaries. I've had several already in my house and I've
decided to get a dog.' She turned to Gary, knowing he
would refuse, knowing he would see her as the enemy
who had taken his mummy away to hospital. 'Would
you like to come with me and help with the puppy?' she
asked him.

To her immense surprise he began to nod.

Linda sat very still and then said, 'Oh, what a lovely
idea.'

Next afternoon Mary came back to the flats. Gary
was ready and waiting at the window.

'Go and fetch your coat, Gary,' called Linda. As he
ran from the room she said shyly to Mary, 'I hope he'll
be all right and not play up. He's been so difficult lately.'

'Oh, I'm sure everything will be fine,' said Mary,

hoping it would be.

'Mum and Dad live in the flat above us,' said Linda. 'Dad's been so ill and it has been the church folk who have visited him regularly and helped us all. Now you've come.' She looked down at her knees. 'And I read that magazine you left yesterday.'

Against all expectation Mary and Gary had a wonderful day. They sang choruses in the car, went on the beach, had ice-creams on the sands, and collected Sophie, the five-week-old puppy. Gary held her tightly all the way home. He was so thrilled and somehow the day out helped him so much that he never looked back. He was soon at school again and every day when lessons were finished he called on Mary, visited the puppy and took her for walks.

Soon afterwards the whole family began coming to church.

At about the same time as Gary was recovering his confidence an article in *Crossroads* said,

The nation needs to hear the word of God and see the love of Jesus through the church. Sometimes the church is mistakenly thought of as a building. There are even some who expect to find God dwelling in certain buildings. *However God dwells in a people. The word 'church' means 'a called-out people'.* We in the church are people from every background, race and nation who have been born again into the family of Jesus Christ.

19

Healing at St Mark's

For to me, to live is Christ and to die is gain.
Phil. 1:21 NIV

Jeffrey Fewkes drove steadily down the road. He glanced at his watch and relaxed slightly. He was going to be just in time so there was no need to worry. He never liked to keep Ray Austin waiting: it was important for a sick man to know exactly when his prayer partners were coming. The others would not be late, he felt sure of that. And there was a possibility today that Elmer Darnall and even Jean might be coming. Jeffrey slowed down at the lights and waited his turn in the queue. As the moments ticked by he caught himself wondering just why he was so sure that praying for Ray to be healed of cancer was the right thing to do. Jeffrey knew that it was a rare thing for him to feel so sure about someone's healing, but in Ray's case for some reason, he almost had an inner compulsion to pray. This was special. He did not know why. All he knew was that he and a few others would gather at Ray and Carole's flat every day at the same time and pray earnestly for Ray's healing. Then they left. This had been going on for a month now, but it seemed a small thing to do when Ray was fighting for his life.

Jeffrey arrived at the flat, parked his car and rang the bell. Once inside he followed Carole into the bedroom and sat by Ray's bedside. Ray's eyes smiled but he did not speak. Jeffrey knew and Carole knew and all the others knew, that St Thomas' Hospital had discharged Ray because there was nothing more they could do for him. He had been allowed out to die in the comfort of his home surroundings. But Ray did not know any of this. He knew of course that he was very ill and had had asthma, and emphysema, and had had a collapsed lung twice. But what he did not know was that he also had incurable cancer in his lungs. His wife forbade any mention of that dreaded word. It was hard to believe that this desperately ill man in the bed was the same as the smiling young man in the wedding photograph, taken only a few months earlier.

Jeffrey did not say much. But his mind was filled with the memory of what Ray had talked about only recently: the unbelievable agony of trying to breathe; the pain in his chest; the desire that came more than once to die and be done with all the pain. Ray had been anointed with oil, the ancient practice of the Church, some weeks before. Instead of being healed immediately he got worse and had to be readmitted to hospital. And there was Carole, so faithful, so pretty in her wedding photograph, and now, a bride of only a few months, facing the ultimate in pain as she watched the man she loved suffer. She knew he had only a few weeks to live but carried on bravely and kept the knowledge from him.

So why were they here, Jeffrey asked himself as the other few prayer partners arrived and gathered round the bed. He did not know. All he did know was that he felt he *had* to come, and despite all the evidence to the contrary he believed, in a way he was rarely able to do, that Ray was going to be healed. Ray himself had whispered one day, 'I believe. I *know* God is going to heal me, even after that anointing and nothing happening. I *know*.' And the strange thing was that there was no aura of hopelessness around Ray. Helpless he might be. But despairing, no.

As the second and then the third month slipped by

Jeffrey and the others persisted in the prayer and the visiting. Nothing sensational happened.

Yet one day Carole said, 'He's not actually lost any more weight lately.'

Jeffrey looked at Ray. It was true. Ray did not look any thinner. And he was actually looking the same as the week before. A little spurt of excitement tingled in Jeffrey's brain, but he stilled it. All right, so Ray was looking no worse. That was cause for praise, but there was still much prayer needed. He touched Carole's arm, 'It's good. I'll come tomorrow.'

Another week went by. And then another. They all began to notice that Ray seemed infinitesimally plumper, and pinker, and his eyes were more alert.

'He's gained a bit of weight,' was all Carole would allow herself to say.

So it was that a man for whom medical science had done its all and acknowledged failure, and had been sent home to die, got up one day after three months at home.

'Carole,' he said, 'I feel so much better. I want to go back to work!'

Carole stared at him. Back to work in that W. H. Smith stall on Waterloo Station. Back to work!

When Jeffrey and the group found out they were delighted. Ray had to return to hospital for further tests and the results were all good.

His doctor said, 'You appear to have been healed. We can't give any rational explanation for this...'

And eventually Ray went back to work at the bookstall. That was over nine years ago. For the past five years he has worked for the Church of England Children's Society. He and Carole have run the Traidcraft stall at church; he has helped in counselling, ministry and discipleship groups, with the church flowers, and has formed a Christian Fellowship group at work.

One Sunday a few months after Ray's recovery he found himself standing in the church service next to a consultant, Chris Bartley. Afterwards Chris said to Ray,

'You shouldn't *be* here!"

'Why not?' and Ray laughed. He laughed even more as the conversation developed. Chris had not heard of Ray's recovery and had naturally assumed he had died. Now he found himself standing next to Ray in church; a fit and obviously well Ray.

'I heard of you at St Thomas',' said Chris. 'You were the talk of the hospital – but I didn't put two and two together!'

This healing greatly encouraged the whole fellowship at St Mark's. The healing ministry and the laying on of hands was, and is, offered every Sunday after morning and evening services. Other spiritual gifts too were used increasingly: tongues, interpretation, words of knowledge, prophecy, singing in the Spirit, administration, helping and teaching. But these gifts were somehow a part of a greater wholeness, not just sought after and used as an end in themselves. They were part of the whole worship at St Mark's: gifts accepted from the Lord and dedicated back to him. Indeed many people said, and say, that it is during the worship at the church that they feel lifted heavenwards, and especially during the music and singing. The inner life of St Mark's has a breath of healing and wholeness about it; at its best like the healing and affirming atmosphere of a family where all the members can be more and more themselves, free and true to themselves, free and true to each other and free and true to God.

Mary Boak, wife of Don Boak, who was then St Mark's church administrator, found this to be true.

'The first prophecy I ever heard that directly appertained to me,' she said, 'was words to the effect that all the treasures of my heart and all the things I'd learned after being a wife, mother and grandmother for over twenty-five years, were going to be used. I was going to be able to minister to young women... well at that time there didn't seem to be any opportunity, but later Don took up a post at the Bible Society in London and we joined St Mark's. At my very first evening

service a young man called Robert Ward bounded up to
me. He told me he had a 'word' for me – and it was the
very same as I'd heard before! Such a confirmation was
quite wonderful. In the weeks that followed I was
approached by some young mums and eventually I ran
a mother and toddler group at the church for nearly six
years. I had a lot of help from Marigold in the crèche.
We began with six people and ended up with about
twenty-five plus all their children! In a church where
the average age was twenty-seven and Don and I were in
our fifties you can see that we did have a role to play. I
loved being a career mum and I loved my proxy
daughters and grandchildren in the group. Some of
these young wives were from broken home backgrounds. They had never known how a mother should
and could behave in the home and I was able to be a sort
of Christian role model to them.

'By the time we left for Don to take up ordination
training, I realised what a healing experience St Mark's
had been to me. The whole of our time there had healed
me: and I realised something I'd never known for over
fifty years. That I was a woman called by God, with a
recognised ministry. I was encouraged and appreciated
by the St Mark's leaders. This was fulfilling and deeply
affirming.'

Mary helped too as a worship leader. She took over
this role from a young man called Trevor Stuart who
was moving from the area and who had made a good job
of leading the musicians and the worship in his time.
Now it was Mary's turn. She played the organ too upon
the retirement of Frank Lewis, the original organist
when Nicholas first came. Mary found herself as a
worship leader, and three decades older than many of
the excellent and professional young musicians who
came to St Mark's and wanted to play and sing. Several
came from the Royal College of Music hostel down the
road. Into this excellence Mary moved. There were
other people in the congregation who wanted to join in,
more in the line of gifted amateurs. Somehow Mary had

to unite the quality and perfectionist standards of the one with the homespun, spontaneous offerings of the other. This made for tension but Mary was determined it should be a creative tension. She wanted a church service to be neither a quality performance nor a slipshod unrehearsed time. It had to contain the best out of professional and amateur alike. There was a rota of different groups singing and playing each week. The worship of St Mark's, and in particular the music, became well known in South London and was truly an offering to God, anointed by the Spirit; lifting people, as they said, heavenwards.

It was about this time in 1980 in the newly restored church that Nicholas and the other leaders decided to stop wearing robes, except for weddings and other special services. They did not want in any way to appear separate from the people in the congregation. There was no longer a pulpit, so preachers preached from a small dais and then sat at one side with all the rest of the congregation. This helped to further relax the atmosphere.

However, as Jeffrey Fewkes recalled, a relaxed atmosphere was wonderful, but there had to be order and structure in the background. The trouble with St Mark's was that it was a like a tree in springtime: bursting out with growth all over the place. At times the growth seemed uncontrolled, and yet it was wonderful. It was impossible at times to keep up with it all. The previous curate, Hugh Wakeling, told Jeffrey that the congregation had grown from between fifty and seventy to a hundred and eighty. In 1981 during Jeffrey's own time it more than doubled to four hundred and fifty. When Marc Europe did a survey of St Mark's they discovered that the average stay of a person at the church was two years and seven months. There was a constant turnover of people, especially young people. So the growth peak in 1981 did not comprise altogether the same four hundred and fifty that were counted in 1986. People were constantly joining the church, becoming

Christians, maturing and then leaving for new jobs and so on. Some became missionaries in hard and difficult places like Thailand, Niger and Uganda. Some joined missionary societies that worked at home. Ten went on to ordination training. Many opened up their homes and welcomed in needy people, including one man who helped many young Irishmen.

Jeffrey smiled when he thought about St Mark's. 'In all this,' he said, 'a particular strength was needed, so that you didn't worry about the chaos all round you! Helen Clark was marvellous. She spent a lot of her time following Nicholas round with the diary and writing it up for him every day.' Jeffrey laughed. 'My wife Noriko and I loved it though. The love and care were tremendous. People really mattered at St Mark's. And the one man who really held it altogether administratively, quietly in the background, was Don Boak. He did a great job, and had a big influence even though he didn't have an up-front ministry. He was on the preaching rota, a churchwarden and an elder, during the two to three year period after I left when St Mark's had an eldership. The eldership was the right thing for a while but as the work continued to grow it was disbanded in favour of more lay workers and a corporate leadership.'

When asked why he had come to St Mark's Don smiled and sloughed off the praise. 'We'd read an article in *Renewal* magazine called, "The Spirit's call to the hard places", written by Douglas McBain. A lot of pastors and people like that had a burden for South London and St Mark's was right in the middle of that area. With all the rubbish and graffiti and tin cans rolling round the pavements it was quite a contrast to Bath, where we had lived before. But we felt God calling us and so we came.'

He noticed the importance of what he called the threefold cord in the life of St Mark's in the first half of the 1980s. YWAM, Bethany Fellowship and St Mark's all had close links and this formed in itself a creative tension. St Mark's people often went to YWAM Discipleship Training Schools at Holmstead Manor and elsewhere; and in its turn YWAM held monthly rallies at St Mark's. Colin Urquhart of Bethany Fellowship was a spiritual-director figure to Nicholas; and Nicholas himself was a trustee of Bethany. Many other organisations too used St Mark's for meetings.

All this fertilised and cross-pollinated the life of St Mark's, helping it to deepen its identity as a place of wholeness and healing.

Don remembers that Nicholas eventually shared what was happening at the church with the three local bishops: Ronald Bowlby, the new Bishop of Southwark, and the two suffragan bishops of Kingston and Woolwich. Don wrote a paper on the structure of the church's activity for them to read. He recalls that they were very interested, even when the paper made clear that as far as baptism went babies were baptised or dedicated and adults immersed if they so wished. The bishops were not critical at all, but on the contrary were very commendatory. One thing they did advise on was the subject of deliverance. Nicholas must be kept informed of everything that went on at the church and in the case of a serious need the diocesan exorcist should be called in. There were to be, quite rightly, no unwise hole-in-the-corner dealings in deliverance.

After the healing of Ray Austin's incurable cancer it must have seemed to the folk there that God's special healing grace was present in the church. After all Wallace Bird had had a vision for healing in the early days after the war. Noriko, Jeffrey's wife, and Marigold became special friends and often prayed together about people's healing. Jeffrey too found himself being healed in an unexpected way, in which it had never occurred to him he needed any healing or making whole. When he arrived at St Mark's for his first service he had a moment of panic. This place, he thought, is just too high-powered for me. I'm only a working-class country boy at heart. All this praying and preaching is too much! I'm simply a good old Anglican minister with charismatic beliefs. I'm even nervous of the traffic and noise of London, I'm so unused to it! But as he got to know Nicholas he marvelled at the way he accepted him. Nicholas, with his baronetcy, whom normally he would never have met, nor moved in his circles, could now sit with him and talk freely. My father worked in a quarry and Nicholas's father was a Vice-Admiral, thought Jeffrey. Nicholas inherited the baronetcy from his uncle, but it makes no difference to him. Nicholas is a completely classless person. He truly believes in people's equality.

He watched Nicholas. He saw a man who often appeared hesitant, unwilling to take the limelight; desirous of putting other people forward and enabling them to be released into ministry. He saw a man of great strength, both moral and physical, who would preach openly against sexual sin and the sin of greed and would command violent men to drop their knives. A man who would sit with his head bowed while street men, and occasionally women, tramps swore and cursed at him in his office. He would not react but simply murmured, 'Bless you. Bless you.' He saw a man who worried about his own failure, as he saw it, when everyone else knew he was saintly. And all this healed Jeffrey into a new freedom, authority and maturity.

He grinned. There had been the time when he and Noriko, his Japanese wife, and their little daughter Saya were due to come to London and take up the curacy post. But there had been nowhere for them to live. Nicholas was quite sure the Lord would provide accommodation: and the family waited. Every time they rang it was the same story: the Lord will provide. Finally their leaving date was confirmed, the removal van booked, and still there was no flat to come to. Eventually and hair-raisingly a flat did become available ten days before they were due to arrive. It was painted by church members over the weekend. That had really tested their faith, despite Nicholas's assurances, safely and securely housed as he was at the BMMF flat! Jeffrey shook his head and grinned again. How good it was that Nicholas and Marigold were not simply saintly – and therefore unapproachable. It was good that they were warmly human, with their own strengths and weaknesses like everyone else. And of course Nicholas had been right. A flat had become vacant after all.

So St Mark's developed into a place where people in all sorts of conditions were healed and helped into wholeness of being. So much so that when a woman member called Mary King developed cancer the church felt able to pray for her in faith that she would be healed. A small pastoral group covenanted to pray for her with what they called 'soaking' or persistent prayer. This they did, often meeting in the Emmaus side-chapel to do so. Mary King was a personnel manager and was well-spoken, her bell-like speaking voice beautifully clear and articulate. It seemed inconceivable that she with all her gifts and personality should die. But she got no better. Ray Austin was part of the core group that prayed for her. He was so sure that as the Lord had healed him, so he would and could heal Mary King. Obviously he could, but would he? It seemed impossible that there should be any question or any doubt.

On Sunday evening the pastoral group got up and led public prayer from the front of the church for Mary King. They prayed earnestly and claimed her healing. Mary Boak went up quietly to join them, grieved that such a young woman should die and longing to add her own prayers to those of the core group. As she gave herself to prayer Mary Boak tried to visualise Mary King as well and whole.

All at once, right in the midst of all the asking, claiming, soaking prayer, Mary Boak seemed to hear a voice. She knew it was not coming from behind her but was within her head. Yet it was so clear, so distinct, so unexpected. Mary concentrated. The voice said, 'But I'd rather have her at home with me.' Mary stood quite still. That voice was almost – no, it couldn't be – but it was. It had a quality of wistfulness about it. Could it really be the Lord, intimating that it was time for Mary King to go home, to return to the Father of all? Mary Boak raised her head and glanced round quickly. The claiming prayers were mounting up. But she knew now that she could not say Amen to any of them. Perhaps I lack faith, she thought without conviction. She opened her mouth and then closed it again. Perhaps I'd better not say anything just now, she said to herself. For what she thought was out of tune with what everybody else was asking. She thought of Mary King so white in her bed. Of course it was right in general to pray for the sick. It was a command of scripture. God answered such prayer so often. But if she were honest it would be embarrassing to share such a new prayer publicly.

Later she told her husband Don. He told Nicholas the next day. Nicholas was quiet at first. Then he raised his head. He said, 'So Mary had a check in her spirit, Don. That's very interesting. Someone else has said the same thing to me as well.' He sighed. It was so difficult to understand the mystery of God's sovereignty; and the mystery of suffering. They needed the gift of discernment so much. Undoubtedly the greatest healing was in death. Eternal, radiant life in heaven was a clear teaching of the Bible.

Finally Mary King was admitted to hospital. The church continued to pray for her, but she grew weaker and weaker. She was visited regularly and Nicholas tried to help her prepare herself for death. He said, 'In her last few days she had a revelation of Jesus and felt his presence with her in the room. She was filled with joy and peace and died victoriously. Maybe all that was a result of the terrific prayer. For surely no prayer i wasted.'

Poor Ray Austin felt terrible. He had been told eventually that it was cancer he had been healed from and this only increased his praise and his faith. So he wa doubly sure that Mary King's cancer could therefore b healed. He had longed and believed for her healing. What did her death then mean? Why should the Lord have saved him and not her? It didn't make sense. And later when the news of David Watson's death came through, Ray felt even worse.

'Why should the Lord save me' he said, 'when my impact on the world for proclaiming the gospel is so limited, whereas someone like David Watson had a preaching and teaching ministry over the whole world? Logically it would be far more beneficial for him to live on earth and not me.

'I had to accept that my divine appointment, as it were, was not yet fulfilled. Yet for David Watson and for Mary King and many others, although they could have been used a lot more, God chose not to. I had to accept that it was God and God alone who decided how long a person should live. I had to come to terms with the fact that God *knew* these things and they weren't my concern, except in the sense of being obedient and available to serve him. I had to accept that God knows the future of every single one of us.'

He paused and was thoughtful. Then he said, 'Yet I believe we should pray for healing – and yet it doesn't weigh up in the logical sense. It has got to be what God wants in a person's life. So I pray according to my faith and belief in what the Lord is saying in a particular situation. It's not so much my problem if that person is healed in the body or healed by going to heaven. It's all God's timing.

'I had to accept that God's ways are not our ways. His purposes are different to ours. His perspective on life, on death, is different. As Paul says, "For to me, to live is Christ and to die is gain."'

20

People Matter More than Programmes

Then I was brought into St Mark's: that so helped
me and so changed my thinking about people,
especially about white people, seeing as I am a black
guy, it so changed my thinking about middle-class
people. As a working-class guy you pick up a lot of
stereotyped images as to what middle-class people
are all about, you know. And to go to a church like St
Mark's where middle-class people accept working-
class people and not only that but different nations
accept each other for who they are and there's no
barriers, you know that made such an impact.

I realised I'd been so helped by the love and the
care and I wanted to show that ONLY through Christ
do we receive wholeness and life in abundance: to the
fulness as they say on the back streets round here. To
the fulness. And I wanted to share it with other
people, especially young people.

Steve Drummond
Youth Worker

A very tall, very black teenager called Steve Drummond
sat down in St Mark's church and managed to fold his
long legs under the pew. It was not a bad church, as
churches go, he thought. He had enjoyed the few times
he had been since that first occasion when his sister
Maxine got married here. No one seemed to turn round
and stare because he liked wearing lots of bracelets and
rings that jangled when he moved. No, it wasn't a bad
church. Everyone was friendly and said 'Hello!' with

such beaming faces. He settled back and waited for the service to get under way.

But today was different. There was a silence and then a rustling. A lot of people began getting to their feet. Steve glanced round. What was going on, he wondered? Gradually he became aware of a humming, a throbbing almost, as a song started to take shape in the air. Yet it was unlike any song he had ever heard: the music was clear and bell-like, weaving in and out round a simple melody. Most of the folks had their eyes shut and their faces seemed to glow. And there was another thing. They must be singing in Welsh or some other funny foreign language because he could not recognise any of the words. But before Steve could wonder any more he began to feel a burden on him; not a physical weight exactly, but a burden of sweetness and joy, like a presence hovering round him and resting on him, weighing him down with its own majesty. Nothing in his life up to that point had ever prepared him for this. He had never had any experience like it; but he knew he wasn't imagining things because it was simply too real. His heart was beating rapidly and he realised he was afraid. For in that moment as the singing soared around him, he suddenly knew there was something big in the universe; someone, and that someone wanted him and that someone was God...

Steve buried his head in his hands: he would have to decide. He knew it instantly. He would have to make decisions concerning this God. He knew instinctively he could not pretend that nothing had happened, and get up and walk away at the end of the service. I want what these people have got, he thought in a sudden agony. I must have it. Oh yes, he had become a Christian when he was about ten years old, but all the way through his early teenage years he had more or less forgotten about that commitment. Now however the decision had to be faced. And taken. Yet even as the singing died away to a beautiful echo he knew he had already made it. What and whoever he had met that day, he was determined to follow until he knew him for himself. Later he discovered people called the presence that had so over-whelmed him the Holy Spirit.

Not long afterwards the church was closed for the building renovations and services were transferred to the Montgomery Hall. At the end of the final service everyone picked up a piece of movable furniture and carried it in a long straggle down the road to the hall. Steve went along, a British citizen born in Dulwich of Jamaican parents. A few Sundays later he cross-questioned Dave Elliott, the lay reader, after he had preached the sermon.

'Dave, can you speak in this here tongues thing?'

'Yes.'

'Can you speak it now?'

After a moment's silence Dave did as he was asked and Steve's eyeballs nearly dropped out of their sockets. As he listened Steve knew what he was hearing was not gibberish. It was a language with distinct words being said in a foreign tongue and he knew it was not a language Dave had learnt.

'I'm bowled over!' said Steve and all his bracelets twinkled in the sunlight as he raised his arms in the air to emphasise his point.

Later on Dave and another friend, Carl, prayed for Steve. He waited and waited to be filled with the Holy Spirit. Nothing happened. Yet deep inside him he felt something bubbly, like a stream. He did not know what it was, but he knew something was there and he longed to speak in tongues. But nothing was coming from his lips. Oh no, thought Steve eventually, God's passed me by and he doesn't want to know. Carl and Dave persevered in their praying. Then Dave touched Steve's chin and said firmly, 'In the name of Jesus I command you to speak in tongues!'

Steve never quite remembered what happened after that. One moment nothing was happening. The next minute he was speaking in tongues. Words were streaming out of him and he had no knowledge of where they were coming from. He felt like a fountain bursting and bubbling within and there was a great joy and release.

As he said afterwards, 'I went on a high for about a couple of months. Then there was a bump and I came back to earth! I had to find the reality of daily living, of walking in the Spirit. That's when my journey, my spiritual journey really began.'

Day after day he continued in his job in the warehouse of a fur business, run by two elderly Jews. But he felt there was another calling, a different career he should pursue, and so he persevered in prayer, trying to discover what it was.

'I'm willing to stay in the fur trade or come out, Lord,' he said. 'I'll do either!'

After some time a day came when Roger Bagge asked if he would like to help out at the Sixteen Plus Friday Club at the London City Mission Caine Hall Centre. Steve agreed. He enjoyed it and knew at once that this was the sort of work he should be doing in life. He decided to enrol for a part-time ILEA course for youth workers. One day they were told to draw the area as a map and write on it all the schools, flats, homes, shops, centres and services, and so really get to know the place well. He tramped round the streets in the pouring rain, determined to do the job properly. And as he did so the realisation grew in him that this work with young people was what he should be doing. This was to be his career. He was a grass-roots type of person and he longed to be involved with his own kind of people. He was filled with a burning desire to reach young people with the Good News of the gospel. It became his vision and his goal: to work with them in groups and youth clubs, help with unemployment projects and teach teenagers Christian basics.

He said, 'God has taken me out of a rut and a vicious circle that I'd have been swallowed up in if I hadn't got to know Christ at that age of eighteen. I'd have been in the rut of sex, drugs, partying; in the world of no

standards, no purpose, no awareness of what a man or a
woman is really about. I'd have known nothing, nor
how to behave with people. There are a lot of young
people like that.'

Eventually Steve worked part-time at Caine Hall.
Roger and Nicholas saw his potential and how good he
was with the rough gangs of teenagers, often unemployed. So after a further two years he was given a
full-time job, shared between St Mark's and Caine Hall.
It was hard for Steve to wait those two years, not
knowing whether there would be any full-time opportunities at the end. But waiting puts root and character
into a person.

Today he is still working for the Caine Hall Family
Centre and for St Mark's, as well as being near the end
of a course at Avery Hill College to become a fully
qualified youth worker. The wind of the Spirit had
blown on Steve and changed him from an impression-
able teenager, through much perseverance to a mature
man of twenty-seven, able to help and deal with all the
challenges of inner-city London youth work. The Holy
Spirit set Steve's feet on the path of discipleship and he
loved Christ and rose to the challenge.

Others too at St Mark's were being tested and refined
by the Spirit as they tried, however stumblingly, to
follow on behind Christ. But it was one thing to long for
the wind of God to blow through England in general,
and upon St Mark's in particular, as David Lamb had
called out to God to do. It was quite another thing to put
oneself in the way of his refining wind. And then to obey
him; which they did as a church in the question of giving
and of street evangelism and home visitation. This was
costly. But then it was another thing again to cope with
the results of the wind of God.

None of them had really thought of that. For as the
number of new converts slowly grew, so did the tensions
in the church of working out the structures in which to
nurture them all. In the four years between 1978 and
1982 when the congregation had grown to four hundred

and fifty, many of the new members were young and single. There were very few mature families brought in. Very few natural leaders seemed to emerge. The number of discipleship groups mushroomed.

As Roger said, 'It was a job to keep abreast of it all. There was so much growth! Our weakness was a lack of leaders and we weren't training them to be disciples and leaders. We decided that St Mark's was growing too big for a part-time eldership. A new pattern had to emerge. We decided to have a full-time staff to take the responsiblity of running the church. This seemed right to all of us elders and we eventually disbanded. Also Caine Hall had just won a grant of a quarter of a million pounds from the Inner City Partnership and was to have an extension and be developed into a Family Centre. My wife Margie and I have still been able to keep the links with St Mark's and ninety per cent of our staff come to the church. Much of our work is with the elderly, youth, pre-school and unemployed and we can often help St Mark's: either with their needy people coming to us, or sometimes with employing people from St Mark's. Our links with this church are sustaining and we love coming.'

But still the structures in the church, or rather the lack of them, caused tension. Arthur and Elizabeth Cunningham took over the running of the vicarage household for six years from Graham and Maureen Ashdown. Immediately Arthur, as lay pastor, was plunged into trying to discover the perfect structure within which St Mark's could function most efficiently. First he kept the commitment to handing out free sandwiches and coffee at the back door of the vicarage before ten in the morning *only*. He changed the 'open door' policy.

'We've got to be realistic with the resources and people available,' he said. 'We can only offer ministry to certain types of people in a residential sense, but we do have an outreach in the crypt, where sandwiches and coffee are served. And we can send on needy people to other agencies.'

Would the time ever come when there was a mercy ministry at the crypt with some beds and a permanent warden? That was a vision for the future. He knew the original vision for the crypt had begun with Hugh Wakeling, the previous curate. It was a good vision and they were expanding it. Who knew what the future might hold?

Then Arthur turned his attention to the problems, glorious though they were, of growth in the church. With the encouragement of all the other leaders he devised and ran a six to eight-week course called The New Life in Jesus Group. This was held in the vicarage, which meant that his wife Elizabeth could be a co-leader. The course was for new Christians and took them through the basics in the faith: salvation, assurance, prayer, fellowship, renewal in the Holy Spirit, obedience and so on. In six years four hundred and fifty people went through this course. At one stage forty to fifty new Christians were coming along. It all worked well.

Then Arthur saw the need for many more discipleship group leaders to be trained, because the existing network of twelve groups was not big enough. So in 1983 he began a training course for the new leaders and forty or fifty people came along to that over about two years.

Throughout all this growth one thing stood out for Arthur. It was something to do with Nicholas and at first he could not work out what it was. Nicholas hasn't got an administrative gift, he thought, and he's the first to recognise it. He's seen the need to bring in other people to do this and we are more efficient as a church because of it. But, he shook his head. Still the structures were not exactly right. He thought back to the churches he had visited or known where everything was super-efficient and hyper-organised. He had never felt fully at ease in them. Over-structuring could lead to a lot of surface froth and not enough substance, he decided. Certainly it wasn't enough to have only the right technique or method or procedure or formula. Probably the perfect structure did not exist and certainly the Lord had not allowed it to happen at St Mark's. At least the Holy Spirit had room to move when things were more flexible.

He chuckled. The structures at St Mark's had never been right. Ever since he had known the church, people had been saying things ought to be changed. St Mark's was never settled. It was like a family, always changing and its needs always changing. But obviously people came because their needs were being met. Like a family, he thought. Perhaps the secret lay there. For Nicholas held the family ideal highly.

The truth was that the St Mark's structures had grown out of a concern for people, not the other way round. Get the methods right and then slot people into them, no; at St Mark's people mattered. First and foremost it was people. Nicholas was a people person, almost to a fault, if such a thing was possible. People always came first with him. And surely that was right. 'God so loved the world that he didn't send a committee!' as it says on a fun poster.

But the family idea was, he was sure, part of the key to the life flowering at St Mark's. On the whole people felt loved and cared for as if they were in a real family. Prayer was another key; many people, Nicholas included, had formed a life-long habit of constant, regular prayer. Worship too was another key: there was a willingness to be flexible with the liturgy and follow the leading of the Spirit and at the same time be under the authority of the bishops of the Church of England. There was no personality cult at St Mark's. People did not say 'I'm going to Nicholas Rivett-Carnac's church', but 'I'm going to St Mark's'. Nicholas had the vision for corporate leadership: one vicar expressed through four leaders. Personalities were down-played and there was teaching of submitting to each other, sharing and serving. Leadership was taught as being service. The Lord had protected St Mark's from becoming a celebrity-type church and given their leader the humility not to seek, or even want to seek, his own glory.

There is another key that St Mark's people won't admit to readily. It is the key of sacrifice. Jesus said, 'he who saves his life shall lose it, but he who loses his life for my sake and the gospel's, the same shall find his life' (Matt. 10:39). Many people sacrifice living in the country or in safer suburbia, for the inner city of Kennington. Some have no choice, obviously. But some have. Yet most of those interviewed for this book said that the joy and happiness they found in being part of the family of St Mark's far outweighed any sacrifice in the area of housing and schooling. For the word 'ministry', which means 'service', is people in the end. People rather than programmes.

For Arthur and Elizabeth Cunningham there was sacrifice in living at the vicarage, much as they enjoyed it. Seven or eight times thieves broke down the doors with pickaxes. Sometimes they clambered up the drainpipes as well. All Elizabeth's jewellery was stolen. No insurance could be got for the house. Once lighter fuel was pumped through their letter box. The inner-city London life was unpredictable in the extreme.

Arthur and Elizabeth led the vicarage household and were used in evangelism. They helped in the crypt as well, which was now used as a coffee bar for the unemployed and for youth work, and for the showing of good films on a weekly basis.

It was against this backcloth of inner-city life that in April 1983 the YWAM team was invited to lead a mission in the area, as a culmination of all the visiting that had been done. Steve Drummond happened to be in the church one day when he met a young Mauritian who had come along because of the witness of a St Mark's member at his place of work. The Mauritian was so amazed by everything happening at the church; so struck by the quality of the worship and the music, that he decided to become a Christian. He then brought his mother-in-law who was dying of a haemorrhage condition. Doctors had been unable to help her and she had even been back to Mauritius and seen a

witchdoctor. Dave Lamb and Nicholas laid hands on
her and prayed for her and her bleeding stopped. Over
the weeks that followed it became obvious that she had
been healed as there was no recurrence. She then began
bringing her family along one after another, and many
Mauritian friends too, who all eventually decided to
become Christians.

'Signs and wonders!' laughed Dave Lamb. 'Why do
people worry so much about them? In this case it's had a
snowball effect for the gospel. It's done nothing but
good!' He grinned. 'There's quite a community of
Mauritians down in the East End. Fancy them
travelling all this way to come to church. Amazing!
Amazing what an international church we are, with all
the Nigerians, West Indians, Ghanaians, Ugandans,
Malaysians, Asians, Chinese, Indians, Pakistanis, Euro-
pean and even a Lebanese chap, a converted Muslim
and now these Mauritians! There are some English of
course: if they can squeeze in!'

The YWAM mission was remarkably led by two
Africans, one a black man from Zimbabwe called Oliver
Nyumbu, the other a white South African called Wade
Roberts. It was deeply moving to see these two men
sharing a platform, embracing as brothers. Everything
political in Wade's home country was dead against him
being in any position of equality with a black man. But
in Christ they were brothers and behaved like brothers.
The royal law of love far and away superseded the
narrow cruel law of apartheid. Even so, one day at a
meeting Wade Roberts had the grace and humility to
say that he would not have wanted to share a platform
with a black man before his own conversion to
Christianity. There were many converts.

In commenting on YWAM's support to St Mark's
Dave Lamb said, 'We got a lot from YWAM, in seeing
their lifestyle, teaching, leaders and fellowship.'

Following this in May of the same year a week of
meetings was organised by Colin Urquhart and the
Bethany Fellowship. In August 1983 Luis Palau came to

Wembley and then Clapham Common, and many of St
Mark's members and their friends were able to hear and
enjoy him. Again there were a number of converts at
these meetings.

A few miles away from St Mark's was the Stockwell
YMCA building. For several years this was run by
Michael and Thelma Cheney, who were members of St
Mark's. They accepted and helped many needy people
there. Many of these people came along to St Mark's
and some of St Mark's members took services at the
YMCA.

One evening a staunch Hindu, Mr Dasannamaly
from Singapore, who was studying for a law degree and
living at the Stockwell YMCA, saw St Mark's Church.
He was deeply unhappy at the time because he had lost
his wife and on an impulse he came into the church.
Jackie Pullinger was preaching, a woman who had lived
and worked in Hong Kong for many years. As Mr
Dasannamaly, Das as he came to be known, listened to
her words and saw the joy on the faces in the church,
heard the music and experienced the worship, he quite
simply and suddenly gave his heart to the Christian
God. He must have talked about this at the YMCA
because at Christmas time he brought to a service fifty
Polish dissident sailors who were members of Solidarity
and had jumped ship at Tilbury. St Mark's rose to the
occasion and welcomed these Catholic men, many of
whom were in tears, and gave them coffee and food in
the crypt. Nothing it seemed could stop the Good News
from spreading.

Yet great trees grow from tiny seeds, taking time and
weathering storms. Great events in God's kingdom have
usually been heralded by long silent years or secret
sacrifice on the part of God's servants. For God looks on
the heart and not the outward appearance. Such a
person was Peggy Thompson, the former housekeeper at
St Mark's vicarage household. Little did she know then
as she left her job at the Ministry of Defence, how God
was going to train and use her, nor what ministry he
would give her. By 1978 her old mother needed help and

Peggy temporarily left St Mark's and went back to Wales and helped her sister to look after their mother. She was away for two years. Then in 1980 her mother died and Peggy came back permanently to Kennington.

On her first Sunday back she wondered why she felt so empty. But then she had come back to nothing: no work at the Ministry of Defence, no housekeeping at the vicarage, absolutely nothing. The church was due to go on a PCC away-day at the Hyde, home of the Bethany Fellowship, so Peggy went too, feeling quite broken and useless inside. If this was what was meant by absolute brokenness, she thought, it was jolly painful. Not to be needed, not to be able to work, that was awful. She went for a walk round the grounds, determined not to give in, but feeling bad all the same.

All of a sudden she rounded some rhododendron bushes and came face to face with Nicholas. They began to talk and then he listened as she told him how she felt. He was silent. Then he said the last thing she expected to hear. 'Of course you are in a marvellous position because you've got nothing. Absolutely nothing. And the Lord has got something for you.'

Peggy looked at him, the question large in her eyes.

'He has,' said Nicholas gently. 'There is something for you.'

Later as she looked back to that day she saw that Nicholas's word had been prophetic. Out of her brokenness and feelings of uselessness and nothingness grew her counselling ministry, and her ministry of inner healing. It became a whole new way of life.

As the church grew and trebled its numbers and bulged at the seams, it was good that there were people like Peggy who were warriors in the faith and in life, able to listen, able to counsel, and by the power of the Holy Spirit able to follow in the steps of the Lord and 'bind the broken-hearted and set the captives free'. So many of the St Mark's converts were bruised by broken homes, unemployment and worse, that they needed inner healing and deliverance. And the Lord had led Peggy on a long path of preparation.

21

Take the Problems to the Cross

A personal care centre will be open from November
7th, Monday, Tuesday, Thursday and Friday
6.30–9.00 p.m.... If you'd like to talk over
confidentially any problem related to stress in
marriage, relationships, involvement with the occult,
drug addiction, loneliness, depression, divorce etc.,
drop into the centre or make an appointment...

Advertisement
Crossroads
(October 1983)

As Peggy thought back over the years she could see the
ways in which the Lord had led her. Nicholas had
introduced her to the healing ministry at Brompton,
where she had heard George Bennett. She had been to
conferences on the subject and lapped up the teaching.
She had become keen on the concept of inner healing
and took any opportunity to be involved. Then as
housekeeper at the vicarage she found that people often
cried on her shoulder and she could help them by
listening and praying. But it was only after she left that
she began to realise she had a ministry of her own and
people began coming to her informally.

One evening at the church it was suggested, almost off
the cuff, that anyone who wanted to help with
counselling should go up on the carpet by the altar, meet
there and pray. A variety of people went up including

Stuart Checkley and Peggy Thompson. For about six months the group met once a month and talked about some aspect of listening. Stuart began to feel a little frustrated. 'We needed to move on to other things,' he said, 'but the Lord didn't want us to!' Eventually numbers dropped until a core remained, still meeting and still prepared to wait. Then they realised that the group had become a listening team.

At the first of the counselling evenings after this someone had a picture in their mind's eye during the opening worship: it was of a rock opening up and in the middle was a grain of wheat. The interpretation given was that God wanted to plant the word into the depths of personality, and that their team ministry was to be involved in this delicate and deep work. The spirit of a man is the candle of the Lord. But it is easily broken and hurt, distorted and damaged. It needs kindly and delicate hands, patient, gentle and scarred, to bandage another's wounds.

In time Anthea Dimitri, Peggy and Stuart discerned the structure of what came to be known as the Free to Be course. This derived from a course originally formed out of the John Wimber Vineyard Fellowship teaching in the United States, which involved inner healing using the Bible. They started with a weekend led by Peggy based on the Wholeness through Christ teaching. Then on five Thursday evenings at fortnightly intervals Stuart taught on inner healing, sin and separation, suffering and rejection, the father heart of God, and forgiveness. On the alternate Thursday evenings they divided into small groups for sharing and prayer, and a member of the team led each group. This made a ten-week course. About fifty church members attended, and Nicholas was so pleased with the results that future courses were planned and took place. 'You can lead one whenever you like,' he said to Peggy.

Stuart and Peggy wrote in the booklet, *Every Member Ministry at St Mark's*:

Alongside the Free to Be course, a pattern of counselling evenings has developed. The team counsel in twos and threes in different rooms at the church with a central back-up intercessory prayer group going on at the same time. We are still learning how the Lord wants us to work, but the structures that he has given have been blessed...

One evening Stuart was trying to counsel a very intellectual man. In the end he realised he wasn't getting anywhere and went upstairs to ask the back-up team led by Anthea to pray. 'I'm stuck,' he said. 'What shall I do?' As they continued praying Sarah Richards, a churchwarden, had a picture in her mind's eye of the man concerned being like a little curled-up baby. Then someone else gave a word of knowledge. 'This is a battle of fear in the person. It is a fear of abandonment.'

Using this extra knowledge Stuart gently persisted in counselling the man. It emerged that he had had such an identity with his mother as a baby that he could not break free and this had hampered his personality development. All at once it came to the man that God had not even spared his own Son for him. Even as Stuart listened to this the man burst into tears – something he had never done before as an adult, as he had been cut off from all emotional feeling. So his healing began. Stuart bounded upstairs, very thrilled, and interrupted the prayer group to tell them. Anthea smiled and said, 'Yes. We knew in spirit. The Lord revealed it to us! We all felt it.' The man came willingly to further sessions and if not completely healed immediately, was very much better.

Stuart's wife too is gradually testing and using her gift of interpreting dreams and helping people to hear what God is saying to them in this way – a way much used in the Bible.

The key to inner healing is at one and the same time quite simple and quite profound. Stuart explained, 'Nicholas understands this and uses it in counselling. It is simply this: help someone to take their problems to the

Lord. Take the problems to the cross. Each time we see that the problems are already there: sin, separation, pain, rejection, death. They are already there. Jesus Christ has quite literally gone through them. He has taken them on the cross; he has borne our griefs and carried our sorrows. That realisation is the healing point. Once the revelation of *that* strikes, you can let the Lord do the work in a person's soul.'

One Monday Sarah Richards, a long-standing member of St Mark's and a health visitor by profession, heard about something that stopped her in her tracks. 'I simply can't believe it,' she cried. But it was true. All the money collected during the previous day's services had been stolen from the church safe. How on earth could it have happened? About £2,000 went through the church every Sunday in the offerings. A careful procedure of keys had been set up and everyone connected with the receiving and counting of the money was meticulous. The system should have been foolproof. But obviously it was not, because now this had happened. Sarah was distressed and angry with herself. It was not her fault but as churchwarden she felt the responsibility keenly.

'Oh, Nicholas,' she cried, 'what can we do?'

He was calm. 'We'll pray,' he said. 'Four of us can pray.'

'But I'm very upset,' she cried.

It was difficult for Sarah to compose herself to pray. Yet in a few moments the habit of years steadied her. And then in those minutes of silence she 'saw' a picture in her mind's eye. She 'saw' a man and how he took the keys. She 'saw' his hand going down into the safe. She 'saw' his face and its colour and features. As she shared this, all at once a different silence fell. Each person there guessed who the thief was from her description. But what could they do? With no proof they were powerless. All they could do was pray. After all, in British law one is innocent until proved guilty.

The following Thursday she had a surprise phone call from another church member called Andrew Baker who ran a coffee-and-drop-in centre in the basement of his house in Richborne Terrace.

'We've got a man here with bunch of keys,' he said. 'He's pretty wild and two of the lads are holding him down.'

'Is he white?' she asked.

'Yes.'

'I'm coming.'

She tore round to the basement, certain the man was the same as the man in her 'picture'. Once there she was less sure. The man was angry, all tense and elbows in his seat and she realised that the bunch of keys jangling in his fist was not the church safe key-ring. They gave him a choice. Either they would call the police or he could wait to see Nicholas. He would not look at them but muttered something about Nicholas. So an uneasy truce followed and she was beginning to wonder what to do next when all at once he slumped back and relaxed in his seat. She looked up, surprised. Then she saw Nicholas standing in the doorway. He had an indefinable air of spiritual authority about him, so much so that all the fight had instantly left the man.

'Will you come with me?' said Nicholas.

Like a lamb the man got up and followed him out of the door.

Later Sarah discovered that Nicholas and Marigold had taken him late at night to a café and talked. Next afternoon he had gone, not unwillingly, to the altar in St Mark's, knelt down, said he was sorry, and given back half the money. He plonked it in a dirty plastic bag on the altar. 'I couldn't keep it,' he said. 'It were 'oly money.' The other half, it turned out, had been given in a Robin Hood-like gesture to his sister, who was a single parent.

The following Sunday Sarah saw him watching her and she steeled herself. But quite calmly he came up and asked her to tell him what she had 'seen'. She described it in detail.

'Was that how it was?' she asked.

He stared at her, quite bemused. 'Yes,' he said at last, looking now at his boots. 'That was how I did it. I put my hand down into the safe.'

Then he turned and walked away, no trace of belligerence in his hunched shoulders. He knew that God and the church had forgiven him and this helped him to face the court case.

From that time the church set up an even stricter system of keys to make theft impossible. But thefts of handbags and other items continued to occur in the church from time to time. Sarah had to smile when, after a bag was snatched one day, the same man found her and said solemnly, 'It weren't me! Did you "see" anyone else?'

She shook her head. She still felt and feels amazed by the relevance and detail of her 'picture'. It was after all an unusual occurrence.

All the church leaders knew that professional burglars sized up the church from time to time and would drift in at the back during services. The staff tried to be extra vigilant, warned the congregation and had people on duty at the back. What were they to do? Nicholas decided that he would continue to hand out sandwiches and even money sometimes to the down-and-out people who came in and asked for help. Even though in the future a corporate decision was taken not to do this, yet when the moment came Nicholas could not help himself.

'I'd rather err on the side of giving than not,' he said. 'How much damage has been caused in the past by the church appearing to be hard and unloving? It is after all a place where people expect to find God. A place for the prodigal son. Obviously Christians aren't meant to be conned and there is a need for discernment, but on the whole,' he said emphatically, 'I'd rather give than not give.'

Despite the excitement of the night of the keys, Andrew Baker, who was a doctor at St Thomas' Hospital, continued to run the basement of his home as a

Christian eating centre, where anyone could drop in for food and friendship. Eventually he married Clare and in 1985 they had a baby, Simon. In 1986 the family left for a four-year assignment with Tear Fund in a Muslim country helping to set up a community health project on the edge of the Sahara Desert. St Mark's has strong missionary links. About twenty-six missionaries and their families have prayer and financial support at present. They come from several different missionary societies.

Nicholas feels that one man in particular has helped St Mark's to become an international church, a body of people with a burden for the worldwide church, especially in the Third World and Africa. This is Rob Martin, an accountant, who joined the church in 1971 and became a PCC member and eventually the church treasurer. One day Rob took his courage in both hands and challenged Nicholas about how much the church was giving away.

'It's hardly anything,' Rob said, 'except to support church functions at home and for local outreach.'

Nicholas really listened. 'What shall we do then?' he asked.

Finally it was decided by the PCC to form a Giving Committee and look at the challenge of biblical stewardship.

As Rob looks back he sees the formation of that committee as crucial. 'It was the turning point,' he said, 'as we realised how much God had given to us.'

In 1972 the giving at the church was about £2,000 a year. This went up eightfold, so that by 1977 it was £16,000. Now, in 1988, the giving is about £150,000 a year. Perhaps the secret of this phenomenal giving from a congregation mainly made up of poorer people is that the church itself covenants to give from its income. At least a tenth, the biblical tithe, is given away to outside missions and charities, and often this figure is nearer fifteen to twenty per cent. The more the church gives the more it receives.

Rob then married and in 1977 he and his wife Sue went to Kenya. The man who had preached giving became himself a gift to the church in Africa. He was the accountant for the Anglican diocese of Mount Kenya East. Rob and Sue, and the three sons born to them there, stayed in Africa for ten years and have only just returned to England.

Meanwhile Nicholas and Marigold continued on at the flat, enjoying their late marriage. The main pressures they experienced came from outside circumstances and not from themselves. At the moment a young man called Cameron lives with them. 'It's a joy to have Cameron,' says Marigold. But a thread running through all this hurly-burly of trying to re-parent young people who stay with them, is one of sadness. Marigold in particular loves children. She helps in the church crèche and mothers the congregation. One of her special joys is to help young brides at the many St Mark's weddings. But she always hoped she and Nicholas would have a baby of their own one day. Even Nicholas, who had been so adamantly against having children in his younger days, knew now that it *was* possible to give a child a rich Christian heritage in a conflicting world. Yet no baby came along.

They both realised as the years went by that they certainly could not have done the things they both have done, and together too, if they had had a child of their own to care for. How could a baby have been brought up in a home where the phone or the doorbell often rings at night? Another crisis has to be dealt with; another person in desperate straits needs to be invited in and the sofa made up into a bed by Marigold in the small hours of the morning, while Nicholas, grey with tiredness, counsels and listens to a story of anguish and despair.

So God has not given them a child. This is a cross to bear but not an overriding one.

'When people ask me how many children I've got,' says Marigold, 'I joke and reply, "Oh, five hundred or so!" I don't feel desperate for a baby. I only hoped for a

long time. The truth is I am satisfied and fulfilled in the
Lord's work. I gave this marriage to the Lord. And
before that I was prepared to be single, although I still
longed for a husband in my heart of hearts. Since then
I've known the joy of such a wonderful husband that the
issue of not having any children is relatively un-
important.' She waited and then she said seriously, 'The
concept of the family of Jesus is very real to us.'

One day, unknown to anyone at St Mark's, a fire
broke out in a London flat. The young mother managed
to get her two older girls outside to safety. By then the
flames had taken a hold but without thinking of herself,
she plunged back inside to rescue her third, handicapped, daughter of five. Tragically it was too late. The
mother and the youngest child died later in hospital.
When Bill Stranaghan, her common law husband, was
told he rushed over immediately to take care of the two
older girls, Nicki and Susie. It was very hard for him. He
felt guilty that he had not been living at home at the
time; he felt sad about his common law wife Elizabeth,
whom he had loved; he felt anguished about the dead
child; and he had the task of telling the girls about their
mother and little Debbie.

He left his labouring job, which was a hard thing to do
because he had a pride in it, and began to look after the
two girls. He came to live in a flat in Lockwood House in
the Kennington Park council estate, just a stone's throw
from St Mark's and Nicholas and Marigold's flat. For
those first six months he was there alone with the girls.
He felt he had nothing and no one left except them.

In that time he coped. Somehow. The girls had
terrible memories of the fire and he tried to help them
over this, worried and wondering all the time why he
himself was unable to grieve properly. They all missed
Debbie very much. She had been mentally and
physically handicapped. Bill and Elizabeth had taken
turns, hours at a time, to care for her and to stimulate
her. She was such a courageous and positive little girl
and Bill had noticed that ever so slowly she was

improving. She had learned to sit up and walk a few steps and was beginning to make a few noises. 'She gave us so much love,' he said. And left in all their hearts was an aching space.

One day in the middle of struggling with washing, ironing and wondering what to give the girls for supper, he heard a knock at the door. He stood still for a moment. Hardly anyone ever came. He went to the door and opened it on to the balcony, five storeys high, and looked blankly at the two people standing there with smiles on their faces.

The young man said, 'Oh, hello. We're from St Mark's church and we wondered if you'd like a copy of our magazine, *Crossroads*.' He held out the magazine and Bill put his hand out for it automatically.

'Er, thank you,' said Bill in his soft Irish accent.

Then the girl spoke. 'My name's Giovanna and this is Bill Gordon. He works in the crypt of the church. Doing youth work and helping with the unemployed.'

Bill Stranaghan looked at the other Bill. Was it possible that anyone really bothered about the unemployed? He stood back and opened the door wider. 'Why don't you come in,' he said, 'and have a cuppa tea with me?'

It was the beginning of a friendship. They shared with him about their faith and he listened. It was painful to hear about a God of love after the fire, but somehow he accepted it, partly because they were kind and really listened to him when he told them about the accident.

'Can I call again' asked Giovanna, 'and then you can tell me about your girls?'

'Oh yes. That'd be nice,' he said.

Giovanna kept her word. She often came and chatted to him and heard about Nicki and Susie and how they were doing at school and that Susie wanted to go to St Mark's Church School. Then one day Giovanna said, 'Bill, it'll soon be Christmas. And, well,' she went pink and her words came out all in a rush, 'we're having some special Christmas parties at church. Our Discipleship

Group is having one in a member's home. There'll be
prayers and things, but we'd love you to come.'

'Oh,' said Bill. 'Well, all right then. If I can.'

When the Friday night of the party came, it was
throwing it down with rain. Bill hesitated. Should he go
out and leave the girls? But then again, it was the only
invitation he'd had that Christmas. At last he made up
his mind and, putting his collar up and turning his head
into the wind, he made his way up the road to Clapham
Common. I'm only going because I wanted to get out,
he thought; and because I was fed up with sitting about
in that flat. And I know what'll happen when I get there.
It'll all be talk about God and Jesus and religion and
that. But he kept on. It was very dark and it took him
about half an hour to find the place. By the time he
arrived and was standing outside the door he was
soaking wet and felt terrible. He took a deep breath and
rang the bell. Inside it was as he expected. People were
praying and he did not really know what it was all
about. But a quietness stole over him. It was a deep and
great quietness, such a feeling as he had not had in all
the months since the fire. He sighed and sat down and let
the quietness wash over him. At some point during the
evening, when it was he didn't know exactly, he knew he
had met a new person, a person whose name was
familiar to him but whose nature was not. From the
heart of that quietness came a feeling of love; love for
him, loved as he was, accepted just as he was, despite his
past. He bowed his head, oblivious of the prayers being
said all around him. He's accepted me, thought Bill
quietly. And I want to follow him.

It was quite simple. Bill had made up his mind. There
would be no going back.

As he slipped away at the end and walked down the
noisy streets his head was no longer bowed. And he had
the most unusual feeling. It's strange, he thought. It's
just as if I've been born, born a second time. As if I've
been born again.

In the weeks that followed Bill found himself being

drawn into the life of St Mark's, particularly into the work of the crypt. He started going to the B1 Club held in the Crypt for the unemployed during the day from Tuesdays to Fridays. He met Bill Gordon again there and he met Ruth Gardiner, the new dynamic Scottish community social worker based at St Mark's.

Right from the start Bill found he was good at relating to the wide variety of men who came, some very lonely and needy. He played snooker, table tennis and darts. He played TV games; until the TV was stolen. He helped to welcome people and made coffee and sandwiches. He listened. He stayed for the Bible study at half past three. He was able to direct men with questions to Ruth, who knew all about the different agencies in the community and how to cope with the ins and outs of the social security system. Without realising it Bill became a voluntary worker. Finally he took over the church workshop in the crypt, repairing and painting chairs. This was a way in which he felt he could repay some of the kindness shown to him. It wasn't a fully-fledged business; the facilities were not big enough; but perhaps one day it could be – if the Montgomery Hall was ever done up, as he had heard people say. For the time being he was content to work quietly, and to teach anyone else who was interested. Even though some of the men who came down were most difficult Bill liked to listen to them and show them how to work with wood.

Slowly and quietly as the year wore by the little family settled down. Eight-year-old Susie had joined St Mark's School, which was near enough for her to walk to, and nine-year-old Nicki enjoyed her school in Brixton. Their father gave them a key and they let themselves into the flat after school. They made their own cup of tea and watched TV or played out until their father got home. Bill did his very best for them. He watched them playing one day from the balcony. Susie's hair needed cutting and Nicki's coat was too small. He sighed. What they really needed was a mother. He had loved Elizabeth, their natural mother, but now he had

joined St Mark's he was beginning to know what real
love was. And it was a much deeper, finer and more real
thing than he had ever known before. He looked at his
hands, roughened with work. Would the Lord answer
his prayers and send him a wife? A woman he could
truly love and cherish as a woman should be loved?
Could he indeed make up for the past? He did not know.
And anyway, would any woman want to come and live
in the Kennington Park estate with its bleak walkways
and curved red-brick façades? Some people bravely
kept their flats spick and span. Some did not. But always
there were vandals, graffiti, broken bottles, tin cans and
windows boarded up. He sighed for the second time.
Rubbish poured out from the rubbish chutes and spilled
all over the stairs. To get to his balcony you sometimes
had to tramp over yolks of eggs and smelly cabbage
stalks.

But as he turned to go back indoors the quietness
gently held him again.

22

Divine Appointments

For the kingdom, the power, and the glory
   are yours
now and for ever. Amen.

The Lord's Prayer ASB

On the Thursday morning after Easter 1985 Geoffrey
Smith got on the train at Horsham and settled down in
the corner. He opened his briefcase and took out a copy
of *Anything You Ask* by Colin Urquhart (Hodder &
Stoughton, 1978). He found the place and began to
read. Immediately the chapter heading arrested him: 'I
have appointed you...' He knew the famous words of
Jesus by heart, yet today they held his eye, sank into him
and spoke to him with intensity. 'I have appointed
you...' He looked up and gazed unseeingly out of the
window. It was amazing really that he should read these
of all words on this day. For today he had decided was to
be the day he gave up his job in the City and applied for
the new administrator's job at St Mark's, Kennington.
'I have appointed you...' He read on, smiling a little.
There was no way he was going to tell the St Mark's
people the import of these words until after the
interview. That is, if they gave him an interview and
offered him a job at all. Yet this verse held his attention
so strongly that he could almost say he was sure they
would.

As the train sped along he settled back to read, but

before he got to the end of the first paragraph the events of the last few days came flooding back into his mind. Their strength and power were so great that he suddenly found himself bowing his head and reaching for a handkerchief. And the hand that held the handkerchief trembled slightly. So engrossed was he with his memory of those events that even the book lost precedence for a few minutes. He scarcely looked up as the train stopped at station after station. He was hardly aware of sombre-suited men and shopping women as they entered and left the train. His mind was still so vividly aware of what had happened to him on Easter Sunday. It was so few days ago, and yet an experience of such magnitude that he knew his whole life had been changed. It had been altered in perspective; as if he had been a diver all his life in a watery kingdom, suddenly surfacing and seeing the light, the glorious light, for the first time. Oh yes, he had perceived the light of God before, transmuted, as it were, through water. But now he had seen a vision of that true radiance of unutterable light and – his hand again trembled slightly.

Things had not only begun last Sunday. Really events that began in childhood had culminated then. The train gathered speed, rattling along the great curve of the line. Geoffrey read on a little, taking in Colin's words. But at another level his life flashed before his eyes: he had been a Christian since boyhood; gone out as a teaching missionary in Tanzania; then on to the University of Papua New Guinea; come home and worked for the Commonwealth Secretariat in London; then taken up a post as deputy secretary of a national charity, where he was at present. Yet running through all this had been a thread, a general sense of call to work for the Church in some way. And he had postponed it. It had always been 'next time, Lord'. Then, only recently he had caught himself saying, 'When I retire, Lord, then I'll accept your call and work for the Church.' So it was that the still, small voice of the call was always postponed.

Now he was no longer young, a mature man, sitting in a railway carriage. And at last he was willing to answer that call. The train stopped at Gatwick. People spilled out. Others clambered in and sat down. Geoffrey hardly saw them. He remembered his lack of interest only a month ago when his wife Margaret had casually mentioned a job at St Mark's. Now he was on his way to phone them.

She had taken him to a meeting of the Bethany Fellowship. In fact he had been several times, at one point even talking to Michael Barling about the constant sense of call. 'I feel called by God,' he had said, 'but I'd have to leave a great deal behind.' He had shaken his head, anxious and troubled – anxious to obey the Lord and yet troubled because it would mean, as he thought, giving up too much. He said to his wife in the car afterwards, 'I feel like the rich young ruler. I *know* I ought to be following this call, even though I don't know what the call's really to, or where it might lead.' He had bowed his head. 'I can't do it, Margaret. There's too much to give up.'

So much to give up. He thought of it now in the train as it neared London. A salary bigger than the Archbishop of Canterbury's; a lovely home; the lifestyle that went with it. Then there were the little trappings of power; the uniformed porters who opened the door for him and said 'Good morning, sir'. He felt he could not lose all this after a lifetime of building it up. But the call only increased its burden upon him. He thought of it constantly for he truly loved God and wanted to serve him.

What was the reality, he wondered? Was it the joy of Christians as he sat with them at evening meetings, who had so little that they had to pray in the money for next year's budget? Or was reality the daytime meetings in the corridors of power where the charitable organisation for which he worked had millions behind it to pursue its necessary and very *good* and important work? Which was reality and what did money mean in all this?

There was another problem too. He half smiled
remembering it now. He had not felt altogether at ease
with the Bethany meetings and often went simply to be
with Margaret. He did not question their love for God
and their dedication. But from his background in
education he really knew so much about psychology
that he was sceptical of some of these so-called
charismatic manifestations. He felt emotion was worked
up by the singing of repetitive choruses. He had seen
people falling down. Were they resting in the Spirit? Or
was it simply a result produced by explicable psycho-
logical factors? He doubted if some of these manifestations were from the Lord. The strange thing was that
he did not feel unhappy in the meetings or rebellious.
Only the genuine questioning of his intelligence
concerned him. He knew he needed an answer to satisfy
himself.

The train sped on. He would be in London soon. He
looked at his watch and calculated he had time to finish
the chapter: 'I have appointed you . . .'. Strange that he
was at peace now and had been ever since he made up
his mind to follow the call. Once decided the conflict
died away, leaving this peace in its wake. It had been
difficult to write that letter to Michael Barling the week
before Easter; but so right. The call had beckoned so
insistently that in the end it was irresistible. In the letter
he had simply written that he was willing to give up his
job and come to Bethany, with no apparent future work
beckoning, and join the fellowship with no financial
support, if they agreed. He had made up his mind in
which arena his reality was to be found, and he did not
regret it.

Nothing however had prepared him for Easter
Sunday. Immersed in his thoughts, he forgot the train
and did not notice the dismal suburbs or that his book
slid off his knee. That Easter Sunday morning, only a
few days previously, had rocked him to his foundations,
had for ever altered his view of reality. He thought
about it now. He and Margaret had arrived late at

Bethany and slipped into the back row. Colin stood up and began his sermon by saying: 'Let's look at the evidence for the resurrection.' As Geoffrey heard Colin's words, other words seemed to superimpose themselves over them. 'Come and see,' said a gentle voice in his ear. Instantaneously Geoffrey was lifted in spirit, whether actually or in vision he never knew. He found himself in that moment taken to the empty Easter morning tomb in the garden. The tomb was cut out of rock and the stone rolled to one side. From the tomb shone a light so bright and brilliant it seemed a million times brighter than the sun. Geoffrey could see this radiance, such a weight of Glory that he could not get any closer to it. 'I could scarcely dare look at it, I was filled with wonder. I could see the glory, the glory.' Even in memory, tears wetted his eyes. For the glory was so other, so real, so immense, all he wanted to do was fall down and worship. For this was the God John wrote about: the light of the world, the light of life, with whom we walk in the light. This was the ultimate vision of who God is, when the curtain is lifted in *Revelation* and we see his majesty and are filled with awe – and see the true backcloth to all the puny doings of sinful and evil mankind.

Geoffrey began to search through the gospels to see what had happened when the disciples got to the tomb. Had they seen the glory as he could see it now? Please let this continue, Lord, he prayed. And so it did. For about half an hour. Surely John the apostle must have seen it as his gospel has so many references to light. Geoffrey could hear Colin's words in the background, but his own heart and mind were filled with the awesome light. After a time the weight of light was so powerful that Geoffrey found himself saying, 'I can't stand this any longer, Lord. I don't want to see the glory again until I die.' Slowly the intensity of the vision faded. A hymn was sung. The bread was broken for the Easter communion. Geoffrey was unsteady on his feet as if truly he had just returned from the empty tomb.

He could not speak of it to anyone, not even to Margaret. He drove home, went into the kitchen and peeled potatoes at the sink, for the family were coming to Easter Sunday lunch. Margaret put her hand on his arm, 'Can you speak about it, dear?' she asked. Dumbly he shook his head. After the potatoes were done he went outside to their caravan to be alone. He lay on his face and found his body shaken by weeping. After a while he said, 'I'm sorry, Lord, only the family are coming and...' Graciously that otherness, that presence, that Lord of all glory and all the universe, intimated that he knew all about festival lunches and vegetables. Geoffrey knew he was allowed to leave the caravan and go and help Margaret with the carrots. This he did. Margaret did not say anything. He knew she understood. She had known the baptism in the Holy Spirit many years before and was willing to wait until he was ready to speak to her. The day passed and in the evening when the children had gone home she said again, 'Can you talk about it, dear?' He shook his head. 'No,' he said, 'I can't. I'm sorry.'

Then she phoned Colin and they went over to see him. His first words were an enormous help to Geoffrey. 'Don't be afraid,' he said. Suddenly Geoffrey relaxed. He had needed to hear that. 'It was the absolute otherness of the glory', he said 'that left me so overwhelmed.' Colin prayed. He felt the Lord had something special for Geoffrey to do and counselled him not to resign from his job or even think of joining them at Bethany, until he had waited and seen what it was. Geoffrey agreed. But he could not eat for three days. His stomach churned over tea and coffee and all he had was water.

The train shuddered and slowed down. Geoffrey looked out of the window. Clapham Junction already! Soon he would be at Victoria. He picked up the book, glanced at its message 'I have appointed you...' and put it away in his briefcase. When the train came to a halt again he was first off. He strode hastily down the

platform, his mind busy with his thoughts. He would
phone St Mark's this morning, even though the closing
date for applications was yesterday. And if he got the
job, then he would leave the charity. He felt no conflict
now. No regrets. For the experience of the glory on
Easter morning had lifted him into such an awareness of
true reality that all other factors put together were as
nothing.

He tried phoning St Mark's but no one answered. He
tried again. He sighed. When eventually he got through
he smiled to himself. It appeared that no one had
answered the phone because all the staff had downed
tools and gone off to pray earnestly that the Lord would
send them an administrator!

It was after the interview at the church, with the job
offered and accepted, that Sarah Richards came up to
him and said, 'There's a special verse I believe is for you
today. It's John 15 verse 16: "I have appointed you..."'
It was only then that Geoffrey told them he had read
and believed this same verse the previous week.

His salary was to be a mere quarter of what it had
been. In fact he realised that last year he had paid more
in taxes than he would be earning this year. The
adjustment was not easy: he and Margaret had to let go
of a lot of their lifestyle. But they did it willingly. They
knew they were in the right place for them and at the
right time. He knew too that many people in the church
on low incomes tithed their money and this helped them
to see things in perspective. One day he met a man
crossing the road at the traffic lights outside the church.
The man handed Geoffrey a brown envelope and said,
'Oh, this is my tithe. Please can you hand it in for me? I
didn't manage to get it in yesterday.' Geoffrey took it
and thanked him. He watched the man walk away,
knowing he was unemployed and that the tithe came
straight from his dole money.

The first Sunday after Geoffrey took up his
appointment in August 1985, it was announced that the
church had not got enough money to pay its bills.

Geoffrey sat stock still. The contrast between the job he had just left and the job he had come to could not have been greater. Yet here, in this church and among these people, was reality for him. Three years later he was able to say that the average yearly church budget was £150,000: an average weekly giving of £3,000.

On top of this of course was the money needed to restore the Montgomery Hall. He learnt lessons too in how the Lord provides. As the Montgomery Hall project got under way the church decided to tithe the sacrificial offerings for the restoration. In February 1987 they began the fund and by the end of May it stood at £20,000. So the Giving Committee of the PCC, which met four times a year, allocated £2,000 as its tithe from the Faith Fund. They rejoiced to give away £1,000 to a project in Israel and an equal sum to another project in Uganda. Geoffrey was glad to do this but he could not help thinking how much they as a church needed that £2,000 they had just given away. But to his amazement and joy when he came in on the Monday morning there was a cheque for £2,000 in the letter-box. It had been posted the previous Friday before the meeting by someone who could not possibly have known about their need. God had provided before they had even given away. That, Geoffrey knew, was a spiritual lesson to him and one that Nicholas knew much about. 'Give, and it will be given to you. A good measure, pressed down, shaken together and running over, will be poured into your lap (Luke 6:38 NIV).'

It was not only in the area of finance that Geoffrey was seeing new things. When he first arrived he wanted to get to grips with the way the staff was organised. It would have been easy to reorganise with one person in charge of teaching, one evangelism, one preaching and one administration. But as he discussed it with Mike Marshall the curate, Arthur Cunningham the lay pastor, and with Nicholas, they realised the Lord was calling them to share their lives together in a corporate leadership, freed of departmental roles. Nicholas explained that a corporate leadership had gradually been developing over the years from Jeffrey Fewkes's time; then they had had the shared eldership; now the corporate leadership. This was difficult for Geoffrey as he knew that no organisation he had worked in before had had the fluidity of plural leadership. Unless roles were clearly defined confusion, friction and chaos were the result. Yet as he shared with the others and the bonds of friendship grew and he knew they all had a deep desire to hear God, then strangely enough it did work. It was costly in time as the four of them shared together and made decisions corporately, rather than letting a business agenda rule them. He knew that such a way of doing things would not necessarily always be right for them or for other churches all the time. But it was right for St Mark's now.

He read deeply in Luke's gospel and saw how the Lord shared his life at a profound level with three of the disciples. In the light of this Geoffrey wrote in the church magazine that the congregation was now at the five hundred mark, but not the same five hundred as three years before. Peter Brierley of Marc Europe helped to collect information that Geoffrey used in the article. Two-thirds of their people were in the nineteen to thirty-four age group and (as a reflection of life in South London) there was a fifty per cent change of faces in the congregation over a three-year period. There were further facts too: half the congregation had been coming for less than two years, and four out of five had been coming for less than five years. One in ten had not attended any church before. Over half the regulars in every age group were unmarried. If the growth rate continued the congregation would double by 1990. Half the regulars lived in the immediate neighbourhood. A quarter came from up to five miles away. Also, he was able to write, there was, 'an exciting mix of people: C of E, Baptist, RC, Methodist, House Churches, URC and others come at times, showing powerfully that people from widely contrasting backgrounds can have genuine fellowship with each other.'

Geoffrey realised as he collated and wrote this
material that in an expanding congregation and staff it
was impossible for one person to share his life with them
all. So out of the closeness of the four leaders came a new
concept of pastoring based on the Paul Yonggi Cho
idea, at whose church in Seoul, South Korea no one
person was responsible for more than ten to fifteen
people.

Now at St Mark's each of the four leaders is
responsible for one of the four Care Groups and its
leaders. Each Care Group leader is responsible for his
quarter of the Discipleship Group leaders. They in turn
are responsible for the small groups in their care. This
means, at least in theory, that no one at all in the church
need be without a friend and someone to turn to if the
going gets difficult. It means many young people are
being trained as leaders. In fact there are so many
leaders that they themselves go away for a Leaders'
Weekend. There are too many people in the congregation for a normal Parish Weekend to work. So
smaller groups go away together instead.

Nicholas says, 'The main qualification for a leader is
that they should have a shepherd's heart. A heart of love
for those they are leading and a heart of love for God.
They must be open too to share and to serve. For
leadership at St Mark's is taught as service.'

Geoffrey saw also that Nicholas took the lead in
mutual submission in the meetings between the four of
them. He refused to become a lone Moses going up the
mountain and bringing down the vision. It had to be a
shared vision and until it was, they would wait for it.
The four leaders met at length once a week to pray,
share and if necessary check one another. This was
costly and difficult at times.

'It is part of the way of the cross to follow the Spirit
and become moulded together into a body,' said
Nicholas.

And then once every two or three months the four

men and their wives would meet together as 'The Mixed Eight' and further sharing would take place.

A quotation from the booklet *Christ Incarnate at St Mark's* says clearly how the church views leadership:

> Leadership is not a role or status but an opportunity for service. The task of leadership is to prepare God's people for the works of service, expressing his compassion and mercy to the lost and hurting, so that the body of Christ may be built up. This is the Lord's commission as he prepares his Church to be the instrument through which God brings his rule on earth.

This excited Geoffrey who had written the booklet, which was the fruit of the four leaders' shared vision. Many churches fell down on not having medium-sized groupings and St Mark's was getting this right. In his reading of Luke 9 he had seen a leadership of four on the Mount of Transfiguration. Previously in the same chapter Jesus briefed the twelve disciples. They were appointed and sent out to preach and to heal. Then he organised and fed the five thousand by seating them in groups of fifty. At the beginning of chapter 10 he read, 'The Lord appointed seventy-two others to go out and to preach and heal'. Geoffrey could hardly sit still, he was so thrilled by all this. Here was Jesus using groups of four, twelve, fifty, seventy-two and five thousand. Jesus was using numbers with understanding, knowing that you could do different things with different sizes of groups.

'All this makes sense,' he told Nicholas. 'We've got the intimate friendship level at church; then the small Discipleship Group; then the middle-size Care Group; and then the very big grouping in a Sunday service. People who can feel lonely and lost in a large service should, in theory at least, know some other people and have learned to feel more at ease in the middle-sized group.'

But St Mark's was no different from any other church in one respect. It had a multiplicity of meetings in the evenings, so many that folk began to drop off from attending. What was the answer? Was there in fact an answer for people tired out after a day's work? Is there ever any answer to the problem and pressures of meetingitis for the Christian, other than cutting him or herself off from the necessary fellowship and therefore not helping or relating to others?

St Mark's had already come up with one radical answer, in that lay workers had been appointed, so releasing laity from a lot of burdensome evening church meetings. Now the church came up with another radical idea. They decided to organise their life in a four-weekly rota. In Week One the middle-sized Care Groups met on Monday, Tuesday or Wednesday evenings. In Weeks Two and Four the smaller Discipleship Groups met on the same night. Week Three was to be left free for ministry/service teams.

The idea of a week free for a totally different structuring of people was new. It meant a Discipleship Group leader with a lot of responsibility at work and in the church could, if he or she wanted, have a rest. Or they could join one of the twenty ministry teams and do something quite different. This ranged among practical helps: care of altar linen and preparing communion; sewing; knitting, making clothes; car parking; catering; carpentry; decorating; gardening; chair moving; driving; flower arranging; maintenance (general odd jobs); building, plumbing; electrics; legal matters; bicycle repairs; car repairs; car servicing.

There were communicating skills teams including: book centre; public address system; reception desk; tapes; videos; and Bible reading. Office skills included: typing; shorthand/speedwriting; telephone receptionist; clerical work; duplicating; book-keeping/accounting.

Outreach in the parish included: coffee bar; counselling; intercessory prayer on request; visiting homes

'Open Airs'; visiting schools; visiting local community centres/facilities; King's Club; Fishers' Club; home-based evangelism; and visiting the elderly. Creative Gift Groups included: artwork (Posters); dance; drama; music and instruments; writing; singing; and mime.

People could serve the church family in: crèche; junior church; teaching children; teaching teenagers; and babysitting. Finally hospitality could be offered in your room, flat or house, whether: tea/coffee/biscuits; occasional lunch/dinner; regular meals; short-term accommodation; medium-term accommodation; or finally, long-term accommodation.

The aim of all these groups was to serve. No one need ever be redundant and unemployed in the body of Christ. As the St Mark's booklet *Every Member Ministry* says:

> The central and clear teaching of every member ministry is that we all have gifts, talents and abilities whether natural or supernatural which we can use to build up and extend the church of Jesus Christ. No one is too small; too inadequate; too hopeless. All can and should be included and involved.

Everyone has a divine appointment in ministry and service.

The basic organisation is described in *Christ Incarnate at St Mark's*:

> Structures are needed to provide ways of relating to one another in a large family or organisation and mobilising resources to achieve a common purpose. The structure we use is not important in itself. What matters is that it enables us to care for one another and to express the love of Christ in building up the body and serving him. Among the structures in the Bible are three especially useful models. The first is group-based: when God's people left Egypt and were marching through the desert to the Promised Land,

capable men from all Israel were appointed as leaders
of thousands, hundreds, fifties and tens (Exod.
18:24–26).

Geoffrey Smith had also noticed the way Jesus used
different groupings:

> The second pattern is gift-based. In the Old
> Testament we find this in preparation for the building
> of the temple, e.g. Carpenters, Stonemasons, Silver-
> smiths and Singers. In the New Testament we find it
> in the different ministries within the Church, e.g.
> Evangelists, Teachers, Pastors and Administrators.
>   A third pattern is neighbourhood and home-based.
> Under the old covenant the Israelites connected
> particular places and neighbourhoods with the
> worship of God. Jesus released us from this restricting
> localism, but he used homes as a base for caring and
> ministry, e.g. the home of Mary, Martha and
> Lazarus; and in his instructions to his disciples in
> Matthew 10:11–14.
>   The pastoral structure described in this booklet is
> group-based in Care Groups and home-based in
> Discipleship Groups. The ministry teams are gift-
> based. Let us be sure we build upon the rock which is
> the only sure foundation... 'for no-one can lay any
> foundation other than the one already laid, which is
> Jesus Christ' (1 Cor. 3:11).

Geoffrey put down his copy of *Christ Incarnate* and
thought deeply. Yes, he felt sure St Mark's had got it as
right as any church could. But the challenge would
always be there. Unless they built at all times upon the
rock of Jesus Christ they would fail. Unless they built on
his words their building would collapse. And of course
everyone was aware that people were people and that
within the different groups it was relationships and
commitment that counted. The church structures must
always be the servant, albeit an efficient servant, of the
people. People were the most important.

God has our lives within his hands. He has work, gifts, places and people appointed for us. He even had Rebekah 'appointed' as a wife for Isaac in the Old Testament story.

But Bill Stranaghan, the man who tramped every day from his flat in Lockwood House to help Bob Uden at the crypt and the B1 Club, wondered very much if God had any appointments for him. Would there ever be a job and would there, could there, ever be a wife? Someone appointed just for him and the girls who would love them all? Until he knew the answer to that, he realised he was simply going to have to wait and see.

Meanwhile he played snooker and table tennis. He worked in the workshop restoring chairs. He enjoyed the summer festival in June, which included 'Get to know you' parties in homes; a flower festival; theatre groups in schools and the open air; sixty people from YWAM calling on every home in the parish; a Saturday Fun Afternoon for children which Nicki and Susie enjoyed; films, talks, coffee bars, women's meetings and live music and drama at the youth night. He remembered that earlier in the year the drama group developed an update of the medieval morality play, *Everyman*, and later performed drama sketches at the Brixton Festival. He heard that Syd Ravatte, a Mauritian, was appointed as caretaker of St Mark's, John Keung took over the bookstall ministry, John Everett was the evangelism secretary and Gareth Thomas, a carpenter, was appointed the church's maintenance manager.

There was so much life going on around him and he was part of it and involved in it and was deeply thankful. But if only, he thought, one day I could meet someone and get a proper home going in the flat for the girls. He sighed. There was nothing for it but to carry on steadily with what he was doing. He put his coat on and buttoned it up firmly. He had to get back home and get the girls' tea ready.

But God's appointment was just round the corner.

23

Muggers' Mile

St Mark's, Kennington is a very mixed neighbourhood of about 6,100 people. 9 of the 21 Census
districts making up the parish are among the most
deprived 10% in the country, as classified by the
Department of the Environment in 1981. It is an area
of widespread poverty and unemployment, where at
the 1981 Census 15% of the young people aged 16 to
24 in the labour market were out of work. There are
also many nurses, students craftsmen, and young
professional families in the area, where at least 4
MPs, including a cabinet minister, have homes.
    ... It is an area with a strong sense of locality.
Many who live here are powerless to live elsewhere;
others live here for a few years while undergoing
training; and still others live here because they have
chosen the inner city. Among this last group was
Paul Chadeyron, a young solicitor who came to the
neighbourhood in order to work with young
offenders, and who was murdered in 1986 on his way
home from St Mark's, where he was an active
member of the Church Council. Members of the
church have thus shared in the pain of the area. Out
of the ten staff supported by the church, three were
mugged on the street in 1986, two others assaulted,
and two held at knifepoint.

Geoffrey Smith
from *A Parish Consultation*
Report on the restoration of
Montgomery Hall (1986)

Bill Stranaghan carried on helping out at the crypt.

Ruth, the social worker who pioneered the work, had left to get married and eventually Bob Uden was appointed as a youth and community worker in her place. He consolidated the work she had begun. The mending of furniture in the workshop was going well. Someone had suggested they make some toys to give away to Caine Hall at Christmas and Bill was looking forward to getting stuck into this. He carried on with his voluntary work conscientiously, glad to be able to give, glad not to be cooped up in the flat alone all day, glad he had found a new faith and a new meaning in life.

One afternoon he began clearing up some of the dirty mugs from the coffee bar. All at once he stopped. He swallowed as the unfamiliar lump gathered again in his throat. He felt sad quite a lot lately and could not understand it. His girls were doing fine. The flat was fine. He was fine and had a whole new circle of friends at St Mark's. He and the girls had put the fire and the deaths behind them now. After all they had to live again.

But the grief worried him. At a counselling session Nicholas gently pointed out to him that he was still mourning the loss of his common law wife and little Debbie. Bill stopped for a few minutes and stared at the soapy water in the sink. It was strange, but he had forgotten until now how concerned he had been after the fire that he felt so little grief. Perhaps that was a necessary stage because he had had so much to do. Now things were much more settled the grief seemed to be coming out. He bowed his head. No doubt it was for the best. He emptied the bowl and swished the water away. Carefully he began drying the mugs and putting them on the shelf. Better not start getting sorry for himself though. Better not start thinking about being lonely, longing to share his life and...

'Hello,' said a voice behind him.

He spun round. 'Why, hello Dawn,' he said, his soft Irish voice breaking into a smile.

The young woman on the other side of the counter

smiled back.

'Just on your way back from helping at the Playgroup?'

She grinned. 'That was with Barbara Sidwell this morning. No, in the afternoons I help Roger and Margie Bagge with the elderly at the Day Centre.'

'Oh, yes.' He smiled at her and she smiled back.

She said, 'Some of the St Mark's elderly people come to Caine Hall for lunch each day. It's great isn't it, the links between St Mark's and Caine Hall. It helps everybody.'

Bill turned his back to her and began to fill the kettle. 'I thought you might not be coming down today.'

'Oh, I always like dropping in here, especially for a cuppa coffee!' She went and sat at a table. 'You having one?'

'Er, yes.'

When the drinks were ready he said, 'Where did you work before?'

She pulled a face. 'I was a chambermaid in a big club off Park Lane. But I didn't like it at all. They expected so much of you and you had to be so quick as well. And then on Sundays it was such a long way back from church and I was scared of being mugged and Nicholas and Marigold were so kind and used to drive me back sometimes after the service.'

'Where are you living now?' he said quickly.

'Well, I'm looking for somewhere, actually.'

He said in a rush, 'If you want to look round, I'll come with you. It's not safe on your own, especially at night.'

'Oh, thank you.' She smiled gently at him.

Later, when she was gone and he still had some tidying up to do, he found himself praying. As in all his prayers he came straight to the point: 'She's nice, Lord. I fancy her, but I'm not sure. At least *I* am sure, but would a relationship with her be your will, Lord?' He sighed. He had prayed this before and it was rather hard to know what answer the Lord was giving. Yet he was determined that any friendship with Dawn was going to be built upon the rock of Jesus. He had loved his common law wife after his own fashion, but since becoming a Christian he realised he had never really known before what love was. Not to the full extent of the word. If anything was to develop with Dawn it was going to be very different from the past. Jesus would have to be the head of their love life – and that meant a properly conducted relationship and a marriage in church. Automatically he glanced round. Everything was neat. He shook his head. It was early days to be thinking of marriage, especially when he still felt upset about the past. Or did he? Wasn't it simply the buried grief coming up to the surface and him being healed in the process? That's what Nicholas said during the counselling. And he always felt good after a chat with Dawn.

Another part of his mind said, 'It's Monday. King's Club down here for the nines to thirteens. Nicki and Susie would be coming. Then tomorrow Fishers' Club was here for teenagers from the area and he would be helping. He came regularly to church too and brought the girls to junior church. He also helped with young people at a community club on the Kennington Park estate. He was well known now and well respected in the council blocks of Lockwood and Alverstone Houses. Life was quite full. Some of the teenagers at the Fishers' Club had become Christians, though there was no pressure. They sometimes joined the church Youth Club, which catered more for the spiritual side of life. Down here in the crypt though, and in the Fishers' Club, there was often a lot of aggression. Sometimes it seemed to Bill that violence, threats, noise and destruction bred in the very streets of Kennington and South London. But he was not afraid.

Yet as he locked up and set off back to the flat, his mind grappling with the problem of what to buy the girls for their tea when his dole money was running so low, he thought again about Dawn. Whether or not marriage was in the air, nothing was going to stop him accompanying her in her search for accommodation. Life was too dangerous on the streets for women alone.

At half past twelve in the morning on June 30th 1986 the phone rang in Nicholas' and Marigold's flat. Marigold was still up and she answered. After a few moments she managed to say, 'I can't believe it. Just a minute, I'll get Nicholas.'

She put the phone down on the table and stumbled into their bedroom. He was already awake. 'What is it, beloved?'

'It's . . . it's Paul Chadeyron. He's . . . been murdered!'

For a few seconds neither spoke. Then Nicholas was flinging on his clothes. She went back to the phone. 'We'll come at once,' she said.

A few minutes later, still numb with shock, they were on their way to Kennington Police Station, where they met three of Paul's friends who had found him before he died and were intensely grieved and shocked. The superintendent too was shocked when he met them later at the hospital. But it was too late. Paul Chadeyron, a young solicitor from St Mark's Church, was dead.

When they were able to piece together the story, it turned out that Paul had been coming back from church at about half past ten that Sunday evening. He had called at a friend's flat for coffee on the way and was on foot because it was so near his own flat, down the road off the Clapham Road. He was mugged, obviously by people who wanted money. They left him to bleed to death but he managed to crawl to his own doorstep and cry out. His flat mate Robert Mills heard him and dashed out, along with two girls from the flats nearby. It was very terrible for them as they found Paul falling unconscious and crying out, 'Lord, Lord, Lord.'

Nicholas felt this tragedy deeply. Paul had felt called to work in the inner city and joined St Mark's through the recommendation of his friend, Robert Ward. He was a solicitor in the Brixton Road and had a burden for the West Indian kids in the area: they often roamed the streets in packs and Paul felt called to help them. He was firm, stern almost, in his dealings with them, but that sternness sprang out of his concern. He was well thought of in the area among his fellow solicitors and social workers. One social worker rang up Marigold and said, 'Paul was very conscientious and willing to go the second mile with his clients. He often visited them in prison or in their homes and sometimes prayed with them.'

'It was a martyr's death,' said Nicholas, 'and he'll receive a martyr's crown.'

But his murderers have not up to now been caught. John Everett wrote this in 'Hope for Murderers' Mile', an article for *Crossroads*:

We all have a responsibility... for the creation of an environment in which hatred, violence, rape and murder are so widespread, and we all need to lay our hearts and lives bare before God if there is to be any significant change!

The police and the enforcement of law can go a long way towards repressing crime, but they cannot change the seeds of murder which lie in all our hearts. Jesus Christ told us in the Sermon on the Mount, 'You have heard it said, "Thou shalt not commit murder", but I tell you that whoever hates his brother has committed murder.' (Matt 5:21-22)

The news of Paul's murder shocked everyone in the church. Up to then, although they were in a dangerous area where people were mugged and held up at night, nothing serious had happened to them. Everyone had been protected. The St Mark's leaders began to warn the congregation to stick to the main roads, avoid side streets, go around in groups and give each other lifts in their cars. They were to take great care, even during the day. Then the parish secretary, Charlotte, was mugged in broad daylight outside the supermarket two weeks before her wedding. Her handbag was snatched. And even before Paul's murder John Everett was held up one evening by three youths with knives. He handed over his wallet, which was empty. The thieves were angry but he kept on walking away. A few minutes later he was home and telephoned the police. It was a dangerous incident.

'Nevertheless we believe the Lord is sovereign,' said Nicholas. 'Nothing can happen to those who believe, without his permission and promise to bring good out of it. Even in this terrible situation the Lord wants to release us from fear. However hard it may be to accept at times, Romans 8:28 (NIV) puts it clearly: "And we know that in all things God works for the good of those who love him, who have been called according to his purpose."'

And as Nicholas tramped around the area he saw much that was heart-warming. A coloured man stopped his car to let him cross the road, waving him over with a beaming smile. An elderly woman, waddling across the forecourt of the Lockwood House flats, hailed him by name and smiled all over her face. Shopkeepers often had a real warmth, a ready smile and were willing to go out of their way to help a person. People offered up their seats on the Tube. And hundreds of people at church had never been harmed in any way.

He saw a young black British friend from the church and waved. It was Lloyd Appollos, wearing a track suit with an enormous badge on it which blared out in white letters THERE IS NO GOD! Underneath was a picture of a court jester; above in tiny letters was the phrase, 'The fool has said in his heart'.

'Why do you wear that badge?' asked Nicholas, intrigued.

'Well, it's great for street evangelism,' said Appollos. 'And I've got other badges too!'

Nicholas knew that after his baptism about twenty people had been brought into the church through Appollos. One said, 'I watched Appollos for two years since he became a Christian. It must have been rea because he laid aside violence. He never hit back or fought back. This spoke to me and I decided to give my life to the Lord as well.'

Appollos was not afraid, not since he had seen a large gang of youths wielding sticks and knives in Kennington Park turn and run away from his own gang of eight or nine friends.

'They were afraid of the Christians!' he said and whistled. 'I don't know how or why! But they turned and ran. And they've never gone for us again! They must have been afraid of who was in us!'

Nicholas smiled. It sounded a bit like an Old Testament encounter. But the fruit in Appollos's life and the lives of those he was influencing was true and good. No, there were many decent and good living people in the church and in the area. The problem was that at times evil threatened to take over. There was only one answer in this flawed world. And Nicholas knew who it was. He knew too that prayer was the great key.

One good thing that developed out of his, and many people's, concern for the South London area were the half nights of prayer, held at St Mark's on the first Friday of the month. They prayed for revival in South London and asked to be workers with God in building his kingdom. In 1986 many other churches and groupings joined in with this: Lynn Green of YWAM; Roger Forster of Ichthus; Philip Mohabir of the West Indian Evangelical Alliance; Dave Tomlinson of Teamwork; Les Isaacs from the black Apostolic Church; Clifford and Monica Hill (St Mark's members) of the Prophetic Word Ministries; Mike Woods from Streatham Baptist Church; and several other Anglican vicars joined in as well.

The two hundred or so children at St Mark's School were doing well too, and prayer was at the heart of it. Jean Parker, the headmistress for fourteen years, said, 'We have many children from problem families. Some are disturbed, many are poor and deprived and live in overcrowded housing with nowhere to play. But at the

moment I can't think of any bullies in the school. This is
amazing. And a real support to the school is that once a
term any of the Christian parents and teachers who
want to, and the St Mark's leaders, get together and
pray for the school. Some of the parents help too with
the reading groups and the church leaders often pop in,
so the children have got to know them. The church
leaders take assembly on Tuesdays. And we have great
support from our governors, who are almost all from the
church.' She laughed. 'They must be about the only
governors in the country who pay for all us teachers to
go out for a meal together once a year!

'Lloyd Appollos is a general assistant and helps with
Ricki, a ten-year-old with muscular dystrophy. This
year we invited the elderly folk from the Day Care
Centre at Caine Hall to a carol service in the church.
They came in a converted ambulance-cum-coach.
Afterwards the children gave them bags of food, and this
was instead of a harvest gift.'

Marigold laughed with Jean. 'What about the school
pantomime!'

Jean smiled. 'Oh, yes! We did *Punkerella*. I was
Baroness Hard-up, the wicked stepmother! The children adored it. They absolutely roared with laughter! I
think it does them good to see their teachers letting their
hair down a bit!'

Marigold grinned. 'Yes, I remember. Susie Stranaghan was in stitches.'

Nicholas had to smile too when Marigold told him
about it. So much good and wholesome fun and
laughter went on in Kennington; and a lot of it, though
not exclusively, emanated from Christian sources.

The year slowly passed. Peter Batiste, along with his
wife Jocelyn, came as the new lay pastor and together
they ran the vicarage household, as far as possible as a
family unit.

Peter said, 'In an area where accommodation is

increasingly scarce we see the vicarage as a real home for single church members where they can experience love and support and yet enjoy at the same time freedom and fellowship.'

He also wrote the church booklet, *Every Member Ministry*.

Nicholas and Marigold visited the conference ACTS '86. Out of the great feast of teaching there, however, he noticed one imbalance. The fact was that there was only one woman speaker, and she was put at the end of the last night. Because the previous speaker ran late many people left without hearing her. This somehow highlighted the imbalance to Nicholas. He thought about the ministry of women at St Mark's. Jean Darnall often came in and preached and ministered. Peggy Thompson spoke in and led smaller groups. Other women from the congregation and outside had spoken on various occasions. Several were Care Group leaders, and many others were Discipleship Group leaders. Two women from the congregation wanted to become deacons in the Church of England.

Later, when Keith Sutton, Bishop of Kingston, asked what he thought about the issue of women's ministry, Nicholas replied spontaneously, 'Anthea Dimitri is a member of our congregation. And as far as I'm concerned she can preach any time she wants. The point is that she always preaches under the anointing of the Holy Spirit. And surely that should be the seal of anyone's preaching, whether male or female; the anointing of God. Nothing less will do. The church appreciates her enormously and so do I. People often say, "When is Anthea going to preach?"'

As far as a woman taking on the organisational and spiritual role of leading a whole church was concerned, Nicholas was not so sure. But for any woman: if she was born again and a child of God, and called by God into a certain ministry, then it was disobedient not to release her into that ministry. Disobedient and selfish.

While all this life and activity were driving forward,

Bill Stranaghan continued his daily work at the Bl Club in the crypt. One wonderful day the Manpower Services Commission gave him a year's paid job there helping Bob Uden. Bill loved it and worked hard. But the main joy in his life was that he and Dawn had got engaged.

In May 1987 their wedding took place in St Mark's church. It was made even happier by being a gloriously sunny day. The previous weeks had been filled with a glad rush of shopping and Marigold helped with getting Nicki and Susie ready as bridesmaids. It was a beautiful wedding. Dawn was radiant in white and Bill proud and standing tall with a grin on his face. Finally came the honeymoon in an annexe in Shropshire belonging to some friends of Nicholas and Marigold's. The couple had a wonderful time. The girls remained at the Lockwood House flat, looked after by friends, but longed for their father and new mother. And at last Bill and Dawn came home and settled down with Nicki and Susie. Life was full and rich for them. And when in August Dawn told them she was expecting a baby, the little family was thrilled. And so was the bigger family of the church. Perhaps this new baby will finally heal the aching gap left in all their lives when their mother and little Debbie died in the fire, thought Marigold. Judging from the way they were all so excited, it certainly seemed so.

24

Who is My Neighbour?

'Love the Lord your God with all your soul, and with all your strength and with all your heart and all your mind', and, 'Love your neighbour as yourself,' said the questioner in Luke 10:27 NIV. Jesus replied, 'Do this and you will live.' But the questioner asked Jesus, 'And who is my neighbour?' And Jesus told him the story of the Good Samaritan (vv. 28–35 NIV).

The people in this report are our neighbours, and neighbours one of another. The way to life remains the same. Love God and love your neighbour.

... the hall should be a place to develop and strengthen family life. If should not just provide another programme of activities like any community centre, with a Christian gloss, but it should be a radical alternative – a place where the family of God expresses God's love in a quality of relationship that attracts people to the family, and helps build up their family life.

Is the church in the inner city weak and in decline? The people of St Mark's, Kennington refuse to accept that the gospel has nothing to offer in areas of great human need. In fact Jesus himself spent much time with the poor. The church is determined not only to offer the saving power of the gospel but also to work in a practical way to build the life of the local community.

Tim Anderson wrote: 'The words of James (2:17 NIV) have been on our minds: "Faith by itself, if it is not accompanied by deeds, is dead."'

from *A Parish Consultation*
Report on the restoration of
Montgomery Hall (1986)

Tim Anderson was not looking forward to going to the PCC meeting that evening in 1987. As members of the Development Committee for the Montgomery Hall project, he and the others, out of integrity and responsibility, felt some new information that had come up about costings had to be pointed out. He ate his evening meal alone in the flat but his mind was only half on his pizza. He knew the Montgomery Hall was built in the 1950s when the vicarage was first put up after the war. But due to a local council Compulsory Purchase Order that had hung over the building in the 1970s, the hall was now in a poor state of repair. Meetings were still held there occasionally, but all the 'church hall' type of meetings were in the church itself. The trouble was that the Montgomery Hall was not ideal as it was across a very busy road and quite a walk from St Mark's. Now the Compulsory Purchase Order was lifted and they were left with a dilapidated and run down hall. And yet, after all it was *there* and could be used.

Early in the 1980s the PCC had had the vision for the hall to be a servant in the neighbourhood; a distinctively Christian family centre; a drop-in centre for the unemployed and the over-sixties; a leisure centre; an advice centre or a venue for a playgroup or for day and evening classes. The ideas were many. Linking them together though, the overriding feeling was that it should not become merely another social services type of help, very necessary as that was. It must be used somehow for the glory of God; prayed for; and be a servant to the needy, poor, old and frightened in Kennington. It was not enough to wish your brother to be warm and dry and then forget him. Love meant action too. Words and preaching on their own were not enough.

Tim sighed and stood up. He took his plate to the sink and watched it slowly subside into the washing-up water in the bowl. Coffee, he decided, was next on the agenda. He would clear up later. As he drank the coffee and relaxed he wondered what the PCC was going to say this evening. He and the others were completely at one about the vision for the hall and for the real opportunities it offered for love and evangelism and sacrifice; nevertheless the PCC would not be prepared for, or like, what they were going to hear tonight from him and the Development Committee. Tim thought, I'm almost quaking in my boots, a thing I never usually feel. He put his mug down carefully on the mat and stood up, determined. Whatever any of them on the committee felt, they had to go through with it now.

One by one, the members of the Development Committee explained why they no longer felt able to support the original view of the PCC that a renovation of the hall was all that was needed. Well over £10,000 had been spent already on plans.

'But we thought that renovation would give us twice the size a complete pulling down and rebuilding would,' said Tim. 'We thought we'd be getting twice the space for the same money. Now we've found out that, going into all the costs, the renovation and the rebuilding will give us more or less the same floor space. And it will cost an equal amount.'

In other words they could have a brand new building for the same money and the same size as the renovated building.

The architect was in favour of the new building idea, because a renovation might discover dry rot or any number of problems not as yet apparent. There was a better idea of costs too with a new building and advances in building technology since the 1950s meant it would be a much sounder construction.

So the Development Committee put forward the view that the PCC should change tack, even though the church was already a certain way down the road to renovation.

There was silence for several moments. Then heads began to turn. Tim glanced at Geoffrey Smith. He knew Geoffrey had done a vast amount of work drawing up his report on the area, a green *Parish Consultation*, and how

useful the hall could become. Geoffrey had only recently
written in *Crossroads*: 'The Montgomery Hall would be
brought back into use as a Family Centre supporting
family life in the parish. It would express the love of
Jesus through the family of St Mark's and be a place
where people can find friends, refuge and a new purpose
in life. This is our faith.'

Geoffrey had organised a campaign of visiting local
residents; an opinion poll; and forms had been left in
shops and banks. Anyone in Kennington could write
down what they wanted in the way of amenities in the
Montgomery Hall. Good results had come from it, even
to realising they needed some forms printed in Urdu,
some in Bengali and some in Spanish. It had been an
enormous task and Geoffrey had spent a lot of time on it.
Now, having listened and digested the new information,
Geoffrey was concerned.

'Rebuilding will delay things so much,' he kept
saying. 'I feel it urgently that we shouldn't delay. We
might lose the whole impetus, lose the whole vision.'

Several people began talking at once. Many expressed
the view that the PCC had not commissioned a new
building because they thought renovation was cheaper;
also that much money had already been spent on plans.

Peggy Thompson stood up. 'Look,' she said, 'the
foundations are already laid in the Montgomery Hall.
It's basically a sound building...'

Someone interrupted, 'We think it is. But we can't be
sure!'

She carried on, 'and surely we should build on those
foundations and not go back on it. Wallace Bird had the
vision for the future when the church was in ruins after
the last war. Those people then had the faith to rebuild
and pray in the money. And by the same token we ought
to repair the building. Carry on the vision of Wallace
Bird!' She sat down.

Jonathan Jackson, a professional man used to
handling large projects like this, said calmly, 'I am a
great supporter of having a new building.'

Yes, thought Tim, logically a new building is the best thing. But emotionally people will find it difficult.

'Well I'm NOT!' someone burst out.

Tim said, 'The Development Committee reports that a new building is more sensible and that the PCC should give it due consideration.'

A low murmuring began to run round the room. It gathered in intensity and Nicholas, who had said nothing so far, heard it. He looked quickly round the room and saw the discontent, the unhappiness, the lack of ease on people's faces. He knew that rebellion and disobedience were in the air. He drew himself up and without knowing what he was about to say, opened his mouth.

'I'm very much afraid that as a Development Committee you had no authority to change tack in mid-stream! We'd gone forward in faith for the renovation. Perhaps you have been disobedient in considering this option. In fact you had no right to do it! Even though I'm sure you did it in good faith.'

He sat down. Every eye was fastened on him, some shocked, having only known the soft hand of pastoral love from him, and unaware of his inner steel-like determination to go the way he felt was right. The silence was total, the atmosphere electric.

One by one a different murmuring began. It was people saying, 'I'm not in disobedience. I'm not in disobedience. Not in disobedience.'

Nicholas stared at his Bible and wondered what would happen next. In all his life he could not recall ever having spoken like that before. But the church hall project was as nothing to disunity. He sat quite still with his shoulders bowed and waited. A vote was about to be taken. Any disunity over such an important issue would be heartbreaking.

Tim felt upset, as if others were about to steamroller him. He had only acted out of integrity and yet – then he remembered it was the habit of the PCC to pray together at the beginning and end of each meeting. He looked up quickly.

'Please, can we pray in silence together for a while,' he asked. 'At least then we'll be giving God his chance to have his say before we take the vote.'

The tension eased and folk began nodding in agreement. Nicholas smiled at him and Tim said, 'We are after all handling the rudder of a very big ship.'

So for ten minutes they sat in silence, heads bowed, lips moving silently. At first people seemed all elbows and tension, but gradually, as Nicholas sensed without opening his eyes, a peace was coming. It was slow at first and then came more quickly, as the Holy Spirit moved amongst them bringing unity to brothers and sisters. He knew the atmosphere was genuine and he also knew that what was happening was important. Tim sat quite still. He felt completely calm, no longer upset in any way. He felt as if a load had been taken off his back; he relaxed back into his chair, his hands open on his knee.

In the different silence that followed the prayer everyone relaxed in their seats.

Then Danny McGill, a builder and a down-to-earth member of the council, said, 'Well I don't know what anyone else thinks, but the Lord's been showing me that we've got to have confidence and believe he is in all the plans.'

Each person then shared what they felt the Lord had said to them during the quietness of the prayer time.

Jonathan Jackson said he had changed his mind. 'We should press on with the renovation.'

Tim looked round. Everyone's head was nodding including his colleagues' on the Development Committee; including his own. There was absolutely no question now. Everyone was united in feeling the renovation was right. The Spirit had given them unity, even though he could not explain it or explain why he felt so much at peace with the new decision when only ten minutes ago he had felt so upset.

Then the chairman and former churchwarden John Harries said, 'I came here tonight with the thought we should definitely be going for a new building. It was more satisfactory in practical terms. But the Lord has shown me quite clearly he doesn't want that.'

By the end of the evening there was complete unity on the PCC. The vote in favour of the renovated building was unanimous. Nicholas knew a deep joy about this. And he discerned, correctly, that because everyone was so certain that the Lord had broken in on the meeting, as it were, then new vision and purpose for the Montgomery Hall project would be the result. This is now the case. And any who were reluctant and half-hearted before are now wholly in favour. The whole church is united in prayer and seeking to raise the almost half a million pounds necessary. Nicholas was deeply glad about this. If there had been disunity their desire to be good Samaritans in the neighbourhood would have been wrecked. The desire to reach out to their neighbours would have been lost in a storm of controversy. It would have been no good wondering who their neighbour was if they could not even agree on an initial plan for the building. The enemy of souls had tried to lead them into disunity but the Lord had overruled. But only at the request and agreement of the members.

As Tim walked home he felt very different from when he had set out. He recognised, as did many of the others, that no pretence had been made at the meeting to suggest that the case had been argued. There was no question that rationally it was not a sensible decision. But surely in the end, he thought, if a PCC is trying to hear God, then it must be willing to take irrational decisions; or rather to obey God if he led that way. Tim knew that God had made the mind and reason, and that Christians were called to love God with all their minds. But then man was more than rationality. He was heart too. And soul. Much in the New Testament was beyond reason; or rather was in obedience to the higher law of love. Was it rational to feed five thousand with five loaves and two fishes? Was it rational to heal the sick

with a word of command? Was it rational to rise from
the dead? Tim smiled and then yawned involuntarily. It
had been a long day. But still his mind would not rest.
He knew the only qualification Nicholas looked for in
PCC members was that they should be filled with the
Spirit. They were not necessarily the most able or
qualified people. Many were, of course. But it wasn't the
be-all and end-all.

Yet reason was used in the PCC too; not simply a
godly intuition on its own. Membership was open to
anyone and nominees were elected in the usual way.
The meetings were carefully prepared. People did not
groan over them, but all came with Bibles and a desire to
find out what God wanted. Even he really looked
forward to the meetings, and that said a lot! He guessed
all this was quite rare in the Church of England, but it
need not be. One sadness was that the members tended
to be white and middle-class, even though the church
preferred, and worked very hard to encourage, the
black church members not to be diffident and to allow
themselves to be put forward for election.

He let himself into his flat and yawned again. It was
no use, his alert mind would not let him go to sleep; he
would have to stay up. So he put a record on and sat on
the settee. His mind raced forward to the architect's
pictures of the new Montgomery Hall. Would vandals
spray the new building with paint and kick the doors in,
he wondered? Would people on drugs abuse the
hospitality there? He did not know. But it would all have
to be faced in the next stage. God was calling the church
to a new and sacrificial chapter in its history and in that
of Kennington. A new kind of evangelism was going to
be expressed through the body of Christ in the
Montgomery Hall. It was exciting and on that note he
climbed into bed. But even then his thoughts still ran on.

He had come to St Mark's in 1982 from St Aldates in
Oxford. He had been bowled over by the mix of people
in the church and by the love and quality of
relationships and the quality of the worship. This was a

church that 'worked', where needs were met, where it wasn't all words. People mattered at St Mark's, more than programmes. He felt so happy there that he moved into the inner city and bought a flat nearby, for, as he realised, people mattered more than places too. As a single person, St Mark's was in many ways like his family. He loved it and felt at home and at ease there.

Yet he had to admit it wasn't perfect. St Mark's had a high view of the scriptures and of faith, but sometimes one's critical faculties and appraisals could get thrown out of the window. People could be under pressure not to question. St Mark's was like all other charismatic churches in this respect, he guessed. Yet despite the danger that a group could be manipulated because people longed to agree and because they put peace and unity high on the agenda and wanted to please the leaders, that had not happened at the PCC meeting tonight. It was very hard to be manipulated after being silent together before God. No, that meeting had been subject to God himself, from the first to the last member. It really was quite remarkable. And of course the integrity of Nicholas meant that people had not been, nor felt they were being, manipulated.

Tim remembered a 'picture' of some crossroads that had been given at a previous church meeting some time ago. 'The church is at a crossroads,' Dave Lamb had said. 'There is blessing down both roads. We can choose. One road is marked "Comfortable". And one is marked "Sacrificial". But God is saying that there is far more he wants to do down the road marked "Sacrificial".' Tim knew this was a true picture of the dilemma a church like his faced. They had reached a certain size and momentum, so that it had become quite easy to keep going. But it was harder to be that radical body of Christ that they all wanted to be. And perhaps it was a word in season to the whole of the Church as well.

They had failed terribly at St Mark's in a way. He knew there were lonely people in the church. There were needy people in the church. And there were people living very comfortably while others lived in hardship. And the one knew nothing about the other's needs. They simply did not know.

But as sleep came Tim knew he did not want to criticise St Mark's. Because although they had failed, they had failed in something that most churches did not even try to do. Despite the dirt, vandalism, noise and burglaries, the community spirit and love here at St Mark's meant so much to him that with all his heart he wanted to live nearby and be in the parish. Yes, that was it in all its simplicity. He loved the people in the church.

Finally, sleep overtook him in the top floor flat down a side road near St Mark's Church.

25

The Least of These

I sat back in my chair and thought I might turn the lights off, but when I opened my eyes there was no light. I was praying, but there seemed to be a dazzling light. It was getting brighter, as bright as the sun. It wasn't fluorescent at all, but a healthy light. A healing light. A source of light. I gazed and gazed and it was breathtaking.

Then the centre of the light changed and became a crown of thorns. Then it was the glory of light again. It made me realise the close connexion between glory and suffering... Afterwards I was spellbound and silent, full of joy, overwhelmed, unable to speak much.

> A vision of light given to Andrea Leonard as she was praying with her eyes closed, upstairs at St Mark's

Nicholas stood at the window of their upstairs flat and gazed down at the Kennington Road. His face was troubled and he hardly noticed the prunus trees in the tiny square below with their burden of delicate ruby-red blossoms. Marigold was in the kitchen preparing a late lunch and Cameron was at work. She had realised that Nicholas felt tired and oppressed again so she decided to try and cheer him up.

'Think of Cameron,' she said. 'It's been good having him live with us this year.'

'Oh, yes,' said Nicholas emphatically. 'It has. And

I'm thrilled he's working at last for the London
Electricity Board.'

She said, 'He's done very well to get that job as a
clerical assistant in the drawing office. I'm proud of
him.'

Cameron had spent his earliest years in a children's
home. When they first met him as a teenager of nineteen
he was going to Derwen College for the Disabled in
Wales and spending part of his holidays at the Stockwell
YMCA. It was there he met a Christian friend and
eventually found himself at St Mark's where he became
a Christian too. Later he helped Ruth in the parish
office for a year on a Manpower Services Commission
(MSC) scheme. On weekdays he was on reception duty
at the church, welcoming visitors or answering the
phone. Now he was living for a while with Nicholas and
Marigold, who had recently supported him through an
operation on his foot and the subsequent recuperation.
He was born with spastic diplegia, and was blind in his
right eye and slightly deaf in his right ear.

Marigold came in from the kitchen carrying a carton
of orange juice. She crossed the room and put her free
hand on Nicholas's arm.

'Cheer up,' she said. 'Think what Cameron is coming
to terms with.'

Nicholas nodded. Every morning he prayed with
Cameron before he went to work and Nicholas knew
that the young man said that he would rather be
disabled and know the Lord, than able-bodied and not.
Cameron believed he was healed in heart and soul and
that God loved him just as he was and... Yes. It was
good to have Cameron with them. Nicholas was glad.

But the trouble was, Nicholas thought, as he gazed
unseeingly at the traffic and half registered a siren as an
ambulance tore past, he continually had doubts. And
however much he and Marigold and the church had
done for others, and willingly, it did not dispel his
underlying sense of oppression. It was there all the time,
sometimes so faint as to be almost unnoticeable and at

other times, as now, a burden. Perhaps it had begun in his Bermondsey days. Perhaps the Lord allowed it so that he would always know what others in the world felt. He did not know. But still after all these years he felt oppressed by a sense of failure and guilt. He was burdened by what he felt he had not done. He felt the church had failed the uniformed organisations: the Scouts, Guides, Cubs and Brownies. These had been strong in the early days but now the links had grown tenuous. He longed to welcome them again and see them grow. He felt condemned really, because when he came to St Mark's all those years ago he had had such vision of what he believed the Lord wanted him to do. A vision for the family of Christ, for households, for evangelism, for the down-and-outs; yes, even a vision for himself. That they might all be transformed, changed, metamorphosed by the glory of the Lord. And so much of it now, as he saw, had not happened. So much had failed. No, he had failed.

Marigold rushed in again with a tray of cutlery and some plates. She put these on the table and then put her arm round him.

'I love you,' she said quietly.

Immediately he brightened. Slowly he began to smile, responding to her. As ever she could bring him out of himself.

She said, 'When are you going to see Colin next?'

'Oh, fairly soon.'

'Good. It always does you good to see him.'

Suddenly her hand flew to her mouth and she dashed away. 'The potatoes! They must be burning! I can smell them!'

He smiled. Perhaps if he shared his feelings at one of his twice yearly visits to Colin Urquhart that would help. But he knew in his heart of hearts that he had carried around a burden of oppression for so long that probably nothing would change it. It simply must be that the Lord was allowing him to feel the oppression of the area, of a fallen world, of people's pain. So shoulders slightly stooped, he went and sat down at the table and waited while Marigold rescued the potatoes.

'Have you done the drinks?' she called.

Oh, no! He had forgotten again. The juice was out but there were no glasses. He hurried into the kitchen and then had to wait while she tore past him with both hands full. He reached for the glasses. The doorbell rang and then the phone. She stopped dead in the tiny hallway and stared at him rather desperately. He took charge. 'You carry on. Leave the phone for a moment. I'll answer the door. It'll be our guest for lunch.' So a tray in one hand and the phone ringing in the background, he opened the door and welcomed yet another person to eat lunch with them.

Later when calm was restored and the lunch plates washed, Marigold sat down for five minutes.

'That was Norman on the phone before,' she said. 'I must visit his wife in hospital. And I've got to go down to the church to arrange the flowers.'

They worked out arrangements between them. Nicholas saw how tired she was and said, 'Can't you rest more?'

She nodded. 'I'll try. But I've got so much on.'

There was silence between them for a few moments and then she said, 'We could never have looked after a baby of our own here. Our lifestyle is too hectic. It's probably God's wisdom that we didn't have one. And anyway,' she went on, 'I do have a family at church! And Cameron . . . oh!' She jumped up. 'Must dash to the shops and get something for his supper. And ours!' And off she raced.

It was hard, Nicholas knew, for them both. The pace never slackened. It was hectic and urgent all the time, one pressing demand after another, never ending. It was a good thing they were both physically fit and well. And Sunday was the biggest marathon of all, although the most rewarding and joyful of all days too. He walked to the church for some exercise as usual and went via the council flats. On the way through he thought of what

Ben and Andrea Leonard, the present full-time
evangelistic team leaders, had said recently: that
something was needed on the dark barren world of the
estate. Evangelism was a creative growing thing. Since
the upsurge in the early 1980s under Dave Lamb, work
on the estate had become difficult again. People had
forgotten the night of the bomb scare and some of them
did not like being visited. Ben's new idea was to build up
some kind of community meeting there, where people
could bring their dogs and their babies and not feel
threatened by a middle-class way of doing things. He
wanted there to be plenty of singing at such a meeting
and Nicholas knew this was a good idea. This along with
the Montgomery Hall project meant there would be
plenty to stretch the St Mark's folk in the foreseeable
future. Thinking of this gave him a lift in spirit.

As he neared the familiar classical front of the church
his old feelings of failure came back in full force. Wasn't
it true that now at the church they did not know enough
about each other's needs to be a covenant family and
fellowship? It was easy, he knew, for a committed
member of St Mark's not to have enough money for food
that week. It was possible also for an equally committed
member to have a house and garden, a car and a good
job and not even know about the other's needs. He
sighed deeply. It was not the fault of the congregation. It
was his failure as a leader, as a communicator, as a
person. He had failed his people. And he had failed his
Lord.

The next day was Sunday. Nicholas decided to spend
the whole day and evening at the church. He preached
in the morning and Marigold helped in the crèche.
Then there was a big farewell lunch upstairs with an
American family. Then Marigold dashed off to the
hospital, promising to be back by six, in time for the
prayers before the evening service.

After she was gone Nicholas remembered he had
forgotten to tell her about Solomon, the Ugandan.
Solomon had been visiting the church and had come up

to him at the end of the morning service and reminded
him of an incident some years before. At that time
Solomon had been friendly with a fellow Ugandan
called Peter. Peter began coming to St Mark's and one
day asked to see Nicholas. Nicholas was shocked by his
gaunt appearance.

'You see,' Peter had explained, 'because Idi Amin is
in power my Railway scholarship money has inexplic-
ably stopped coming through.' He shrugged. 'I came to
England on that scholarship knowing I'd eventually get
a good job in Uganda. But now I've no money left. I
can't send anything to my wife and four young children
and I don't know what to do.'

Nicholas and the elders had promised to pray and
then they allotted him a grant. But they were pressed
with so many needs and so few of their own members
were wealthy. Although living a simple lifestyle was
preached and many gave and gave, yet the needs
around them were enormous.

When Nicholas got the phone call to visit Peter in
hospital he was again shocked – and guilty to think that
the church had not helped this struggling anxious man
with more money. Shortly afterwards Peter developed
leukaemia and died. Nicholas and the elders immediately sent a sum of money to the widow and she wrote
and thanked them deeply, her words showing her faith.

Now on this particular Sunday Nicholas was
confronted by Solomon, Peter's friend, and he was
telling him that the widow, Josephine, was flying to
Heathrow and arriving that afternoon. She had
husbanded the church gift so carefully that it had lasted
all these years, but now with the very last of it she was
coming to England to try and bring out the remaining
Railway scholarship money legitimately owing to her
from her husband. Nicholas spent a few moments taking
this in. Uppermost in his mind was amazement that a
family of five had lived for nearly ten years on the
modest church gift. He looked at Solomon, knowing
what was coming.

'Can you put Josephine up for the night?' he begged. 'I've no flat and I'm living on a friend's sofa and Josephine only just phoned me on Friday and said she was coming!'

Nicholas smiled tiredly. He knew Africans did not have the same concepts of timing as Europeans.

'Yes, of course,' he said.

'I'll bring her to the service tonight then,' said Solomon.

So while Marigold was visiting the hospital Nicholas arranged some accommodation. He did not worry too much that he had not told Marigold as she had not known Peter, who was before her time at St Mark's. He could have snatched a quick word with her after the evening service, which ran late, but by then he had forgotten again; his mind was filled with the numbers coming forward for ministry. He noted fleetingly that Solomon and Josephine had not come to the service and by nine thirty he decided they were obviously not coming. Someone else came up with an urgent need for accommodation and so he transferred Steve and Caroline's kind offer for Josephine to this other lady. Then he turned back to the group who were offering prayer with the laying-on of hands. Many were there asking for help. It was wonderful afterwards to see them walk away with such peace on their faces. And such joy. But one woman was still in great need and he could see Marigold was spending a lot of time listening and ministering to her. His heart ached to see his wife looking so white and tired, still gallantly giving of herself at eleven thirty at night.

At long last everyone went home. Slowly Marigold trailed upstairs to the church kitchen to find some food covered up there, left over from the farewell lunch and which she knew would do for Cameron's meal the next day. She managed to get herself downstairs.

'I'm so tired,' was all she was able to say.

'Come on,' said Nicholas and took her arm. 'I'll make you a cup of tea at the flat and you can rest.'

He locked up, then they rounded the corner of the church building on the way to the car. By now it was getting on for midnight. Then he stopped dead. It couldn't be! Surely not!

A voice said, 'Oh, Nicholas, I tried to phone you.'

Nicholas gathered himself together. 'The phone's upstairs at church,' he said automatically. 'We didn't hear you.'

He turned to Marigold. 'Go to the car,' he said.

But she stopped and stared. Nicholas went forward. Standing on the pavement were two Africans. One was Solomon. The other was a woman, as thin as Marigold had ever seen. She had a suitcase in one hand; on her legs were no stockings; all she was wearing in the chill spring air was a thin dress and jacket. And even at a distance Marigold could see that she was very tired. However as far as Marigold was concerned these were two strangers who appeared to know Nicholas. Yet she had a sinking feeling. Surely no more was going to be demanded of her that day. Surely not. Her gaze was drawn to the woman again. Ebony dark under the street light, tall and dignified, with so thin a body, she stood stock still. Her eyes were bright and huge in her undernourished face. Marigold watched as Nicholas strode over to talk to them. And she knew before he turned round what his face would say.

Her heart sank even further. I can't cope with this, she thought. It's too much, Lord. A total stranger. And Cameron will be waiting up for us and we'll want to spend half an hour with him before settling him down for the night and now I just know we'll have this lady and we'll have to give out to her as well. And we're going away tomorrow for three nights and I've got to get Cameron's food organised and it's the first time he's been left on his own since the operation on his foot. And I'll need to get the washing hung up so that Florence can come in on Tuesday and iron it, and that prayer ministry for so many was exhausting and this is the last straw!

Yet when Nicholas came over to her and she saw the question in his eyes she knew she could do nothing but nod. So Josephine climbed into the back of their car.

Marigold, overtired and overstretched, said to Solomon who was still standing on the pavement, 'Surely you realise we are not normally here at this time of night! Fancy bringing her as late as this! Why couldn't you have let us *know*,' she kept saying. 'We're going away tomorrow.'

Solomon looked helplessly at her. 'I did speak to Nicholas and her plane got delayed,' was all he said.

'Oh,' said Marigold. 'I'm sorry. It's obviously not your fault.'

She looked at Nicholas and he looked steadily at her. She turned away and bit her lip and struggled valiantly to make herself go the second mile.

'What will you do now?' she asked Solomon.

'Oh, I'll get a late train. I'll be OK. I'm going back to my friend's flat.'

In the car Marigold turned to Josephine, and more in resignation than annoyance said, 'Couldn't you have let us know beforehand? We're going away and...'

But Josephine looked as if she did not grasp the concept of such an arrangement being necessary and stared and smiled at Marigold from her enormous black eyes. Then Marigold remembered that in their culture Africans do not do things that way; they just turn up. She sighed.

'Please help me Lord,' she breathed. 'Help me. Help me to be gracious.'

Back at the flat they talked to Cameron, offered Josephine some tea which she refused, found clean sheets and blankets and made the sofa up into a bed, and put the automatic washing machine on. Then they prayed with their guests. At last Cameron's light went out, and then Josephine in a borrowed pair of tights and a cardigan to stop her from shivering, settled down on the settee. Marigold looked at her watch. It was one thirty in the morning. She opened her mouth to speak to

Nicholas but he got in first.

'Forgive me for not telling you,' he said, 'only it was
all arranged. Then she didn't turn up and I assumed she
wasn't coming.'

Marigold said, 'It's all right. But I feel awful. If only
I'd been nicer to Solomon.'

'Don't worry,' said Nicholas. 'How could you help it?
Just relax now.'

'If the phone rings I'll –'

'I'm taking it off the hook,' he said calmly. 'And I'm
switching off the doorbell as well. Nothing and no one is
going to trouble you, or me, tonight.'

Just before going to sleep he whispered, 'In a strange
sort of way I feel by receiving Josephine tonight, we have
received Jesus.'

In the morning when Marigold awoke she felt better.
The rest had done her good. She waited till she heard
Josephine stirring and then began to make some
breakfast.

'Have a cup of tea,' she said and gave a mug to
Josephine.

Josephine took the tea and gazed at it. Then she
sipped, savouring the taste.

Marigold watched her. 'Do you drink tea in
Uganda?'

Josephine smiled. 'Oh, yes. Well, not quite like this.
It's just tea leaves and water. Water flavoured with tea
leaves. We use them again and again.'

'What? The tea leaves?'

'Yes. And milk is too expensive.'

Josephine ate some cornflakes. They went from her
bowl slowly and she chewed each mouthful carefully.

'Would you like some toast?' asked Marigold.

'Oh, no thank you.'

'Are you sure?'

'Yes. Quite sure.'

'You speak very good English!'

Josephine smiled. 'Yes. I'm glad I understand you.
We learn it at school in Uganda. Most people can speak
English.'

'Well, why not have a banana?' said Marigold and passed her the fruit bowl.

Josephine's eyes widened. 'Oh, no thank you.'

'Don't you like them?'

'Well, yes. But they cost five shillings each at home.'

'But you can have one here then,' said Marigold, puzzled.

Josephine said, 'It would cost twenty-five shillings for my whole family to have one each. I've got four children and I look after an orphan. And twenty-five shillings would be like thousands of shillings to you. We couldn't afford that.'

The words were said without a shred of self-pity or criticism, but with a simple dignity.

Marigold swallowed and put the fruit bowl away. Then she said, 'What do you eat at home?'

'We have one meal a day. In the evening. It's porridge made of millet. Sometimes we are lucky and can grow vegetables and cook them. Sometimes we miss a day.'

Without hope Marigold said, 'Would you like another cup of tea?'

To her relief the large eyes brightened. 'Thank you. But no sugar. Thank you.'

As they drank the second cup Marigold asked her about the children.

'My eldest is twelve and she is in charge until I get back.'

'You left them – alone?'

Josephine's whole body became expressive. 'After the war, and Idi Amin, I had to move. There are no relatives. Only a few villagers left. They'll do their best. But everyone is hungry.' She leaned forward, her old young face tense and determined. 'If I can get this money I'll buy a sewing machine and a typewriter. Then I can make a little business. I can sell things and earn money. And we will survive. My children and Peter's children, they will survive and grow up and be able to work. But I must get that money.'

There was a silence. Then Marigold said, 'Yes, I can see that.'

Josephine relaxed. 'Jesus will help me,' she said simply.

Soon breakfast was over and Marigold found herself getting into a rush again. There was so much to do to get ready for going away.

Nicholas said in the doorway, 'I'll talk to Josephine in the lounge and then you can get ready.'

'Oh, lovely,' said Marigold, her mind concentrating on the two empty suitcases in their bedroom.

Nicholas sat with Josephine in quietness for a while. Then he said, 'Shall we look at the Bible together?'

She sat upright on the sofa. Her face was fine boned and had been beautiful before hunger and bereavement hollowed it. She said, 'I've got a verse from the Bible for you.'

'Oh,' he said. 'Thank you. Please read it to me.'

'It is Matthew 25, verse 40.'

Nicholas waited while she looked up the verse. At last she found the place and read out loud in her African accent: 'The King will reply, "I tell you the truth, whatever you did for one of the least of these brothers of mine, you did for me."' She put down the Bible carefully and looked him straight in the eye.

'Thank you,' she said simply. 'Thank you to both of you.'

Nicholas looked into her face and saw Jesus. 'Thank *you*,' he said.

Later Marigold fixed her up in a Christian hotel near Victoria with a room for two nights; and Geoffrey and Margaret Smith offered to look after her for the rest of the week while Nicholas and Marigold were away. Afterwards Geoffrey was able to report to Nicholas that she had got the money she came for and had gone back to Uganda safely with a typewriter and a sewing machine.

The next week it was time for Nicholas to keep his appointment with Colin Urquhart. When he got into Colin's study he found himself pouring out his feelings of failure and oppression. Colin listened, head resting on his hand. Then he got up and walked up and down. Finally Colin said, 'Look, Nicholas, I believe there is something the Lord wants me to say to you. I've felt it from the moment you arrived.'

Nicholas was surprised. He knew that Colin was not usually so forthright but simply liked to listen and help people to hear God's word for themselves.

Colin began to talk over lunch. In a mixture of prophecy, prayer, conversation and relaxation a message began to come across to Nicholas. It was not the message he had expected to hear. But it was as crystal-clear as running water, and it washed over him and through him. As he listened he knew he was being made different, his mind-set was altering, his attitude changing.

'I feel in my spirit that you are under a sense of condemnation and failure,' said Colin. 'And now the Lord is going to release you from it. But first you must let go of your bondage to helping the down-and-outs. Do not be yoked to them. For I am far more concerned about them even than you are. Let go even of St Mark's Church and all the work. It's the Lord's church and he wants to build it. Let go of everything you wanted to strive for and see happen. Let go, even, of your utter commitment to London. Release the whole of St Mark's in its entirety back to him. Be yoked only to me. For my yoke is easy and my burden is light.'

In the silence that followed Nicholas bowed his head. In his heart he knew he was willing to let go of all these things.

There was a time of stillness.

Then Colin said, 'Now the Lord will release you. He says to you, Nicholas: "I know. I know everything. And within the limitations of your own gifting, within the limitations of the dedication I've given you and within the limitations of the dedication I've given to others, the work at St Mark's has been fruitful and pleasing to me. All the things you think of as failures and sins are forgiven. Despite them and through them I have been working and building my church.""'

Suddenly Nicholas saw everything clearly, in a new light. A great release swept through his body and left him limp, relaxed, at peace, quiet and smiling. Yes. So be it. The Lord had spoken. And he, Nicholas Rivett-Carnac, had heard. And believed. It was the same message he had heard before, only now it came through with a new reality and power. All he had to do was obey. For it was the Lord's church. A whisper like a distant echo seemed to reverberate faintly in the room, a whisper he had heard before. 'This is my church and I want to build it. I love you and I accept you and I will build my church through you.' And he felt he had been given a picture of the Lord choosing and loving to build something true and good through human limitations. Afterwards all he felt able to say was, 'Thank you, Lord'.

When he told Marigold about it, Nicholas said, 'How amazing it is really. When I saw Josephine on the pavement late that Sunday evening, I knew in a sense that it was Jesus. It was as if he was standing there. Even though it was at such a difficult time for us. And when she read about the kingdom of God in the parable of the sheep and the goats and said, "The King will reply, 'I tell you the truth, whatever you did for one of the least of these brothers of mine, you did for me'", I knew it was the Lord speaking. He spoke through a poor Third World widow; and also, as I heard today, he speaks through a man like Colin. Two such different people, but the same Lord.'

So Nicholas was at peace again, this time deeper than ever. After the trauma of his Bermondsey days, after all the longing and striving to see the kingdom of Christ on earth, he knew now that the King of kings had spoken to him again, unmistakably, personally and powerfully. And he experienced a deep sense of being loved and accepted by the Lord.

And what is the secret of St Mark's? Why is a church in the inner city filled Sunday by Sunday with joyful people, their hands aloft and faces radiant? Is it simply that Nicholas has translated his love for his earthly family into spiritual terms? Or is it much more than that?

Roger Bagge spoke out about what he sees as being at the heart of St Mark's: 'What really comes to me is what I sensed when I first came to St Mark's: the love of Christ that was being expressed through the family. And the acceptance. At times it really brought tears to my eyes when I saw down-and-outs feeling able to sit there and not necessarily just coming in for a hand-out. But they were loved. They were treated the same as others, who were perhaps professional people. That's what really thrilled me. It was as if Jesus himself was there.'

And the church will stand upon the rock of Christ right into the next century, when it will welcome a whole new generation, such as the brand-new baby Ruth, daughter of Bill and Dawn Stranaghan.

Epilogue

The Rock

Today many people's lives are in ruins. As they have built their existence around such things as power, popularity and selfishness, the 'storms' of life have come and battered them to the ground, leaving only pain, fear and confusion. Perhaps your experience has been like this.

However, there is a Rock – Jesus Christ – on whom you can build, not your own imperfect life, but HIS eternal, abundant, joy-filled life; and no matter what storms you may go through, HE will always remain firm and strong.

Malcolm Banham on the musical *Built Upon the Rock*
written by himself and his wife Claire
and first performed at St Mark's in April 1988
from *Crossroads*, March 1988

It is evening in Kennington. The light gradually fades over the streets, flats and terraced houses. Boys cycle without lights down Prima Road and yell to each other as they dodge parked cars. In the flats on the Kennington Park estate the balconies are lit up. Always there is the incessant sound of traffic, punctuated by sirens swooping down the main road to Brixton.

Alone in her first floor sitting-room sits Rose Marshall, wife of Mike, the curate. She goes to the window and sees the quiet full moon over the darkened trees in Kennington Park. In these still moments while her three young children sleep she thinks back over her four years in this inner-city parish.

For Rose this time has been costly. There's been cost here, she thinks, in noise, in housing, in traffic, and in a recent post-natal depression. I couldn't get out with the kids. There was no garden. The intensity of life was draining. The truth is, and here she sighs, I know what it's like to be at rock bottom. Why did I crumble when the third baby came? Why do I, like many others, feel an oppression in spirit as we drive back into the area after a day in the country? So many people have helped me, but still it's been difficult. And yet I knew God wanted me here. God met me at rock bottom. I needed to accept God's calling. I needed to know in my heart that God's grace was sufficient for me in this calling. But somehow, although I longed to do so, I didn't really.

She stares out across the darkening park and her face softens. I never believed we'd stay in the inner city. I was sure Mike would become a vicar in a smaller town or in the suburbs. But God seemed to point another way. Eventually, without joy, I said I'd consider moving to another parish only a few miles away. The children were begging for a garden and we had to say we didn't know. And then one Friday evening some people came from the church there to see us. I tried to be pleasant, but in my heart I still couldn't accept it.

I don't know what happened that evening; there was nothing spectacular, only coffee and talk and a few prayers in this sitting-room. Yet by the time they'd gone, and Mike was helping me to clear up in the kitchen, I found I couldn't stop smiling and giggling. Everything had changed. I had changed. My heart had changed. Knowing exactly the cost, I was willing, no, glad to stay in the inner city. It was a miracle. A real miracle of grace. And we found out the vicarage had a lovely garden too!

Before, being in the inner city it was like a Gethsemane to me. But now I've found it to be true in my own experience, that God's grace is sufficient. The gospel is big enough to meet people's unhappiness. I cannot cope alone, but his strength as I now know is made perfect in weakness. And as Mike says, millions of people actually live here. They have no call and no choice. Half the nation lives in cities. We are simply servants going where people are.

It had cost her everything she was, but she had won through, a woman who found Christ to be *her* rock.

Nicholas, in his own flat across the main road and on the other side of the church, thinks about Mike and Rose and how much they had contributed to St Mark's. They both loved the Lord and put him first. Rose had been so hospitable and had become, as Marigold had told him, very friendly with other Kennington mothers. Mike was a fine husband and father; and a man who gave himself whole-heartedly to teaching in the church. Nicholas knew that Mike, like most people at St Mark's, longed for revival, believing that only a revived church could save the nation from disaster. But Mike taught clearly that revival could only come as people were willing to identify with Christ, share his sufferings and pray persistently. Yes, thinks Nicholas, the church was going to miss them both.

Now as he sits on quietly in the evening his thoughts slip back to the recent holiday he and Marigold spent in Tenerife. He sighs and stares unseeingly across the familiar room. You never finish learning, he thinks. For he had learned an enormous lesson only a few weeks before, during that holiday. It had been like a living parable. The church had given them some travel vouchers as a gift, but when Marigold asked him to help her decide which apartment to rent he had not bothered to pray or even discuss it with her. 'Take the cheaper one,' he had said, even though he knew she loved a sea view.

When they arrived they found the cheaper apartment looked over a noisy street. And there was a smell of drains. But when they went for a walk in the evening and saw the apartment they could have had, with its indescribably beautiful view, far more wonderful than either of them could ever have conceived or imagined, Nicholas was bitterly disappointed. That was where they *could* have stayed; but because he hadn't bothered the opportunity was lost. Wasn't that what so many parables in the gospels were talking about: lost opportunities; talents buried; no oil in the lamps; even a place of eternal darkness for those who chose to go their own way? He sighed deeply and stared at the ground. And then it was that he caught a sense of the Lord's presence. A lightness came to him and a tiny joy. The still small voice whispered, 'I love you and I want the best for you. But you must walk close to me or you will miss the best, both in this life and in the next ... teach this to others in the church and outside the church ... to choose me and my words.'

Nicholas thought. Weren't the words of Christ so clear? He said:

Everyone who hears these words of mine and puts them into practice is like a wise man who built his house on the rock. The rain came down, the streams rose, and the winds blew and beat against that house; yet it did not fall, because it had its foundation on the rock. But everyone who hears these words of mine and does not put them into practice is like a foolish man who built his house on sand. The rain came down, the streams rose, and the wind blew and beat against the house, and it fell down with a great crash. (Matt. 7:24–27 NIV)

Nicholas was quieted. He walked back tranquilly; only to discover that, like a tiny miracle, their unlovely apartment had been changed. When they arrived at the new one they found it had a balcony overlooking a semi-tropical garden and pool, with luxuriant palms and exotic pink flowers climbing through the dark green trees. It was a miracle of grace, he thought. And they had a wonderful holiday!

Now, back at the flat, he thinks of his congregation. .

Many had responded to the Lord's call to walk in the way of the cross. For some it had meant the hardships of working near the Sahara Desert in a mission hospital; or the hazards of Thailand refugee camps in the war zone. For others it meant opening their homes to the homeless; or working amid the greed of the city, in a spirit of generosity. For many it was the cost of living in the inner city. But he knew for them all that when they dared to forsake all to follow the Lord, they found he had indeed been their provider, even as Paul promised: 'God is able to make all grace abound to you, so that in all things at all times, having all that you need, you will abound in every good work' (2 Cor. 9:8 NIV).

But what if our hearts fail and we feel unequal to becoming his disciples, of following in his footsteps; afraid of failure, afraid of letting him down, afraid of the inner city, afraid of the cost and of where his footsteps might lead us? That is when God himself runs to meet us and, if we are willing, puts our feet upon the rock. The Psalmist says:

> When my heart is faint and overwhelmed, lead me to the mighty, towering Rock of safety. For you are my refuge, a high tower where my enemies can never reach me... For God alone is my Rock, my rescuer, defence and fortress... Oh my people, trust him all the time. Pour out your longings to him, for he can help! (Pss. 61, 62 Living Bible)

Nicholas smiles. He closes his Bible, crosses the room and sets off to walk to the church. And as he goes he thinks back over his life. How glad he is, how deeply and joyously glad, that Christ is *his* rock. Praise God, he cries, and lets himself in through the side door.